# WRITING SKILLS
# FOR
# TECHNICAL
# STUDENTS

# WRITING SKILLS FOR TECHNICAL STUDENTS

## THIRD EDITION

**DELAWARE TECHNICAL AND COMMUNITY COLLEGE**
English Department, Southern Campus

Prentice Hall, Englewood Cliffs, New Jersey 07632

**Library of Congress Cataloging-in-Publication Data**

Writing skills for technical students / Delaware Technical and
Community College, English Department, Southern Campus: [the text
of this book was written collectively by Sara Drew Lewis,
coordinator . . . et al.].—3rd ed.
  p.    cm.
  Includes index.
  ISBN 0-13-981986-X
  1. English language—Rhetoric.   2. English language—
Grammar—1950–   3. English language—Business English.   4. English
language—Technical English.   I. Lewis, Sara Drew.   II. Delaware
Technical and Community College. English Dept., Southern Campus.
PE1479.B87W75
808′.0666—dc20                                                91-31465
1992                                                              CIP

*The text of this book was written collectively by Sara Drew Lewis, Coordinator;
Harriet Smith, Fred Baker, George Ellegood, Carol Kopay, and Ward Tanzer.*

Production Editor: John Rousselle
Acquisitions Editor: Phil Miller
Copy Editor: James Tully
Prepress Buyer: Herb Klein
Maufacturing Buyer: Patrice Fraccio
Cover Designer: Patricia Kelly

© 1992, 1988 by Prentice-Hall, Inc.
A Simon & Schuster Company
Englewood Cliffs, New Jersey 07632

Printed in the United States of America
20  19  18  17  16  15  14  13  12  11


ISBN 0-13-981986-X

Prentice-Hall International (UK) Limited, *London*
Prentice-Hall of Australia Pty. Limited, *Sydney*
Prentice-Hall Canada Inc., *Toronto*
Prentice-Hall Hispanoamericana, S.A., *Mexico*
Prentice-Hall of India Private Limited, *New Delhi*
Prentice-Hall of Japan, Inc., *Tokyo*
Simon & Schuster Asia Pte. Ltd., *Singapore*
Editora Prentice-Hall do Brasil, Ltda., *Rio de Janeiro*

# CONTENTS

**SECTION TWO**

# TO THE TEACHER

This text is designed for the adult learner who needs a review of grammar and writing skills in order to be able to write clearly and concisely on the job. Its format provides for diagnosis, instruction, and practice in 14 self-paced modules that can be adapted to both individualized and classroom methods. There are 11 grammar modules, a module on paragraph writing, a module on report writing, and a module on business letter writing. Spelling aids are given in the Appendix. Each module consists of a statement of behavioral objectives followed by instruction and practice in small segments with immediate feedback. The examples used throughout are geared to be meaningful and relevant, particularly for technical students. The fundamental principles applied are as follows:

1. Test—find out what the students already know.
2. Teach—explain to them the concepts they need to know.
3. Retest—check to see that they have mastered the objectives. (If not, repeat the procedure.)

The underlying philosophy is that writing skills are built inductively; that is, students learn and practice correct grammar and usage first, then go on to build from the sentence to the paragraph to the report to the business letter.

The materials included in the Instructor's Manual are vital to an effective utilization of *Writing Skills for Technical Students*. The manual contains diagnostic tests for the grammar units, so that you can pretest and exempt students from modules they can already apply. Also included in the manual are module tests (four alternative tests for each module), final grammar tests, applied writing exercises, and extra worksheets for practice when the student does not master the instructional material.

ix

For use with the paragraph, report, and business writing modules, the Instructor's Manual includes checklists to be used by both students and instructors to proofread and evaluate writing assignments and to note the kinds of errors made.

We believe the organization and modular format of this text will provide instructors with a flexible and effective approach to teaching students how to write well.

# TO THE STUDENT

This book presents a self-paced, modularized program to build your skills in grammar and writing. It is divided into two sections. Section One deals with the basic points of grammar and the writing of paragraphs. Section Two covers additional areas in the refinement of grammar plus the writing of reports and business communications.

*Here's how to use the book.* For each grammar module that your instructor requires you to complete, first read the objectives and study the instructional materials. Follow the directions for each Activity. At the end of each Activity, you are directed to check your responses in the Feedback section at the end of the module or to check your work with your instructor. You will also be directed how to proceed after completing the Activity. When you have completed the module, ask your instructor for Test A. If you pass Test A, you will be given an Applied Writing exercise. If you do not pass, your instructor will review your errors, give you a worksheet for extra practice if necessary, and then give you Test B. After you pass a test on each module, be sure to note it on your Student Progress Record (See next page).

The Paragraph Module progresses from the topic sentence to the outline to the writing of four important types of paragraphs. Follow the procedures indicated, checking your work with your instructor when required.

After completing Section One, you will proceed in the same manner through Section Two.

Refer to the Spelling Aids in the Appendix whenever necessary. Keep a list of your particular spelling problem words for frequent review.

Many students have been helped by the materials and methods in this book. We hope you will find it both useful and enjoyable.

# STUDENT PROGRESS RECORD
## Section One

NAME _____

## GRAMMAR MODULES

| | Tests: A | B | C | D | Applied Writing | Review |
|---|---|---|---|---|---|---|
| 1. Verbs | | | | | | |
| 2. Adjectives & Adverbs | | | | | | |
| 3. Phrases | | | | | | |
| 4. Subject–Verb Agreement | | | | | | |
| 5. Clauses | | | | | | |
| 6. Punctuation | | | | | | |
| 7. Fragments & Run-Ons | | | | | | |
| 8. Pronouns | | | | | | |

*Grammar Final*  A_____  B_____

### 9. PARAGRAPH MODULE

| | A | B | Comments |
|---|---|---|---|
| Reasons | | | |
| Reasons & Examples | | | |
| Pro & Con | | | |
| Process | | | |
| *Paragraph Final* | | | |

# GRAMMAR MODULES

| Tests: | A | B | C | D | Applied Writing | Review |
|---|---|---|---|---|---|---|
| 10. Shifts | | | | | | |
| 11. Clarity | | | | | | |
| 12. Acceleration | | | | | | |

*Grammar Final*   A_____   B_____

## 13. REPORT MODULE

| | A | B | Comments |
|---|---|---|---|
| Outlining | | | |
| Technical Procedure | | | |
| Persuasion | | | |
| Interview Questions | | | |
| Interview | | | |
| Recommendation | | | |
| Summary | | | |
| *Report Final* | | | |

## 14. BUSINESS LETTERS

| | A | B | Comments |
|---|---|---|---|
| Request Letter | | | |
| "No" Letter | | | |
| Social Business Letter | | | |
| Resumé | | | |
| Application Letter | | | |
| Memorandum | | | |
| Letter of Transmittal | | | |

# WRITING SKILLS
# FOR
# TECHNICAL
# STUDENTS

# Verbs

OBJECTIVE: This module will give you a good foundation on which to build your sentences.

Upon completion of this module, you will be able:

To recognize action and linking verbs.

To identify helping verbs.

To identify and to use correctly the principal parts of verbs, both regular and irregular.

The verb is the basic part of every sentence. In order to write correct sentences, you have to be able to recognize verbs. There are two types of verbs: *action verbs*, which indicate what the subject is doing, and *linking verbs*, which link the subject with another word in a sentence. Most verbs show action, and generally this type of verb is more forceful in a sentence.

The subject of the sentence is what the sentence is about. It is usually a noun or pronoun. A noun is the name of a person, place, thing, or idea. A pronoun takes the place of a noun.

## PART I: ACTION VERBS

Just as the name implies, *action verbs show action*. You can perform or *do* any action verb, either physically or mentally. Read the following examples and note that the verbs (printed in **bold** type) all show *an action that can be done*.

He **typed** the letter to Dr. Jones. (*Physical action*)

John **read** all of the material. (*Physical action*)

He **studied** every rule. (*Mental action*)

She **walks** to work. (*Physical action*)

Mary **spoke** at the meeting. (*Physical action*)

I **thought** about the experiment. (*Mental action*)

### ACTIVITY 1-A: Identifying Action Verbs

Underline the action verbs in the following sentences.

1. The architect made blueprints of the drawings.
2. The secretary typed the bid specifications this morning.
3. Mary cleaned and oiled the lathe.
4. Their computer operator entered 200 new addresses.
5. Our nurses' program assists the local hospitals with many duties.
6. The hotel offers attractive accommodations for conventions.
7. A new chemical process extracts gold economically from mining residue.
8. Police officers work long hours during civil disturbances.
9. The Help Line volunteer workers saved many lives this year.
10. The prolonged strike hurts too many farmers.

Check your responses in Feedback 1-A at the end of this module. If all your responses were correct, proceed to Activity 1-C. If you missed any, do Activity 1-B.

## ACTIVITY 1-B: Identifying Action Verbs

Underline the action verbs in the following sentences.

1. The auctioneer sold many attractive items at low bids.
2. She drew the most practical plan for the apartment.
3. The Du Pont Company prefers men for some secretarial positions.
4. The electrician installed a new switch on the machine.
5. One of our nurses stopped the bleeding very quickly.
6. In minutes, a computer saves hundreds of work hours.
7. After lunch, the crew assembled the surveyor's level.
8. The Ramada Inn hotel chain sold its Denver branch.
9. Bill transferred to the hospital emergency ward.
10. Doris aligned her truck's front wheels this morning.

Check your responses in Feedback 1-B at the end of this module. If all your responses were correct, proceed to Activity 1-C. If you missed any, review Part I before going on, or ask your instructor for extra help.

## ACTIVITY 1-C: Writing Sentences with Action Verbs

On your own paper, write five sentences containing action verbs. Make sure your verb shows an action that can be done. Underline the action verbs. Check your sentences with your instructor before going on to Part II.

# PART II: LINKING VERBS

Verbs that do not show action are called *linking verbs*. Only a few verbs are in this category: verbs of *being* (**to be, to become,** etc.) and verbs of the *senses* (**to feel, to smell, to taste,** etc.).

Linking verbs express some relationship between the subject and another word that follows the linking verb. (See Module 2, Rule 7, page 23.) This word following the linking verb may be an adjective (a word that describes a noun or pronoun). Its function is to describe the subject of the sentence.

EXAMPLES

S    Adj
John **is** efficient.

S    Adj
They **are** late.

S    Adj
Mary **was** tired.

S    Adj
The test **seems** easy.

The word following the linking verb may also be a *noun* that renames or identifies the subject. The linking verb acts as an equals sign when the subject and the noun following the verb are one and the same.

EXAMPLES

| S | Noun | | S | Noun |
|---|---|---|---|---|
| Joe **is** my brother. | | | Mary **is** class president. | |
| Joe = brother | | | Mary = president | |

The most common linking verb is the verb **to be** in all its forms: **be, am, is, are, was, were, been, being.**

In addition, the following are linking verbs to express a state of being: **become, grow, seem, act, appear, stay, remain.**

Finally, these five verbs are linking verbs when used in connection with the senses: **look, feel, smell, taste, sound.**

Be careful. Some verbs, especially verbs of the senses, are linking verbs when used in one way, but they can be action verbs when used in a different way. You can test it by substituting a form of the verb **to be** in place of the sense verbs.

**Linking Verb Test**

To test whether or not a verb is a linking verb, just substitute **is** or **was** for the verb and see if the sentence still makes sense.

EXAMPLES

The assignment **seems** difficult.
(Can you substitute *is* for the verb *seems*? Yes. The assignment *is* difficult. *Seems* is a linking verb.)
The cake **tasted** good.
(Can you substitute *was* for the verb *tasted*? Yes. The cake *was* good. *Tasted* is a linking verb.)

These verbs are used as *linking verbs*. Here the subject is not doing the action of the verb.

EXAMPLES

This book **looks** good. (The book is not looking. The book *is* good.)
The pie **tastes** delicious. (The pie is not tasting. The pie *is* good.)
This record **sounds** scratched. (The record is not sounding. The record *is* scratched.)
The farmer **grows** tired. (The farmer is not growing; he *is* becoming.)

These verbs are used as *action verbs*. They show what the subject is doing.

EXAMPLES

He **looks** for the memo. (Not He *is* the memo.)
He **tastes** the wine for a hobby. (Not He *is* the wine.)
The foghorn **sounds** a blast. (Not The foghorn *is* a blast.)
The farmer **grows** cabbages. (Not The farmer *is* cabbages.)

---

LINKING VERBS

Verbs of Being

All parts of **to be: be, am, is, are, was, were, been, being.**
**become   grow   seem   act   appear   stay   remain**
*Verbs of the Senses*
**look feel smell taste sound**

---

## ACTIVITY 1-D: Identifying Linking Verbs

Underline the linking verbs in the following sentences.

1. Hog production is second only to poultry production on the Delmarva Peninsula.
2. His typing is the neatest in the office.
3. We are proud of our nursing program.
4. The account appeared complete.
5. The sign on the building seemed too tall for its setting.
6. Many activities for young people are challenging.
7. All the electrical circuits seem to have adequate power.
8. The news reporter remained calm during the interview.
9. Most meals at the plant cafeteria taste delicious.
10. The air-conditioned rooms felt good today.

Check your responses in Feedback 1-D at the end of this module. If all your responses were correct, proceed to Activity 1-F. If you missed any, do Activity 1-E.

## ACTIVITY 1-E: Identifying Linking Verbs

Underline the linking verbs in the following sentences.

1. In this newspaper column, one sentence is as lengthy as a paragraph.
2. Wild cherry trees seem susceptible to web-weaving insects.
3. The judge appears thoughtful.

4. Stale coffee generally tastes horrible.

5. The aroma from that restaurant smells inviting.

6. Our accountant was trustworthy.

7. This electric wire feels hot.

8. Our new generator is much more efficient.

9. I am happy with the new design.

10. He became an excellent keypunch operator in a very short time.

Check your responses in Feedback 1-E at the end of this module. If your responses were correct, proceed to Activity 1-F. If you missed any, review Part II before going on.

## ACTIVITY 1-F: Writing Sentences with Linking Verbs

On your own paper, write five sentences using a different linking verb in each sentence. Underline the linking verb. Check your sentences with your instructor before proceeding to Activity 1-G.

## ACTIVITY 1-G: Identifying Linking and Action Verbs

Underline the verbs in the following sentences. In the space provided, identify them as A (action) or L (linking).

_____ 1. Your comments are valid.

_____ 2. The final paragraph suggests a meeting.

_____ 3. This example supports my viewpoint.

_____ 4. The letters were ready on time.

_____ 5. Each worker seems competent.

_____ 6. Marcia looks capable of good work.

_____ 7. Problems occur in that area often.

_____ 8. An unclear letter causes misunderstanding.

_____ 9. The filing system appears orderly.

_____ 10. All of the reports fell on the floor.

Check your responses in Feedback 1-G at the end of this module. If your responses were correct, proceed to Part III. If you missed any, do Activity 1-H.

## ACTIVITY 1-H: Identifying Linking and Action Verbs

Underline the verbs in the following sentences. In the space provided, identify them as A (action) or L (linking).

_____ 1. All these accounts are current.

_____ 2. We sampled those cultures earlier.

_____ 3. The center also provides responsible day care.

_____ 4. His plea affected my decision.

_____ 5. Pigs are marketable after being weaned.

_____ 6. Justice seems abstract at times.

_____ 7. He listened carefully to the truck's engine.

_____ 8. During the electrical storm, everyone felt tense.

_____ 9. That student carried the engineer's measuring chain.

_____ 10. The secretary prepared an extra copy of our report.

Check your responses in Feedback 1-H at the end of this module. If your responses were correct, proceed to Part III. If you missed any, review Part II.

## PART III: HELPING VERBS

Sometimes the verb is expressed using more than one word. The complete verb consists of a *main verb* and one or more *helpers,* which precede it. When locating the verb in a sentence, be sure to indicate helping verbs as well as the verb they help. In the following examples the helping verbs are in bold type.

EXAMPLES

**has** erased           **might have** been
**will be** coming        **can** say
**should have** gone     **is** finished

Listed below are the most commonly used helping verbs. These helpers may be used singly or in groups with the main verb.

| HELPING VERBS | | |
|---|---|---|
| am | do | must |
| are | had | shall |
| be | has | should |
| been | have | was |
| can | is | were |
| could | may | will |
| did | might | would |

Helping verbs are often separated from the main verb by an adverb such as **not, never, always,** etc. These words are not part of the verb. Likewise, the contraction **n't** on the end of a negative verb (were**n't**, does**n't**, etc.) is not part of the complete verb.

| EXAMPLES | COMPLETE VERB |
|---|---|
| I **did** not **see** you at the safety meeting. | did see |
| He **can** always **type** it again for his boss. | can type |
| **Are** you still **going** to the company party? | are going |
| **Were**n't you **surveying** the lot? | were surveying |

*Note:* When a sentence is in the form of a question, the helping verb is separated from the main verb by the subject.

### ACTIVITY 1-I: Complete Verbs

Underline the complete verb. Remember that the complete verb consists of all helpers and the main verb but does not include adverbs.

1. She is covering the story for the local newspapers.
2. Pat may have already done the internship.
3. Were you planning to attend the seminar?
4. Mary Smith has written the report for the meeting.
5. Mr. Dukes has already proofread the report.
6. We are making several changes in the architect's drawing.
7. Will you complete the experiment before noon?
8. Mrs. Jones's work should have been done earlier than his.
9. He is doing all of the construction himself.
10. I must attend the meeting tomorrow in St. Louis.

Check your answers with Feedback 1-I at the end of this module. If your responses were correct, proceed to Activity 1-J. If you missed any, review Part III before going on.

### ACTIVITY 1-J: Writing Sentences with the Complete Verb

On your own paper, write five sentences with helping verbs and underline the complete verb. Make sure that each sentence uses at least one of the helping verbs listed in Part III, and that each sentence has more than a one-word verb. Check your sentences with your instructor. Then proceed to Part IV.

## PART IV: IRREGULAR VERBS

Learning the principal parts of verbs will help you use the correct verb form. The *principal parts* are the present, the past, the past participle, and the present participle.

The *past participle* is the form that must be used with a helping verb (see the list of Helping Verbs in Part III). Examples of the past with a helper are **has walked, had seen, is given, was ended, were broken, has been sent,** etc.

The *present participle* is the form ending in **-ing,** and it uses a helping verb: **is helping, are writing, is scheduling,** etc.

*Regular* verbs make their past and past participle forms by adding **-d** or **-ed** to the present tense form of the verb.

| PRESENT | PAST | PAST PARTICIPLE | PRESENT PARTICIPLE |
|---------|------|-----------------|---------------------|
| walk | walked | (have) walked | (are) walking |
| hope | hoped | (have) hoped | (are) hoping |
| save | saved | (have) saved | (are) saving |
| polish | polished | (have) polished | (are) polishing |

*Irregular* verbs do *not* make their past and past participle forms by adding **-d** or **-ed** to the present tense verb. Irregular verbs form their past and past participle in various ways: (1) by changing the vowel in the verb (changing *rise* to *rose*); (2) by adding **-n** or **-en** (changing *drive* to *driven*); (3) by making no change at all (*bet, bet, bet*); or (4) by changing the word completely (*bring* to *brought*).


## ACTIVITY 1-K: Verbs

Answer the following.

1. What is the difference between the past forms of a regular verb and an irregular verb?

2. Give two examples of regular verbs.

3. Give two examples of irregular verbs.

Check your answers in Feedback 1-K at the end of this module, Then continue.

9

## Principal Parts of Common Irregular Verbs

Four principal parts of common irregular verbs are given in the following alphabetical list. Consult a good dictionary when you are in doubt about the principal parts of other irregular verbs. Learn the forms below and then do Activity 1-L.

| PRESENT | PAST | PAST PARTICIPLE | PRESENT PARTICIPLE |
|---------|------|-----------------|--------------------|
| begin | began | (have) begun | (are) beginning |
| break | broke | (have) broken | (are) breaking |
| bring | brought | (have) brought | (are) bringing |
| burst | burst | (have) burst | (are) bursting |
| choose | chose | (have) chosen | (are) choosing |
| come | came | (have) come | (are) coming |
| do | did | (have) done | (are) doing |
| drink | drank | (have) drunk | (are) drinking |
| drive | drove | (have) driven | (are) driving |
| eat | ate | (have) eaten | (are) eating |
| fly | flew | (have) flown | (are) flying |
| give | gave | (have) given | (are) giving |
| go | went | (have) gone | (are) going |
| know | knew | (have) known | (are) knowing |
| lend | lent | (have) lent | (are) lending |
| lose | lost | (have) lost | (are) losing |
| ride | rode | (have) ridden | (are) riding |
| run | ran | (have) run | (are) running |
| see | saw | (have) seen | (are) seeing |
| sing | sang | (have) sung | (are) singing |
| speak | spoke | (have) spoken | (are) speaking |
| swim | swam | (have) swum | (are) swimming |
| take | took | (have) taken | (are) taking |
| throw | threw | (have) thrown | (are) throwing |
| write | wrote | (have) written | (are) writing |

## ACTIVITY 1-L: Irregular Verbs

Complete the sentence by supplying the correct past or past participle of the verb indicated.

1. *begin*  I had already _____ to write the memo.

2. *come*  He _____ to the meeting at 10 A.M.

3. *choose*  Has everyone _____ a conference hour?

4. *do*  Norman _____ the work on the computer.

5. *break*  He has _____ his new keyboard.

6. *burst*  The test tube had _____ from intense heat.

7. *do*  They _____ what was required by the job.

8. *burst*  The automobile tire _____ yesterday.

9. *bring*  Have you _____ your lunch?

10. *come*  He had _____ from the other office.

11. *drink*  Have you _____ a cup of coffee yet?

12. *go*  He has _____ to the meeting in Boston.

13. *give*  Don _____ him the check last month.

14. *fly*  He could have _____ to New York in three hours.

15. *drive*  We have _____ the company car.

16. *go*  When the snowstorm came, everyone _____ home early.

17. *speak*  Have you _____ to your supervisor yet?

18. *sing*  The trio has _____ at our meetings many times.

19. *know*  We found that only one _____ the correct procedure.

20. *ride*  A member of the firm has _____ over to see the new property.

21. *see*  Dr. Allen _____ him at the seminar.

22. *take*  She should have _____ the lab reports with her.

23. *swim*  I could not have _____ that distance without help.

24. *throw*  The car swerved and _____ everyone out.

25. *write*  His boss has _____ several reports on this product.

26. *bring*  He should have _____ the safety reports to the conference.

27. *eat*  Last night we _____ at the new restaurant.

28. *lend*  He _____ me his microscope for the experiment.

29. *lose*  We almost _____ our blueprints.

30. *eat*  I should have _____ earlier.

**Check your answers in Feedback 1-L at the end of this module. If you missed any, review the list of Principal Parts before going on.**

## Six Confusing Irregular Verbs

The following pairs of irregular verbs require special attention because they are especially troublesome. First of all, learn the six verbs, their meanings, and their principal parts.

| Present | Past | Past Participle With Helper | Present Participle With Helper | Meaning |
|---------|------|----------------------------|-------------------------------|---------|
| lie<br>lay | lay<br>laid | have lain<br>have laid | are lying<br>are laying | *to recline, rest*<br>*to put, place something* (takes a direct object) |
| sit<br><br>set | sat<br><br>set | have sat<br><br>have set | are sitting<br><br>are setting | *to take a sitting position, to rest in a chair*<br>*to place something* (takes a direct object) |
| rise<br><br>raise | rose<br><br>raised | have risen<br><br>have raised | are rising<br><br>are raising | *to go upward on one's own power*<br>*to lift something; to bring up; to increase in amount* (takes a direct object) |

From the definitions, you will notice that the second verb in each pair (**lay, set, raise**) is a verb of motion that shows *action done to "something."* In a sentence, this "something" will be a *direct object*—a noun that follows the verb and receives the action of the verb. The direct object answers the question "whom?" or "what?" after the verb.

### Direct Object Test

To find out if the verb has a direct object, ask the question "what?" or "whom?" after the verb.

EXAMPLES

Helen laid the book on the table.
   **Laid** is the verb. Laid *what?*
   Laid *book—book* is the object.

The landlord raised my rent.
> **Raised** is the verb. Raised *what?*
> Raised *rent—rent* is the object.

Jim lay down to rest.
> **Lay** is the verb. Lay *what?*
> There is no answer—no direct object in this sentence.

All forms of the verbs **lay, set,** and **raise** can take a direct object. Don't be confused by **lay** (the past form of **lie**), which cannot take a direct object, as we saw in the example "Jim lay down to rest."

When in doubt about the correct form of these troublesome verbs, try the direct object test. It is an easy way to settle the issue.

**Synonym Test**

A second test you can try is substituting the synonym (meaning) of the word in the sentence. Decide which meaning of the troublesome verb fits in the sentence (*rest* or *put? go upward* or *lift?*). Put the synonym in the sentence. Then check the chart to see which form of the verb to use.

EXAMPLES

| | |
|---|---|
| SYNONYM: | I *reclined* on the couch all afternoon. |
| CORRECT VERB: | I **lay** on the couch all afternoon. |
| SYNONYM: | The custodian *lifted* the window. |
| CORRECT VERB: | The custodian **raised** the window. |

When in doubt, the synonym test can help you decide which verb fits the meaning. Of course you must also use the correct *tense* form of the verb (present, past, past with helper, etc.).

## ACTIVITY 1-M: Six Confusing Irregular Verbs

Two verb forms are given in parentheses. Read each sentence carefully and underline the correct verb form. (Be sure the tense fits the meaning of the sentence.) Apply the direct object test and the synonym test.

1. Where did you (lie/lay) the blueprint?
2. The student nurse (rose/raised) a question concerning medication.
3. He asked the technician to (sit/set) the microscope on the counter.
4. The architect had (lain/laid) the drawing in its proper place.
5. When she finished the book, she (rose/raised) from her chair.
6. The custodian (rose/raised) the defective window.
7. Mary was thinking how nice it would be to (lie/lay) on the beach instead of (sitting/setting) in the office.
8. (Sit/Set) the computer on the table next to the desk.
9. Please (sit/set) the T-square on the drawing board when you are finished.

10. We asked the electronics technician to (rise/raise) the amperage.

11. John was asked to (rise/raise) money for an immunization clinic in Los Angeles.

12. In measuring the plot, he had to read the figures on the chart that (lay/laid) on the ground.

13. Andy (rose/raised) the shade after the film was over.

14. Bill (sat/set) at the desk for two hours without getting up.

15. Temperatures will (rise/raise) as summer progresses.

Check your responses in Feedback 1-M at the end of this module. If your responses were correct, proceed to Activity 1-N. If you missed any, review Six Confusing Irregular Verbs (pages 12–13) before proceeding.

## ACTIVITY 1-N: Six Confusing Irregular Verbs

Insert the correct form of the verbs indicated. Apply the direct object test and the synonym test. (Be sure to use the proper tense of the verb, according to the time expressed in the sentence.)

*Lie* or *Lay*

1. I _____ down on the sofa when I am tired.

2. Right now I am _____ on the sofa.

3. Yesterday I _____ on the sofa until noon.

4. All afternoon I have _____ on the sofa.

5. Yesterday I was _____ on the sofa when you called.

6. Where should I _____ the bricks for the foundation?

7. Right now I am _____ the bricks for the foundation.

8. Yesterday I _____ the bricks for the foundation.

9. All afternoon I have _____ the bricks for the foundation.

10. Yesterday I was _____ the bricks for the foundation.

*Sit* or *Set*

11. May I _____ on the chair?

12. Right now I am _____ on the chair.

13. Yesterday I _____ on the chair by the window.

14. All afternoon I have _____ on the chair.

15. Yesterday I was _____ on the chair.

16. Today I can't _____ the menus on the tables.

17. Right now I am _____ the menus on the tables.

18. Yesterday I _____ the menus on the tables.

19. All afternoon I _____ menus on the tables.

20. Yesterday I was _____ menus on the tables.

*Rise* or *Raise*

21. Watch the weather balloons _____ in the air.

22. Right now the weather balloons are _____ in the air.

23. Yesterday the weather balloons _____ in the air.

24. All afternoon the weather balloons have _____ in the air.

25. Yesterday the weather balloons were _____ in the air.

26. Please _____ the window.

27. Right now I am _____ the window.

28. Yesterday I _____ the window.

29. All afternoon I have _____ and lowered the window.

30. Yesterday I was _____ the window every hour.

Check your responses in Feedback 1-N at the end of this module. If you missed any, review Six Confusing Irregular Verbs, the Direct Object Test, and the Synonym Test. Then proceed to Activity 1-O.

## ACTIVITY 1-O: Six Confusing Irregular Verbs

Fill in the chart below with the correct forms of the verbs indicated. Commit the chart to memory, and you will always know which form to use.

In the sentences that follow, replace the synonyms in italics with the correct form of the verb from the chart.

| Present | Past | Past Participle | Present Participle |
|---------|------|-----------------|--------------------|
| sit (*rest*) | | | |
| set (*put*) | | | |
| lie (*rest, recline*) | | | |
| lay (*put*) | | | |
| rise (*go up*) | | | |
| raise (*lift up*) | | | |

EXAMPLE

*set, laid*      The architect *put* the drawing tools on the table.

_____ 1. The nurse asked the patient to *rest* in the wheel-chair, but she was already *reclining* in bed.

_____ 2. Please *put* your printout on the table.

_____ 3. The hot air *went up* to the ceiling.

_____ 4. The secretary *remained seated* at his desk all day.

_____ 5. Have you *put* the ledger on the desk?

_____ 6. The printout has *rested* on the desk all day.

_____ 7. I *put* it there myself.

_____ 8. The weather balloon has *gone up* above the trees.

_____ 9. The athlete *lifted* the weights up over his head.

_____ 10. The nurse had *put* the syringe on the nightstand.

Check your responses in Feedback 1-O at the end of this module. If you missed any, check with your instructor before going on to Activity 1-P. If all your answers were correct, proceed to Activity 1-P.

## ACTIVITY 1-P: Writing Sentences with Confusing Irregular Verbs

On separate paper, write sentences using the following verbs.

1. lie
2. laid
3. lay (*present tense*)
4. lain
5. sat

6. sit
7. set (*past tense*)
8. raise
9. rose
10. rise

Check your sentences with your instructor, who will then give you Test A or extra practice if you need it.

## *FEEDBACK FOR MODULE 1*

**Feedback 1-A**

1. made
2. typed
3. cleaned, oiled
4. entered
5. assists

6. offers
7. extracts
8. work
9. saved
10. hurts

## Feedback 1-B

1. sold
2. drew
3. prefers
4. installed
5. stopped
6. saves
7. assembled
8. sold
9. transferred
10. aligned

## Feedback 1-D

1. is
2. is
3. are
4. appeared
5. seemed
6. are
7. seem
8. remained
9. taste
10. felt

## Feedback 1-E

1. is
2. seem
3. appears
4. tastes
5. smells
6. was
7. feels
8. is
9. am
10. became

## Feedback 1-G

1. L—are
2. A—suggests
3. A—supports
4. L—were
5. L—seems
6. L—looks
7. A—occur
8. A—causes
9. L—appears
10. A—fell

## Feedback 1-H

1. L—are
2. A—sampled
3. A—provides
4. A—affected
5. L—are
6. L—seems
7. A—listened
8. L—felt
9. A—carried
10. A—prepared

## Feedback 1-I

1. is covering
2. may have done
3. were planning
4. has written
5. has proofread
6. are making

17

7. will complete

9. is doing

8. should have been done

10. must attend

## Feedback 1-K

1. The past forms of regular verbs end in -d or -ed. Irregular verbs form their past in other ways.
2. Any verb ending in -d or -ed in the past tense (played, worked, called, looked, etc.).
3. Any verb which does not end in -d or -ed in the past (swam, took, hit, wrote, brought, drove, slept, etc.).

## Feedback 1-L

| | | |
|---|---|---|
| 1. begun | 11. drunk | 21. saw |
| 2. came | 12. gone | 22. taken |
| 3. chosen | 13. gave | 23. swum |
| 4. did | 14. flown | 24. threw |
| 5. broken | 15. driven | 25. written |
| 6. burst | 16. went | 26. brought |
| 7. did | 17. spoken | 27. ate |
| 8. burst | 18. sung | 28. lent |
| 9. brought | 19. knew | 29. lost |
| 10. come | 20. ridden | 30. eaten |

## Feedback 1-M

To help you understand the answers, the meaning is given in parentheses.

1. lay (*put*)
2. raised (*brought up*)
3. set (*put*)
4. laid (*put*)
5. rose (*got up*)
6. raised (*lifted*)
7. lie (*recline*) sitting (*in a chair*)
8. set (*put*)
9. set (*put*)
10. raise (*increase*)
11. raise (*take up a collection*)
12. lay (*rested*)
13. raised (*lifted*)
14. sat (*stayed seated*)
15. rise (*go up*)

## Feedback 1-N

| | | |
|---|---|---|
| 1. lie | 6. lay | 11. sit |
| 2. lying | 7. laying | 12. sitting |
| 3. lay | 8. laid | 13. sat |
| 4. lain | 9. laid | 14. sat |
| 5. lying | 10. laying | 15. sitting |

| | | |
|---|---|---|
| 16. set | 21. rise | 26. raise |
| 17. setting | 22. rising | 27. raising |
| 18. set | 23. rose | 28. raised |
| 19. set | 24. risen | 29. raised |
| 20. setting | 25. rising | 30. raising |

**Feedback 1-O**

| Present | Past | Past Participle | Present Participle |
|---|---|---|---|
| sit | sat | sat | sitting |
| set | set | set | setting |
| lie | lay | lain | lying |
| lay | laid | laid | laying |
| rise | rose | risen | rising |
| raise | raised | raised | raising |

| | | |
|---|---|---|
| 1. sit—lying | | 6. lain, sat |
| 2. lay, set | | 7. laid, set |
| 3. rose | | 8. risen |
| 4. sat | | 9. raised |
| 5. laid, set | | 10. laid, set |

19

# MODULE 2

# Adjectives and Adverbs

OBJECTIVE: In this module you will learn the function of two types of describing words, the adjective and the adverb.

Upon completion of this module, you will be able:

To identify the function of the adjective and the adverb in the sentence.

To use the comparison process for adjectives and adverbs.

Here are eight rules that will help you to use adjectives correctly.

**Rule 1.** *Adjectives describe or modify nouns and pronouns.* They answer certain questions.

EXAMPLES

| | |
|---|---|
| *What kind?* | The **efficient** secretary was hired yesterday. |
| *Which one?* | **That** system is very simple. |
| *How many?* | **Six** men attended the meeting. |
| *How much?* | **Some** coffee was left for our break. |
| | We bought **enough** typing paper for five reports. |

**Rule 2.** *Adjectives usually come before the words they modify.*

EXAMPLE

**The new** typewriter produces **clear** print.

Occasionally, you may use adjectives *after* the word they modify for emphasis or variety. Set these adjectives off by commas.

EXAMPLES

The bank, **old** and **unpainted,** was finally rebuilt.
Billing records, **corporate** or **personal,** are stored in our computer.

**Rule 3.** *The adjectives* **a, an,** *and* **the** *are called articles.* Use **a** before words beginning with a consonant sound and **an** before words beginning with a vowel sound. Go strictly by *sound,* not by whether the word begins with a consonant or vowel.

EXAMPLES

| | | |
|---|---|---|
| **an** egg | **a** factory | **the** keyboard |
| **an** hour (*h* is silent) | **an** upper berth | **the** report |
| **a** union (consonant *y* sound) | **an** envelope | **the** meeting |
| **an** onion | **an** honor | **the** blueprint |

**Rule 4.** **This, that, these,** *and* **those** *may be used as adjectives to point out or identify a particular noun.* They agree in number and are placed directly before

the noun they modify. Use **this** and **that** before a singular noun; use **these** and **those** before a plural noun.

EXAMPLES

| *Singular* | *Plural* |
|---|---|
| this kind | these kinds |
| that type | those types |
| this company | these companies |
| that office | those offices |

Note that a word in a prepositional phrase (a group of words beginning with a preposition and ending with its object—see Module 3) does not change the use of **this, that, these,** or **those.**

EXAMPLES

this kind (of berry) (*singular*)
these kinds (of flour) (*plural*)
that type (of materials) (*singular*)
those types (of material) (*plural*)

**Rule 5.** *Some indefinite pronouns, such as* **each, one, any, many, some,** *and* **all,** *can be used either as adjectives or as pronouns.* As adjectives they are followed by a noun. As pronouns they are not followed by a noun. (*Indefinite* pronouns do not refer to a specific person, place, or thing.)

EXAMPLES

Noun

ADJECTIVE:   **Each** task will be completed in time.

PRONOUN:   **Each** will be completed in time. (The noun *task* has been replaced by the pronoun *each.*)

Noun

ADJECTIVE:   **Many** typists are needed.

PRONOUN:   **Many** are needed. (The noun *typists* has been replaced by the pronoun *many.*)

**Rule 6.** *Two or more consecutive adjectives may be used to modify the same noun. These adjectives are called* **coordinate adjectives.** Notice the punctuation. Commas are placed between the adjectives *but not between the final adjective and the noun.* (If the word "and" makes sense in place of the comma, you need the comma. Also, if you can logically reverse the adjectives, you need the comma.)

EXAMPLES

She is **an industrious, efficient, hard-working** bookkeeper.

He is engaged in **dangerous, exciting** work.

**Rule 7.** *Adjectives are often used after linking verbs.* You will remember that linking verbs do not show action; they *link* the subject to a word that follows the verb. The most common linking verbs are listed below. (For more about linking verbs, see Module 1, Part II.)

<table>
<tr><td colspan="4" align="center">LINKING VERBS</td></tr>
<tr><td>act</td><td>feel</td><td>remain</td><td>sound</td></tr>
<tr><td>appear</td><td>grow</td><td>seem</td><td>stay</td></tr>
<tr><td>be (is, am, etc.)</td><td>look</td><td>smell</td><td>taste</td></tr>
<tr><td>become</td><td></td><td></td><td></td></tr>
</table>

In the following pattern, the adjective tells something about the subject.

$$S \leftarrow LV - ADJ$$

EXAMPLES

        S   LV Adj
The secretary is <u>late.</u>

        S   LV  Adj
The system is <u>complete.</u>

        S   LV  Adj
The test seems <u>easy.</u>

      S   LV  Adj
He feels <u>better.</u>

        S   LV   Adj
The coffee smells <u>good.</u>

Sometimes, as in the pattern below, another word comes between the linking verb and the adjective. That word is usually an adverb, which describes the adjective.

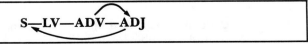

$$S \leftarrow LV - ADV - ADJ$$

EXAMPLES

        S    LV Adv Adj

The secretary is *very* late. (*Very* is an adverb modifying the adjective *late*.)

        S    LV  Adv Adj

The test seems *very* easy.

        S   LV Adv    Adj

The system is *not* complete.

   S   LV   Adv   Adj

He feels *much* better.

       S    LV    Adv     Adj

The coffee smells *extremely* good.

The sense verbs (**feel, smell, look, taste, sound**) are often followed by an adjective. However, sense verbs can also be used as action verbs. When used as action verbs, it is incorrect to use an adjective. (See the Linking Verb Test on pp. 4–5.)

EXAMPLES

                        Adj

LINKING:   You look *sharp* in that outfit.

                        Adv

ACTION:   You should look *sharply* before you plunge in.

An action verb (or a sense verb when it is used to show action) is modified by an adverb, not an adjective.

**Rule 8.** *Nouns can sometimes function as adjectives when they are used to modify other nouns.*

EXAMPLES

I handed in the *book* report.
The *computer* programmer worked on the new program.

---

## ACTIVITY 2-A: Adjectives

---

Underline each word that is used as an adjective. Then draw an arrow to the noun it describes or modifies.

1. Many typists are needed to complete the hard work.
2. The tired nurse was required to chart relevant information.
3. New blueprints were drawn for each of the three architects.
4. Old, broken equipment was to be replaced.
5. The new technician reported all vitally important data to the supervisor.
6. The retired owner of the three motels was honored at a delicious dinner last night.
7. Each supervisor was required to write monthly reports.
8. The new complex computer system is difficult to understand.
9. Report valid test results immediately to the supervisor.
10. A large envelope was mailed without a complete address.

Check your responses in Feedback 2-A at the end of this module. If your responses were correct, proceed to Part II. If you missed any, review Part I; then do Activity 2-B.

## ACTIVITY 2-B: Adjectives

Underline all words used as adjectives.

1. She was in a carefree, gay mood while working on the new plan.
2. These ten processors are in good condition.
3. More people were hired than we expected.
4. Please consider all applicants before the final decision is made.
5. Very old records can be found in the department files.
6. The young, highly educated man was the first one to be promoted.
7. Inform the employees that the newly repaved lot is ready for immediate use.
8. The new green machine in the business office will be used to ease the transmitting of existing records.
9. Control systems are used many times to prevent an excessive buildup of unusable inventory.
10. An introductory tour of the recently enlarged facilities will be scheduled for all new employees.

Check your responses in Feedback 2-B at the end of this module. If your responses were correct, proceed to Part II. If you missed any, review them with your instructor before proceeding.

## PART II: ADVERBS

These four rules will help you to avoid errors in using adverbs.

**Rule 1.** *The adverb modifies or describes a verb, an adjective, or another adverb.*

EXAMPLES

a. *Modifying a verb:*
He speaks **cheerfully.** (The adverb **cheerfully** describes the verb **speaks.** It tells *how* he performs the action.)

b. *Modifying an adjective:*
He speaks in an **exceedingly** cheerful fashion. (The adverb **exceedingly** modifies the adjective **cheerful.** It does not tell *how* he speaks, but *how* cheerful.)

c. *Modifying another adverb:*
He speaks **very cheerfully.** (The adverb **very** modifies the adverb **cheerfully. Cheerfully** tells how he speaks. **Very** tells how **cheerfully** he speaks.)

**Rule 2.** *Adverbs often answer the questions* **when, where, how, how much,** *or* **how often.**

EXAMPLES

| | |
|---|---|
| *When?* | The board met **recently.** |
| *Where?* | John sat **there** in the office. |
| *How?* | Ellen works **fast.** |
| *How much?* | This faucet leaks **slightly.** |
| *How often?* | John drove to town **frequently.** |

**Rule 3.** *Most adverbs are formed by adding* **-ly** *to the adjective form.*

EXAMPLES

ADJECTIVES: swift, slow, warm, cold
ADVERBS: swiftly, slowly, warmly, coldly

*Note:* A number of adjectives ending in **-y** change the **-y** to **-i** before the **-ly** ending of the adverb: **happy** → **happily; easy** → **easily; merry** → **merrily,** etc.

The ending **-ly** is not always the sign of an adverb. Many adverbs do not end in **-ly.**

Examples: **very, much, little, almost, often, there,** etc.

Some *adjectives* end in **-ly:**

EXAMPLES

The **friendly** salesman sold a lovely quilt to an **ugly, lonely** tourist.

Note also that sometimes the adverb and the corresponding adjective have the same form:

EXAMPLES

He had a **fast** grip on the pen. (The adjective **fast** modifies the noun *grip*, answering the question what kind?)

ADVERB:

He held **fast** to the pen. (The adverb **fast** modifies the verb *held* and answers the question held how?)

To distinguish between adjectives and adverbs, use this chart:

| | *Modify:* | *Answer the question:* | |
|---|---|---|---|
| ADJECTIVES | nouns<br>pronouns | what kind?<br>which one? | how much?<br>how many? |
| ADVERBS | verbs<br>adjectives<br>other adverbs | how?<br>where?<br>when? | how much?<br>how often? |

**Rule 4.** *The following words always function as adverbs:*

| ADVERBS | | | |
|---|---|---|---|
| not | very | quite | too |
| never | often | seldom | always |

## ACTIVITY 2-C: Adverbs

Underline each adverb and draw an arrow to the word it modifies or describes.

1. Write all the results accurately and neatly.
2. The police officer slowly approached the quiet man.
3. The committee met recently and quickly discussed the proposal.
4. Slowly pour the solution into the beaker.
5. The newly appointed foreman shouted loudly to his men.
6. Mr. Greer was formerly employed at Sears.
7. He was not very well prepared for the meeting.
8. He is late for work quite often.
9. Jane was very excited about her job.
10. Tilt the vial slightly so that the liquid will flow evenly.

Check your responses in Feedback 2-C at the end of this module. If your responses were correct, proceed to Part III. If you missed any, review Part II; then do Activity 2-D.

## ACTIVITY 2-D: Adverbs

Underline all adverbs.

1. She was in a serious mood while working diligently on the new plan.
2. These typewriters are in extremely good condition.
3. More people have been hired lately than we ever expected.
4. Please consider carefully each applicant before we finally make a decision.
5. Billing records can be found easily in the updated files.
6. The highly educated man was the first one to be promoted.
7. Inform the employees soon that the newly repaved parking lot is ready for immediate use.
8. The very heavy machine in the business office will be used easily in the transmitting of existing records.
9. Control systems are often used to prevent an excessively unusable inventory.
10. Fortunately, a tour of the vastly enlarged facilities will be scheduled later for all new employees.

Check your responses in Feedback 2-D at the end of this module. If your responses were correct, proceed to Part III. If you missed any, check with your instructor before proceeding.

# PART III: "GOOD" AND "WELL"

Two very common words that are often misused are **good** and **well**. As a general rule, use **good** as an adjective; use **well** as an adverb except when it means "in good health."

**Rule 1.** **Good** *is usually an adjective.* It precedes a noun or follows a linking verb.

EXAMPLES

He has a **good** skill.
       Adj Noun

He is **good** in accounting.      The rain felt **good**.
  LV Adj                LV  Adj

**Rule 2.** **Well** *is usually an adverb that describes* how.

EXAMPLES

He speaks **well**. Grapes grow **well** here.
She supervises **well**. They are doing **well**.

**Rule 3.** *When* **well** *means "in good health," it is an adjective and goes with a linking verb.*

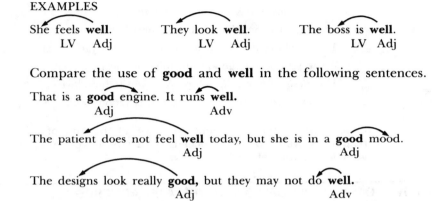

EXAMPLES

She feels **well**.    They look **well**.    The boss is **well**.
  LV  Adj        LV  Adj           LV  Adj

Compare the use of **good** and **well** in the following sentences.

That is a **good** engine. It runs **well**.
       Adj                Adv

The patient does not feel **well** today, but she is in a **good** mood.
                     Adj                       Adj

The designs look really **good,** but they may not do **well**.
                  Adj                       Adv

---

## ACTIVITY 2-E: Good–Well

Underline the correct word and draw an arrow to the word it describes.

1. Because of the move, Sam had to quit a (good/well) job.
2. Each secretary must write and type (well/good).
3. I can type (good/well) if the typewriter works (good/well).
4. If you speak (well/good), you will get the job.
5. The mechanic noticed that the car did not run (good/well).
6. She was late for the meeting because she did not feel (well/good).
7. The new foreman works (good/well) with his men.
8. The staff members ate at Brown's, where the food was (good/well) and prepared (good/well).
9. The nurse told the patient that his pulse was (well/good) and he looked (good/well).
10. The new machine runs (good/well).

Check your responses in Feedback 2-E at the end of this module. If your responses were correct, proceed to Part IV. If you missed any, review Part III; then proceed to Activity 2-F.

## ACTIVITY 2-F: Good–Well

Underline the correct word.

1. She was in a (good/well) mood while typing the memo.
2. These new typewriters are in (good/well) condition.
3. Consider (good/well) each applicant.
4. Personnel records are found easily in files that are kept (good/well).
5. The applicant was educated (good/well).
6. The new parking lot is in (good/well) shape.
7. The machine in the business office works (good/well).
8. We were given a (good/well) tour of the new facility.
9. The new schedule for employees works (good/well).
10. Nurses must learn to give injections (good/well).

Check your responses in Feedback 2-F at the end of this module. If your responses were correct, proceed to Part IV. If you missed any, check with your instructor before proceeding.

## PART IV: COMPARISON OF ADJECTIVES AND ADVERBS

Adjectives and adverbs have degrees of comparison: the positive, the comparative, and the superlative. The positive (base form) describes *one* entity; the comparative is used when comparing *two;* the superlative is used when comparing *three or more.*

EXAMPLES

Frank drafted **new** designs. (*positive*)
His designs are **newer** than Henry's. (*comparative*)
Frank and Henry's designs are **the newest** in the department. (*superlative*)

**Comparison of Adjectives**

The following table shows the positive, comparative, and superlative forms of a few adjectives.

| POSITIVE | COMPARATIVE | SUPERLATIVE |
|----------|-------------|-------------|
| fast | faster | fastest |
| slow | slower | slowest |
| fine | finer | finest |
| happy | happier | happiest |
| careful | more (less) careful | most (least) careful |
| beautiful | more (less) beautiful | most (least) beautiful |

To form the comparative degree, add **-er** or use the words **more** or **less.** For the superlative, add **-est** or use **most** or **least.** In general, long adjectives (over two syllables) do not use **-er** or **-est.** Note that the article **the** signals the superlative in many cases.

Here are some adjectives that are irregular in form:

| POSITIVE | COMPARATIVE | SUPERLATIVE |
|---|---|---|
| good, well | better | best |
| little | less | least |
| much, many | more | most |
| bad | worse | worst |

### Comparison of Adverbs

The following table shows the comparative and superlative forms of several common adverbs. Note that **fast** may function as an adjective as well as an adverb.

| POSITIVE | COMPARATIVE | SUPERLATIVE |
|---|---|---|
| fast | faster | fastest |
| slowly | more (less) slowly | most (least) slowly |
| promptly | more (less) promptly | most (least) promptly |
| carefully | more (less) carefully | most (least) carefully |
| easily | more (less) easily | most (least) easily |

---

### ACTIVITY 2-G: Comparison

Underline the correct degree of comparison.

1. Pat is the (faster/fastest) typist in the office.
2. He spoke (more calmly/most calmly) to his employees than did Ted.
3. That experiment was (more difficult/most difficult) than the last one.
4. Of all the replies, his was the (more prompt/most prompt).
5. Mary was (more dependable/most dependable) than Rose.
6. Who is the (fastest/faster) one to take dictation?
7. The assistant was the (most prompt/more prompt) to answer calls.

8. These results must be tallied (most carefully/more carefully) than all the other ones.

9. Employees who have had the vaccine are (least/less) susceptible to the disease than those who have not had the vaccine.

10. My new job requires more work, and therefore allows me (less/least) time to relax.

Check your responses in Feedback 2-G at the end of this module. If your responses were correct, proceed to Activity 2-I. If you missed any, review Part IV; then do Activity 2-H.

## ACTIVITY 2-H: Comparison

Underline the correct degree of comparison.

1. Jim is the (more efficient/most efficient) of all the electricians.
2. The boss shouted (more loudly/most loudly) than before.
3. The lab results were the (more impressive/most impressive) of all the data.
4. Of the two truck drivers, Sam is (weaker/weakest).
5. Kate was (more effective/most effective) as a receptionist than Belinda.
6. Who is the (faster/fastest) typist in all the offices?
7. The applicant who got the job was (more prompt/most prompt) than his colleague.
8. Evaluate the results (more carefully/most carefully) than you did last time.
9. Molly received the (fewest/fewer) responses of all the graduates to her letter of application.
10. There is (less/least) time for coffee breaks.

Check your responses in Feedback 2-H at the end of this module. If your responses were correct, proceed to Activity 2-I. If you missed any, check with your instructor before proceeding.

## ACTIVITY 2-I: Identification of Adjectives and Adverbs

Identify the italicized word as an adjective (Adj) or an adverb (Adv).

1. The *elderly* patient looks *well* today.
2. *Any* suggestion will be read and considered *immediately.*
3. Our results will be evaluated *quickly* by the *three* technicians.
4. The data machine will function *correctly* when the material is fed *properly* into it.
5. He *recently* compiled the data and wrote a *lengthy* report.
6. Mr. Bonner will respond *adequately* to your *last* question.
7. That man is *less likely* to be promoted to foreman than his *young* co-worker.

8. The building, *dilapidated* and *crumbling,* is to be razed before the new parking lot can be constructed.

9. The *new* blueprint looked *good* to the architect.

10. Please return the *old* printouts to Mr. Grant's office before *late* afternoon.

Check your responses in Feedback 2-I at the end of this module. If your responses were correct, proceed to Activity 2-K. If you missed any, do Activity 2-J.

## ACTIVITY 2-J: Identification of Adjectives and Adverbs

Identify the italicized word as adjective (Adj) or adverb (Adv).

1. The *concrete* bridge was *sturdily* built.

2. *All* plans for the ceremony are being worked out *carefully.*

3. The statistics will be calculated *rapidly* by the *new* computer.

4. The boss was *very upset* about the breakdown.

5. A *skillful* technician is *seldom* unemployed for a *long* time.

6. Mr. Newton will call *later* in response to your *recent* message.

7. *Fringe* benefits should be *carefully* examined when a *new* job is being considered.

8. Marcy's job, *exciting* and *challenging,* has made her *very happy.*

9. The bridge appears *quite sturdy.*

10. The *noon* flight to Dulles Airport was *late.*

Check your responses in Feedback 2-J at the end of this module. If your responses were correct, proceed to Activity 2-K. If you missed any, check with your instructor before proceeding.

## ACTIVITY 2-K: Writing Sentences with Adjectives and Adverbs

On your own paper, write sentences as specified below.

1. Write one sentence using adjectives. Underline each adjective and draw an arrow to the word it describes.

2. Write one sentence using adverbs. Underline each adverb and draw an arrow to the word it describes.

3. Write one sentence with an adjective following a linking verb. Underline the adjective which follows the linking verb.

4. Write one sentence to show the correct use of *a* and *an.* Underline *a* and *an.*

5. With each of the following adjectives or adverbs, write a sentence showing a comparison.
   a. best
   b. better
   c. more
   d. worst

6. Write one sentence using *good* and one sentence using *well*.

Check your sentences with your instructor. If your sentences are acceptable, ask for Test A.

---

### *FEEDBACK FOR MODULE 2*

**Feedback 2-A**

1. *Many* typists
   *the hard* work
2. *The tired* nurse
   *relevant* information
3. *New* blueprints
   *the three* architects
4. *Old, broken* equipment
5. *The new* technician
   *all important* data
   *the* supervisor
6. *The retired* owner
   *the three* motels
   *a delicious* dinner
   *last* night
7. *Each* supervisor
   *monthly* reports
8. *The new complex computer difficult* system
9. *valid test* results
   *the* supervisor
10. *A large* envelope
    *a complete* address

**Feedback 2-B**

1. a, carefree, gay, the, new
2. These, ten, good
3. More
4. all, the, final
5. old, the, department
6. The, young, educated, the, first
7. the, the, repaved, ready, immediate
8. The, new, green, the, business, the, existing
9. Control, many, an, excessive, unusable
10. An, introductory, the, enlarged, all, new

**Feedback 2-C**

1. Write *accurately, neatly*
2. *slowly* approached
3. met *recently; quickly* discussed
4. *Slowly* pour
5. *newly* appointed; shouted *loudly*
6. *formerly* was employed
7. *not, well* prepared; *very* well
8. *quite* often; *often* late
9. *very* excited
10. Tilt *slightly;* flow *evenly*

34

**Feedback 2-D**

1. diligently
2. extremely
3. lately, ever
4. carefully, finally
5. easily
6. highly
7. soon, newly
8. very, easily
9. often, excessively
10. Fortunately, vastly, later

**Feedback 2-E**

1. *good* job
2. write, type *well*
3. type *well;* works *well*
4. speak *well*
5. run *well*
6. she *well* (in good health)
7. works *well*
8. *good* food; prepared *well*
9. *good* pulse; looked *well*. (**Note:** looked *good* is also correct. Either may be used as an adjective following the sense verb *look* when it is a linking verb.)
10. runs *well*

**Feedback 2-F**

1. *good* mood
2. *good* condition
3. consider *well*
4. kept *well*
5. educated *well*
6. *good* shape
7. works *well*
8. *good* tour
9. works *well*
10. give *well*

**Feedback 2-G**

1. fastest
2. more calmly
3. more difficult
4. most prompt
5. more dependable
6. fastest
7. most prompt
8. more carefully
9. less
10. less

**Feedback 2-H**

1. most efficient
2. more loudly
3. most impressive
4. weaker
5. more effective
6. fastest
7. more prompt
8. more carefully
9. fewest
10. less

**Feedback 2-I**

1. elderly (adj.)
   well (adj.)
2. Any (adj.)
   immediately (adv.)
3. quickly (adv.)
   three (adj.)
4. correctly (adv.)
   properly (adv.)
5. recently (adv.)
   lengthy (adj.)
6. adequately (adv.)
   last (adj.)

7. less (adv.)
   likely (adj.)
   young (adj.)
8. dilapidated (adj.)
   crumbling (adj.)

9. new (adj.)
   good (adj.)
10. old (adj.)
    late (adj.)

## Feedback 2-J

1. concrete (adj.)
   sturdily (adv.)
2. All (adj.)
   carefully (adv.)
3. rapidly (adv.)
   new (adj.)
4. very (adv.)
   upset (adj.)
5. skillful (adj.)
   seldom (adv.)
   long (adj.)

6. later (adv.)
   recent (adj.)
7. Fringe (adj.)
   carefully (adv.)
   new (adj.)
8. exciting (adj.)
   challenging (adj.)
   very (adv.)
   happy (adj.)
9. quite (adv.)
   sturdy (adj.)
10. noon (adj.)
    late (adj.)

# MODULE 3

# Phrases

OBJECTIVE: In this module you will learn to identify and use two kinds of phrases.

Upon completion of this module, you will be able:

To define a phrase.

To identify the prepositional phrase and its function in the sentence.

To identify the verbal phrase and its function in the sentence.

A phrase is a group of words serving as a single unit within a sentence and having the following characteristics:

1.  A phrase contains neither a subject nor a verb.
2.  A phrase cannot stand by itself as a grammatically complete sentence but must always be part of a sentence.

There are two kinds of phrases, *prepositional* and *verbal.*

## PART I: PREPOSITIONAL PHRASES

A prepositional phrase is a group of words that contains (1) a preposition, (2) the object of the preposition, which is very often a noun or pronoun, and (3) all modifiers of that object. Like all phrases, it is a part of a sentence, not a sentence in itself.

EXAMPLE

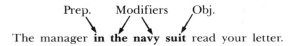

The manager **in the navy suit** read your letter.

In the prepositional phrase "in the navy suit," **in** is the preposition, **suit** is the object, and **the** and **navy** modify the object **suit.**

EXAMPLE

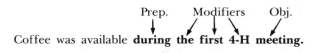

Coffee was available **during the first 4-H meeting.**

In the prepositional phrase "during the first 4-H meeting," **during** is the preposition; **meeting** is the object; and **the, first,** and **4-H** modify the object **meeting.**

*Remember that a word must have an object to be used as a preposition in a sentence.*

**Object Test**

To find out if a word has an object, ask "what?" or "whom?" after the word. If there is an answer, the word has an object.

EXAMPLES

**in the suit**
  (in *what?* in *suit—suit* is the object)
**during the meeting**
  (during *what?* during *meeting—meeting* is the object)

**for my employers**
>(for *whom?* for *employers—employers* is the object)

**He looked above.**
>(above *what?* There is no answer. There is no object.
>*Above* is not being used as a preposition here. It is an adverb.)

Study the following list of some of the more common prepositions. Learn to recognize them quickly so you can identify and use them in sentences.

## PREPOSITIONS

| | | | |
|---|---|---|---|
| about* | beneath | in* | throughout* |
| above | beside | inside | to |
| across | besides | into | toward* |
| after* | between | like | under |
| against | beyond | near* | underneath |
| along | but (*meaning* | of | until* |
| amid | "except") | off | unto |
| among | by* | on* | up |
| around* | down | outside | upon |
| at* | during* | over | with |
| before* | except | past* | within* |
| behind | for* | since* | without |
| below | from* | through* | |

Note: The asterisk (*) indicates prepositions that often begin a *time phrase;* that is, a phrase which answers the question "when?" For example: **about** ten o'clock, **in** the evening, **on** Tuesday.

Some prepositions consist of a combination of two or more words. The following examples are just a few of the many possibilities.

| | |
|---|---|
| accompanied by | in addition to |
| along with | in back of |
| as well as | in front of |
| because of | next to |
| by means of | together with |

## ACTIVITY 3-A: Prepositional Phrases

Underline the prepositional phrases in the sentences below.

1.  I heard about the position from my friend.

2. He moved the car into the shop for repairs.

3. A portrait of the company's founder hangs on the wall of her office to the left of her desk.

4. In the morning, we report for work at the factory.

5. He got the idea for his invention from the supervisor.

Check your answers in Feedback 3-A at the end of this module. If your responses were correct, proceed to Activity 3-C. If you missed any, review the list of prepositions and then do Activity 3-B.

## ACTIVITY 3-B: Prepositional Phrases

Underline the prepositional phrases in the sentences below.

1. The loose bolt fell under the machine.

2. The company's picnic is held every July in the park near the old grandstand.

3. The blueprints are in the top drawer of the gray filing cabinet.

4. The police officer stopped the car that was doing 65 in a 30-mile speed zone.

5. In spring, the horticulture department is busy with planting.

Check your answers in Feedback 3-B at the end of this module. If your responses were correct, proceed to Activity 3-C. If you missed any, review the list of prepositions again before doing Activity 3-C.

## ACTIVITY 3-C: Prepositional Phrases

Supply an appropriate prepositional phrase to complete the following sentence.

1. File the memo _____.

2. The car was stalled _____.

3. The business was located _____.

4. The house _____ was burned.

5. _____, we will write the report.

Check your answers with your instructor before proceeding to Activity 3-D.

## ACTIVITY 3-D: Writing Sentences with Prepositional Phrases

On your own paper, write five sentences using at least one prepositional phrase in each sentence. Underline all the prepositional phrases. Check your sentences with your instructor. Then proceed to Activity 3-E.

## ACTIVITY 3-E: Prepositional Phrases

Underline the ten prepositional phrases in the sentences below.

1. As we watched from the door of his office, we saw the executive.
2. The new computer in the office has been praised by the staff.
3. The retailers have postponed their meeting for three weeks.
4. The decision on the blueprints was made by the committee.
5. The office for the new president will be completed on time by the crew.

Check your answers in Feedback 3-E at the end of this module. If your responses were correct, proceed to Part II. If you missed any, review Part I before going on.


# PART II: VERBAL PHRASES

Like all phrases, a verbal phrase has neither a subject nor a verb. It cannot stand alone but must always be part of a sentence.

A verbal phrase is composed of a verbal, its object (if any), and its modifiers (if any). A verbal is a word that is derived from a verb but that does not function as a verb. There are three types of verbals: infinitives, participles, and gerunds.

---

### THREE TYPES OF VERBALS

(1) INFINITIVES: **"to" plus a verb**
Examples: *to go, to type, to write, to be,* etc.
Infinitives function as subject or as direct object.

(2) PARTICIPLES: **(a) Present Participles ("-ing" form)**
Examples: *going, singing, walking,* etc.
**(b) Past Participles**
Examples: *played, walked, given, heard, lent,* etc.
The participle form by itself, without a helper verb, functions as an adjective.

(3) GERUNDS: **"-ing" form of the verb used as a noun**
Examples: *swimming, fishing, hunting,* etc.

---

The following rules will help you recognize the three types of verbals. You will not have to know them by name. Remember that a verbal phrase does not contain the verb of the sentence. In the examples below, the verbals are underlined, and the verbs of the sentences are in bold type.

**Rule 1.** Present participles and gerunds are identical in form: both end in **-ing.** The difference is in their use.

EXAMPLES

Running **is** good exercise.

(Here running is a gerund, used as a subject of the sentence. It is a verbal, so there is no helping verb.)

He **was running** in the lab.

(**Was running** is the verb.)

The running water **filled** the beaker.

(Here *running* is a participle, used as an adjective modifying *water.*)

**Rule 2.** A participle (or participle phrase) functions as an *adjective* in a sentence. It modifies a noun or pronoun. (The arrow points to the noun modified by the underlined participle.)

EXAMPLES

The running water **has filled** the beaker.

The detective sitting in the car **has reported** for duty.

Standing high on a metal frame, the foreman **shouted** directions.

Having been filled with gas, the car **was** ready for the trip.

**Rule 3.** The past participle is made from the past tense of the verb; however, it is not being used as the verb in the sentence. It usually ends in a *d* or *ed,* such as **talked.** Some past forms of verbs are irregular, such as **sang** or **went.**

EXAMPLES

The Buick, sold yesterday, **was** in good condition.
Broken from mistreatment, the computer **was sent** away for repairs.
The report, written with accuracy, **revealed** many company strengths.

*Note:* There are no helping verbs in front of the verbals.

**Rule 4.** A verbal or verbal phrase that is a gerund must serve as a noun in a sentence. This noun may function as the *subject, direct object, subject complement,* or the *object of a preposition.*

EXAMPLES

Counseling juveniles **has become** my vocation.
    Subject

We **like** doing our work early.
      Direct Object

Through counseling, many students **determine** their job capabilities.
    Obj of Prep

**Rule 5.** A verbal phrase that is an infinitive may also serve as the *subject* or the *direct object* of a sentence.

EXAMPLES

To counsel a juvenile **requires** patience.
    Subject

We **like** to repair cars that need attention.
      Direct Object

*Note:* Do not confuse the infinitive, to + verb (as in **to walk**), with the prepositional phrase, to + noun (as in *to school*) or to + pronoun (as in *to him*).

---

**ACTIVITY 3-F: Verbal Phrases**

---

Circle the complete verb in each sentence so you won't confuse it with the verbal phrases. Then underline any verbal phrases that you spot. Do not worry about which type of verbal phrase you find. Simply look for the verbal signals: *to* + *verb*, **-ing** form without a helper, past form without a helper.

1. They were too timid to ask for more money.
2. Capturing their attention, the speaker referred to their problem areas.
3. Taking care, one can avoid errors.
4. The car, dented in the accident, was the plant manager's.
5. Believing in all their promises was hard for the new employee.
6. Walking quickly, he entered the conference room.
7. To read a report quickly can be a helpful skill.
8. Running a computer requires much skill.
9. Seeing the unsatisfactory results, he tried a new plan of attack.
10. He enjoyed running the machine alone.

Check your responses in Feedback 3-F at the end of this module. If your responses were correct, proceed to Activity 3-H. If you missed any, review the definitions of verbals in Part II and then proceed to Activity 3-G.

## ACTIVITY 3-G: Verbal Phrases

Circle the complete verbs in each sentence so that you won't confuse them with verbal phrases. Then underline any verbal phrases that you spot. Do not worry about which type of verbal phrases you find. Look for the verbal signals.

1. Calling the supervisor, the plant manager requested two more workers for the graveyard shift.
2. The police officers, seeing the speeding car, climbed into their car and drove after it.
3. Hearing the report, the social worker called the agency.
4. Determining the results was the job of the technician.
5. Experimenting with new chemicals can be a dangerous job.
6. To operate the machine can be difficult.
7. Mr. Smith enjoyed working throughout the summer.
8. Speaking with her partner, the president began the new project.
9. Rising early is not much fun for the worker.
10. He liked to calculate the results immediately.

Check your responses in Feedback 3-G at the end of this module. If your responses were correct proceed to Activity 3-H. If you missed any, review Part II before going on.

## ACTIVITY 3-H: Verbal and Prepositional Phrases

Circle the complete verbs in each sentence. Then underline and label all phrases: V for verbal and P for prepositional. (Some sentences contain more than one phrase.) The first sentence has been done as an example.

V

1. He (was) happy to hear the discussion.

2. The man with the briefcase is the applicant.
3. Organizing a conference, state or local, requires detailed plans.
4. Seeing the manager was a pleasant surprise.
5. Gaining her boss's approval was important to Jane.
6. Becoming an architect requires much dedication.
7. The supervisor speaking with the workers encouraged them to finish their job before noon.
8. She became an expert in social work through her job as a counselor in a summer camp.
9. Rising to a towering height, the construction looked beautiful.

10. For many years, the gap between the employer and the employee has been widening gradually.

Check your responses in Feedback 3-H at the end of this module. If your responses were correct, proceed to Activity 3-I. If you missed any, review Part II before proceeding.

## ACTIVITY 3-I: Verbal Phrases

Supply an appropriate verbal phrase to complete the following sentences.

1. He wanted _____.

2. _____, she spotted the accident.

3. His favorite hobbies are _____ and _____.

4. _____, she crossed the street.

5. I asked her _____.

Check your responses with your instructor before proceeding to Activity 3-J.

## ACTIVITY 3-J: Writing Sentences with Verbal Phrases

On your own paper, write five sentences, using at least one verbal phrase in each sentence. Underline each verbal phrase. Check your sentences with your instructor. Then proceed to Activity 3-K.

## ACTIVITY 3-K: Review

Circle the complete verbs. Then underline all phrases and label them in the blanks: P for prepositional or V for verbal.

1. ____ Ms. Banks, will you type an acceptance to the seminar chairman?

2. ____ Taking blood can be difficult.

3. ____ We seldom attend both of the meetings.

4. ____ At the building site, Mr. Blake noticed a broken glass.

5. ____ The employees are allowed to use the administrative lounge.

6. ____ The foremen were encouraged to speak their grievances.

7. ____ Drafting a new plan is difficult.

8. ____ The lawyer was asked to meet the judge later.

9. ____ To cater luncheons is hard work.

10. ____ The staff parking lot is near the main building.

Check your responses in Feedback 3-K at the end of this module. If your answers were correct, ask your instructor for Test A. If you missed any, ask your instructor for extra practice.

---

## FEEDBACK FOR MODULE 3

**Feedback 3-A**

1. about the position
   from my friend
2. into the shop
   for repairs
3. of the company's founder
   on the wall
   of her office
   to the left
   of her desk

4. In the morning
   for work
   at the factory
5. for his invention
   from the supervisor

**Feedback 3-B**

1. under the machine
2. in the park
   near the old grandstand
3. in the top drawer
   of the gray filing cabinet

4. in a 30-mile speed zone
5. In spring
   with planting

**Feedback 3-E**

1. from the door
2. of his office
3. in the office
4. by the staff
5. for three weeks

6. on the blueprints
7. by the committee
8. for the new president
9. on time
10. by the crew

**Feedback 3-F**

1. were *to ask for more money*
2. *Capturing their attention* referred
3. *Taking care* can avoid
4. *dented in the accident* was
5. *Believing in all their promises* was
6. *Walking quickly* entered
7. *To read a report quickly* can be
8. *Running a computer* requires
9. *Seeing the unsatisfactory results* tried
10. enjoyed *running the machine alone*

46

**Feedback 3-G**

1. *Calling the supervisor*  requested
2. *seeing the speeding car*  climbed *and*  drove
3. *Hearing the report*  called
4. *Determining the results*  was
5. *Experimenting with new chemicals*  can be
6. *To operate the machine*  can be
7. enjoyed  *working throughout the summer*
8. *Speaking with her partner*  began
9. *Rising early*  is
10. liked  *to calculate the results immediately*

**Feedback 3-H**

1. was  *to hear the discussion*  (V)
2. *with the briefcase*  (P) is
3. *Organizing a conference*  (V) requires
4. *Seeing the manager*  (V) was
5. *Gaining her boss's approval*  (V) was  *to Jane*  (P)
6. *Becoming an architect*  (V) requires
7. *speaking with the workers*  (V) encouraged  *to finish their job*  (V)  *before noon*  (P)
8. became  *in social work*  (P)  *through her job*  (P)  *as a counselor*  (P)  *in a summer camp*  (P)
9. *Rising to a towering height*  (V) looked
10. *For many years*  (P)  *between the employer and the employee*  (P) has been widening

**Feedback 3-K**

1. P  *to the seminar chairman*  will type
2. V  *Taking blood*  can be
3. P  *of the meetings*  attend
4. P  *At the building site*  noticed
5. V  *to use the administrative lounge*  are allowed
6. V  *to speak their grievances*  were encouraged
7. V  *Drafting a new plan*  is
8. V  *to meet the judge later*  was asked
9. V  *To cater luncheons*  is
10. P  *near the main building*  is

# MODULE 4

# Subject–Verb Agreement

OBJECTIVE: This module provides practical methods for checking subject–verb agreement, one of the most important aspects of good writing.

Upon completion of this module, you will be able:

To identify correct subject–verb agreement by applying practical methods of sentence analysis.

As the first step in mastering subject–verb agreement, you must be able to recognize the subject and the verb of a sentence. In Module 1 you learned about two types of verbs, *action* verbs and *linking* verbs, and you were shown how to recognize them in a sentence.

To find the *action* verb, ask yourself what word shows action, either physical or mental.

EXAMPLES

1. The paint spattered on the drawing board.
   (What word shows action? **Spattered** is the verb.)
2. The technician learned quickly.
   (What word shows action? **Learned** is the verb. Here the action is mental.)

To recognize a *linking* verb, remember that most linking verbs are forms of the verb **to be.** The forms **is, am, are, was, were** link the subject to another word in the sentence, usually a noun or an adjective (see Module 1, Part II, Linking Verbs).

3. I **was** a student. (**Was** links *I* with *student,* a noun.)
4. He **is** competent. (**Is** links *He* with *competent,* an adjective.)

Other verbs of being and verbs of the senses may also be linking verbs. When in doubt you can try the Linking Verb Test: Substitute **is** or **was** for the verb and see if the sentence still makes sense:

**Linking Verb Test**

The assignment **seems** difficult. (The assignment **is** difficult. Linking verb.)

The cake **tasted** good. (The cake **is** good. Linking verb.)

He **tasted** the cake. (He **is** the cake. Not logical; not a linking verb.)

**Subject Test**

Once you have located the verb, it is easy to find the subject. Try putting *Who* or *What* in front of the verb. The answer is your subject. It is usually a noun or pronoun. A noun names a person, place, or thing. A pronoun stands for a noun. Note that most subjects precede verbs. Now let's go back and do this with all the previous examples:

1. What **spattered?** The *paint* spattered. *Paint* is the subject.
2. Who **learned?** The *technician* learned. *Technician* is the subject.
3. Who **was?** *I* was. *I* is the subject.

4. Who **is?** *He* is. *He* is the subject.

5. What **seems?** The *assignment* seems. *Assignment* is the subject.

6. What **tasted?** The *cake* tasted. *Cake* is the subject. (Notice that no action is expressed here. The cake is not doing the tasting.)

## ACTIVITY 4-A: Recognizing Subjects and Verbs

Draw one line under the subject and two lines under the verb.

1. Your reports are due by Friday.
2. I attended the morning conference.
3. The technician went to the lab after lunch.
4. He gave a referral without telling the doctor.
5. The instrument is on the top shelf.
6. Her blueprints needed a few changes.
7. You need to survey the Ladd property.
8. Mr. Raymond requested all of the day shift to attend the meeting.
9. We asked your supervisor to give us a break before midnight.
10. The secretary typed four letters for Mrs. Gableton.

Check your responses in Feedback 4-A at the end of this module. If your responses were correct, proceed to Activity 4-C. If you missed any, review Part I and do Activity 4-B.

## ACTIVITY 4-B: Recognizing Subjects and Verbs

Draw one line under the subject and two lines under the verb.

1. Harry's drawing won the blue ribbon.
2. My secretary ordered new software.
3. The surveyor studied the landscape carefully.
4. The nurse took several vials of my blood.
5. They are Jane's foster parents.
6. The truck driver leased a new tractor-trailer.
7. He bought 50 shares of common stock.
8. We sharpened the blades on the lawnmowers.
9. I replaced the worn-out light switch.
10. A nurse took his temperature this morning.

Check your responses in Feedback 4-B at the end of this module. If your responses were correct, proceed to Activity 4-C. If you missed any, check with your instructor before proceeding.

**ACTIVITY 4-C: Writing Sentences Labeling Subjects and Verbs**

On your own paper, write six sentences, three of them using present tense action verbs and three of them with present tense linking verbs. Draw two lines under the verb. Check your sentences with your instructor. Then proceed to Part II.

## PART II: SUBJECT–VERB AGREEMENT

The subject and verb of a sentence must agree in person and number. In this module you are concerned only with agreement in *number* ("person" is discussed in Module 10). When we speak about "number" we are referring to the *singular* or the *plural*.

A *singular subject* requires a *singular verb*. ("Singular" refers to one.)

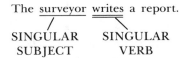

A *plural subject* requires a *plural verb*. ("Plural" refers to more than one.)

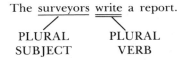

As a helpful guide, remember that all verbs in the third person singular, present tense, end in a single **s**: he *walks*, she *thinks*, it *shows*, he *has*, etc. The ending **s** on a verb signals that the verb is singular and requires a singular subject. The ending **s** on a subject, however, usually signals that the subject is plural and requires a plural verb, one that does not end in **s**. *Note:* This is usually a *present tense* problem, except for such past tense irregular verbs as **was.**

EXAMPLES

The student reports to the class.

S on the VERB indicates SINGULAR.

The students report to the class.

S on the SUBJECT indicates PLURAL.

51

Exceptions to this general guide include the following subjects, which are plural in form but take a singular verb.

EXAMPLES

Mumps is a highly contagious disease.
The waitress has been hired for the lunch shift.
My boss is a fair person.
Mathematics is harder than English for me.
Physics has to be taught well.
Economics is a complicated subject.

A company or corporation, even if it consists of many names, is considered a single body, and therefore requires a singular verb.

EXAMPLES

Williams, Wright, & Wilson is a law firm in Dover.
Chucker, Inc., is a large transportation company.

There are also certain nouns, known as *collective nouns,* which usually refer to a group but use a singular verb. You will learn more about collective nouns in Module 10.

EXAMPLES

The committee is meeting today.
The news is shocking.
The city council meets today.

## ACTIVITY 4–D: Subject–Verb Agreement

Some of the following sentences are incorrect because their subjects and verbs do not agree. Draw one line under the subject and two lines under the verb in each sentence; if the sentence is incorrect, cross out the verb and write the correct verb above it.

1. Mathematics are hard for many people.
2. The boss ride to the construction site daily.
3. The workers are ready to begin laying the bricks.
4. The Riker Company were to call back early this morning.
5. The hotel rooms was to be opened by Memorial Day weekend.
6. The employees were to attend the special program at noon.
7. The two nurses was to be on duty from 3 to 11 p.m.
8. Three people wants to be interviewed for the opening in the Accounting Department.

9. All our employees stays at motels on field trips.

10. Mr. Bruce were to conduct the special meeting for the technicians.

Check your responses in Feedback 4-D at the end of this module. If your responses were correct, proceed to Activity 4-F. If you missed any, review Part II and then do Activity 4-E.

### ACTIVITY 4-E: Subject–Verb Agreement

Some of the following sentences are incorrect because their subjects and verbs do not agree. Draw one line under the subject and two lines under the verb in each sentence; if the sentence is incorrect, cross out the verb and write the correct verb above it.

1. The duties was time-consuming.
2. The late news meets the deadline every day.
3. Allison, Merk & Mann plan to picnic at Crater Lake this year.
4. The whole system drain into the swamp.
5. The eastern farmers was dependent upon subsistence.
6. The computer operators needs to learn how to program the new IBM.
7. On every school day two crossing guards helps with the traffic.
8. Economics is interesting to most people.
9. The drawings show the details of the new addition to the building.
10. Good counseling are necessary to reduce delinquency.

Check your responses in Feedback 4-E at the end of this module. If your responses were correct, proceed to Activity 4-F. If you missed any, check them with your instructor before going on.

### ACTIVITY 4-F: Writing Sentences with Subject–Verb Agreement

On your own paper, write two sentences with singular subjects and two sentences with plural subjects. Use present tense verbs. Underline each subject once and each verb twice. Check your sentences with your instructor before proceeding to Part III.

## PART III: INTERFERING WORDS

When the verb directly follows its subject in a sentence, you will have little trouble making subject and verb agree. Your trouble may come when the subject and verb are separated by other words. Sometimes *prepositional phrases* come between the subject and its verb. Recall that the object of the preposition is a noun or a pronoun. Do not confuse this noun or pronoun with the subject of the sentence. Study the examples below. The subjects are underlined once, the verbs are underlined twice, and prepositional phrases are in parentheses.

EXAMPLES

The performance (of the secretaries) was excellent.
The decision (of the personnel managers) is final.
The supervisor (as well as the managers) was upset about the result.
The employer (together with the employees) does her best.
The President (along with the reporters) is on the way to Washington.

## ACTIVITY 4-G: Interfering Words

Draw one line under the subject and two lines under the verb. To help you locate the subject, put parentheses around the interfering prepositional phrases.

1. The construction of the new buildings was begun yesterday.
2. The computer, in addition to two printers, needs to be repaired.
3. A combination of these procedures is certain to succeed.
4. Mr. Long, together with his associates, attends every business meeting.
5. The firm of McCabe & Walston is able to print the survey results.
6. Politics, along with economics, is a complicated subject.
7. The young men on our shift are going for job interviews next week.
8. John, along with his two assistants, has a promotion to consider.
9. Jane, together with her sister, has a degree in Data Processing.
10. Your contribution, in addition to other people's, fosters the success of the project.

Check your responses in Feedback 4-G at the end of this module. If your responses were correct, proceed to Activity 4-I. If you missed any, review Part III and do Activity 4-H.

## ACTIVITY 4-H: Intefering Words

Draw one line under the subject and two lines under the verb. To help you locate the subject, put parentheses around the interfering prepositional phrases.

1. A secretary for an educational organization needs a broad vocabulary.
2. The interior designs of the house show details of historic value.
3. The engineer of the firm recommends choosing a site before planning a house.
4. The wiring in these houses doesn't meet the specifications.
5. A truck with two sets of dual rear wheels is built for heavy loads.
6. Her weekly articles in our local paper are quite interesting.

7. The serum for the new virus is available at the hospital.

8. Most prisons in the state need to be redesigned.

9. The larger hotels in Atlantic City offer several recreational activities.

10. A medical lab assistant at County Memorial Hospital is usually quite busy.

Check your responses in Feedback 4-H at the end of this module. If your responses were correct, proceed to Activity 4-I. If you missed any, check with your instructor before proceeding.

---

### ACTIVITY 4-I: Subject–Verb Agreement

Draw one line under the subject and two lines under the correct verb. In sentences with a prepositional phrase between the subject and the verb, put parentheses around the prepositional phrase.

1. Employees of the plant (is/are) on strike.

2. Clearness in oral and written communications (is/are) necessary to success.

3. His objections to the proposal (seem/seems) unreasonable.

4. Certain pieces of the equipment (need/needs) to be replaced often.

5. Her skill in dictation (appears/appear) to be her only positive asset.

6. The two therapy rooms (are/is) closed until next Wednesday.

7. Bob's drawing, together with his blueprints, (were/was) submitted for approval.

8. The charts (was/were) to be returned yesterday.

9. The nurses (record/records) the blood type for the doctor.

10. A reporter, because of training and experience, (reports/report) the facts accurately.

Check your responses in Feedback 4-I at the end of this module. If your responses were correct, proceed to Activity 4-J. If you missed any, review Part III before doing Activity 4-J.

---

### ACTIVITY 4-J: Writing Sentences with Interfering Words

On your own paper, write three sentences whose subjects and verbs are separated by a prepositional phrase. Use present tense verbs. Underline each subject once and each verb twice. Also, place parentheses around the interfering prepositional phrases. Check your sentences with your instructor before proceeding to Part IV.

---

## PART IV: INDEFINITE PRONOUN SUBJECTS

When indefinite pronouns (such as **anybody, everyone, many**) are used as the subject of a sentence, students often make mistakes in subject–verb agreement. Indefinite pronouns are nonspecific words, but the way they are used indicates whether they are singular or plural. This is what you need to know in order to make the verb agree in number with the subject.

Most indefinite pronouns are always singular, a few are always plural, and a third group can be singular or plural, depending on the meaning of the sentence.

ALWAYS SINGULAR. Indefinite pronouns that are always singular include:

| | | | |
|---|---|---|---|
| each | one | everybody | someone |
| anyone | everyone | nobody | either |
| anybody | no one | somebody | neither |

The word **everybody** may cause trouble because it seems to refer to several individuals. To avoid confusion, think of **everybody** as "every single body" and you won't be tempted to use a plural verb. The same principle applies to all the words in this category.

EXAMPLES

Everybody (*every single body individually*) who can attend is encouraged to participate.
Everyone (*every single one*) has his own ideas about social services.
Each (*each one*) of the students buys her own book.
Neither (*not either one*) of the technologies is very easy.

ALWAYS PLURAL. The following indefinite pronouns always take a plural verb:

| | | | |
|---|---|---|---|
| both | few | many | several |

EXAMPLES

Several of the members were late.
Few of my friends are on my shift.
Both of your letters are acceptable.

SINGULAR OR PLURAL. Depending on the meaning of the sentence, the following indefinite pronouns are sometimes singular and sometimes plural (this list is not complete):

| | | |
|---|---|---|
| all | most | half |
| any | none | part |
| | some | |

These words are usually followed by a prepositional phrase, and the object of the preposition shows whether to use the singular or the plural. For instance, **all** of something singular uses a singular verb; **all** of something plural uses a plural verb.

EXAMPLES

All of the machine looks clean. (Singular)
All of the machines look clean. (Plural)
Most of the report was lost. (Singular)
Most of the reports were lost. (Plural)

With the words **none** or **any** the choice depends on whether you are emphasizing the singular or the plural meaning.

None of the books *has* arrived. (Emphasizes the singular: *not one book*)
None of the books *have* arrived. (Emphasizes the plural: *no books*)

**ACTIVITY 4-K: Indefinite Pronoun Subjects**

Underline the subject once and the correct verb twice. Put parentheses around the prepositional phrase that comes between the subject and verb.

1.  Each of the managers (grades/grade) the assignments promptly.
2.  One of the experiments (was/were) not finished.
3.  All of our repair work (is/are) done in the back shop.
4.  Every one of my drawings (is/are) too small.
5.  Some of these errors (is/are) careless.
6.  A few of the books (were/was) found.
7.  Everybody in these cities (pay/pays) a municipal tax.
8.  None [*not a single one*] of the supervisors (approves/approve) of our project.
9.  Everyone (is/are) able to complete the assignment.
10. Neither of us (work/works) on Saturday.

Check your responses in Feedback 4-K at the end of this module. If your responses were correct, proceed to Activity 4-M. If you missed any, review Part IV and then do Activity 4-L.

## ACTIVITY 4-L: Indefinite Pronoun Subjects

Underline the subject once and the correct verb twice. Put parentheses around the prepositional phrase that comes between the subject and verb.

1. Each of the secretaries (type/types) sixty words per minute.
2. Neither of the house plans (has/have) a large living room.
3. Most of the information (has/have) been entered into the computer.
4. Everybody at the hotel (like/likes) the new swimming pool.
5. All of the work (was/were) completed by noon.
6. A few of the pine trees (has/have) an unknown disease.
7. Some of the switches (need/needs) to be replaced.
8. Neither of the newspapers (print/prints) news about South America.
9. One of the accounts (show/shows) figures on depreciation of equipment.
10. Each of the truck drivers (own/owns) an eighteen-wheel rig.

Check your responses in Feedback 4-L at the end of this module. If your responses were correct, proceed to Activity 4-M. If you missed any, check with your instructor before going on.


## ACTIVITY 4-M: Indefinite Pronoun Subjects

Draw one line under the subject and two lines under the correct verb. In sentences with a prepositional phrase between the subject and the verb, put parentheses around the prepositional phrases.

1. Both of those supervisors (advise/advises) the others in the shop.
2. The auditors at the state agency (was/were) ready to work.
3. A crate of strawberries (is/are) selling for $12 today.
4. The trucks on our highways (has/have) slowly put the locomotive out of business.
5. Each of the computer operators (was/were) working on a different shift.
6. The technicians in the lab (recognizes/recognize) many molds by color.
7. One of the students (is/are) employed at the Halfway House.
8. Neither of the detectives (choose/chooses) to work alone on the case.
9. A doctor, in addition to a nurse, (make/makes) regular visits in the hospital.
10. The roof, along with the chimney, (need/needs) repairing.

Check your responses in Feedback 4-M at the end of this module. If your responses were correct, proceed to Activity 4-N. If you missed any, check them with your instructor before proceeding.

### ACTIVITY 4-N: Writing Sentences with Indefinite Pronoun Subjects

On your own paper, write the sentences specified below. *Use present-tense* verbs.

1. Write two sentences using singular indefinite pronouns as subjects. Underline the subject once and the verb twice.

2. Write two sentences using plural indefinite pronouns as subjects. Underline the subject once and the verb twice.

3. Write two sentences, one with a singular subject and one with a plural subject, using indefinite pronouns which can be singular or plural. Underline the subject once and the verb twice.

Check your responses with your instructor before proceeding to Part V.

## PART V: COMPOUND SUBJECTS AND VERBS

A *compound subject* has two or more parts, joined by a connecting word such as **and, or,** or **nor.** A compound subject may be singular or plural depending on what the connecting word is.

1. If the parts of the subject are joined by **and,** the subject is plural and takes a plural verb.

   EXAMPLES

   A keyboard and monitor are to be used in every class.
   Tom, Mary, and Clark want to participate in the seminar.

2. If two singular subjects are joined by **or** or **nor,** the verb must be singular.

   EXAMPLE

   Either the manager or the supervisor is ready for the union meeting.

   Note that the sentence does not say "Both the *manager and supervisor are* ready." It says "Either the *manager is* ready or the *supervisor is* ready." It is helpful to take each subject by itself first.

   EXAMPLE

   Neither John nor Jim is to be the new foreman. (John is not, Jim is not.)

3. If the two parts of the subject are joined by **or** or **nor** but one part is singular and one is plural, then the *verb agrees with the subject closer to it.*

EXAMPLES

Either the judge (or) the lawyers are wrong. (lawyers are, PLURAL)
Either the lawyers (or) the judge is wrong. (judge is, SINGULAR)

**4.** If a subject takes two or more verbs, each verb must agree with the subject. Verbs having the same subject are known as a *compound verb*.

EXAMPLES

The secretary types and takes dictation well.
The engineers come to work by bus and leave by train.
A nurse or a doctor is on duty or answers the phone.
Suppliers neither stock nor backorder such items.
The good driver uses judgment and pays attention.

## ACTIVITY 4-O: Subject–Verb Agreement

Draw one line under the subjects and two lines under the correct verbs. Circle the connecting word for a clue to which verb to use.

1. Neither the box nor the wooden crates (was/were) damaged in the accident.
2. Either Sam or his father (is/are) going to drive us to the plane.
3. Neither the supplies nor the book (has/have) been delivered.
4. Private proprietorship and free trade (is/are) aspects of capitalism.
5. Neither Fred nor George (have/has) enough energy to complete the job or (want/wants) to do it.
6. Engineering and architecture (involve/involves) different skills.
7. Randy, his roommate, and his brother (has/have) a new summer business.
8. Either the employees or the employer (is/are) wrong.
9. Neither the college nor the senior high school (has/have) enough lab supplies or (hire/hires) qualified teachers.
10. Either Monday or Tuesday (appear/appears) to be the only time for the interview.

Check your responses in Feedback 4-O at the end of this module. If your responses were correct, proceed to Activity 4-Q. If you missed any, review Part V and than do Activity 4-P.

## ACTIVITY 4-P: Subject–Verb Agreement

Draw one line under the subjects and two lines under the correct verbs. Circle the connecting word.

1. Neither rancher nor farmer (specializes/specialize) in more than one crop or (try/tries) to irrigate the land.

2. On the damaged boardwalk after the storm, the hammering and sawing (was/were) ceaseless.

3. Either dark green or dark blue (absorb/absorbs) more solar heat than black.

4. For example, neither the pick-up nor the station wagons (was/were) built to carry such heavy machinery.

5. Energy and empathy (help/helps) the social worker in many ways.

6. Land, sea, or air (is/are) directly affected by many pollutants.

7. Neither a secretary nor a stenographer (accept/accepts) the responsibility of a report's content and (take/takes) the blame for errors.

8. Science and technology (help/helps) the nurse in many ways.

9. The soil type and the topography (is/are) important when building a highway.

10. In many retirement situations, only a pension and social security (offers/offer) support.

Check your responses in Feedback 4-P at the end of this module. If your responses were correct, proceed to Activity 4-Q. If you missed any, check them with your instructor before proceeding.


### ACTIVITY 4-Q: Writing Sentences with Compound Subjects

On your own paper, write the sentences specified below.

1. Write a sentence with compound subjects which are joined by **and.** Underline the subject once and the verb twice. Use *a present-tense verb.*

2. Write a sentence with compound subjects joined by **or.** Underline the subjects once and the verbs twice. *Use a present-tense verb.*

3. Write one sentence with compound subjects joined by **either . . . or.** Underline the subjects once and the verb twice. Use *a present-tense verb.*

4. Write one sentence with compound subjects joined by **neither . . . nor.** Underline the subjects once and the verb twice. *Use a present-tense verb.*

Check your sentences with your instructor before proceeding to Part VI.


# PART VI: SPECIAL PROBLEMS IN AGREEMENT

When a sentence begins with **here, there, where, which,** or **what,** the subject will follow the verb (V–S order). In this reversed order there must still be agreement of the verb and subject. To check, pick out and state the subject and verb in S–V order, and make sure they do agree.

EXAMPLES

    V      S                      S–V

There <u>are</u> two <u>designs</u> you can make. (Designs are)
There <u>is</u> a job <u>opening</u> at the plant. (Opening is)
Here <u>are</u> the <u>supplies</u> you ordered. (Supplies are)
Where <u>are</u> the <u>plans and report</u>? (Plans and report are)
What <u>is</u> <u>he</u>, the draftsman or the technician? (He is)

*Note:* To be sure what the subject is, mentally rearrange the sentence in the subject–verb order.

Sentences often begin with a prepositional phrase, followed by the verb, then the subject. Again in this V–S order, verb and subject must agree.

EXAMPLES

                           V      S

At the end of the hall <u>is</u> an <u>office</u>. (Office is)

                           V         S

To the right of the desk <u>were</u> three <u>chairs</u>. (Chairs were)

---

## ACTIVITY 4-R: Special Problems in Agreement

---

Underline the subject once and the verb twice. Put parentheses around all the prepositional phrases in each sentence. Mentally rearrange the sentence in S–V order.

1. On the table there (is/are) adding machines and calculators.
2. Here (is/are) the blueprints for the motel.
3. In the lab there (was/were) two Bunsen burners on.
4. Near the filing cabinet there (is/are) some blank forms.
5. At the end of the hall there (is/are) a room to be used for special meetings.
6. There on the desk (was/were) my three reports.
7. Here in written form (is/are) my reason for accepting the proposal.
8. Beside the new lab, there (is/are) a row of chairs.
9. Which (is/are) the new men for the job?
10. Where (is/are) your reports and experiment results?

Check your responses in Feedback 4-R at the end of this module. If your responses were correct, proceed to Activity 4-T. If you missed any, review Part VI and do Activity 4-S.

---

## ACTIVITY 4-S: Special Problems in Agreement

---

Underline the subject once and the verb twice. Put parentheses around all the prepositional phrases in each sentence. Mentally rearrange the sentence in S–V order.

1. Then there (was/were) more printouts for the systems analyst.
2. In the prison compound there (is/are) too many ball games scheduled.
3. There (is/are) many truck body styles.
4. Over here on the table (is/are) the display of portable computers.
5. Near the end of the hall there (is/are) a service desk and an information center.
6. What (was/were) John's temperature and blood pressure?
7. Before you leave, where (is/are) the specifications for this transmission?
8. Which (is/are) your favorite styles of business letters?
9. Where (does/do) the architect and the surveyor research the history of this lot?
10. There behind the door (is/are) the master switch for all the lights.

Check your responses in Feedback 4-S at the end of this module. If your responses were correct, proceed to Activity 4-T. If you missed any, check with your instructor before proceeding.

---

**ACTIVITY 4-T: Writing Sentences with Verb–Subject Order**

---

On your own paper, write the sentences specified below. *Use present-tense verbs*.

1. Write two sentences beginning with the word *there, here, which,* or *what*. Underline the subject once and the verb twice.
2. Write two sentences in which a prepositional phrase comes before the verb. Underline the subject once and the verb twice.

Check your sentences with your instructor. If you feel you have mastered the exercises in this module, ask your instructor for Test A. If not, ask your instructor for additional help.

---

*FEEDBACK FOR MODULE 4*

---

**Feedback 4-A**

1. reports are
2. I attended
3. technician went
4. He gave
5. instrument is

6. blueprints needed
7. You need
8. Mr. Raymond requested
9. We asked
10. secretary typed

**Feedback 4-B**

1. drawing won
2. secretary ordered
3. surveyor studied
4. nurse took
5. They are

6. driver leased
7. He bought
8. We sharpened
9. I replaced
10. nurse took

**Feedback 4-D**

1. Mathematics is
2. boss rides
3. workers are
4. The Riker Company was
5. rooms were

6. employees were
7. nurses were
8. people want
9. employees stay
10. Mr. Bruce was

**Feedback 4-E**

1. duties were
2. news meets
3. Allison, Merk & Mann plans
4. system drains
5. farmers were

6. operators need
7. guards help
8. Economics is
9. drawings show
10. counseling is

**Feedback 4-G**

1. construction (of the new buildings) was begun
2. computer (in addition to two printers) needs
3. combination (of these procedures) is
4. Mr. Long (together with his associates) attends
5. firm (of McCabe & Walston) is
6. Politics (along with economics) is
7. men (on our shift) are going
8. John (along with his two assistants) has
9. Jane (together with her sister) has
10. contribution (in addition to other people's) fosters

**Feedback 4-H**

1. secretary (for an educational organization) needs
2. designs (of the house) show
3. engineer (of the firm) recommends
4. wiring (in these houses) doesn't meet
5. truck (with two sets) (of dual rear wheels) is built
6. articles (in our local paper) are
7. serum (for the new virus) is
8. prisons (in the state) need
9. hotels (in Atlantic City) offer
10. assistant (at County Memorial Hospital) is

**Feedback 4-I**

1. <u>Employees</u> (of the plant) <u>are</u>
2. <u>Clearness</u> (in oral and written communications) <u>is</u>
3. <u>objections</u> (to the proposal) <u>seem</u>
4. <u>pieces</u> (of the equipment) <u>need</u>
5. <u>skill</u> (in dictation) <u>appears</u>
6. <u>rooms</u> <u>are</u>
7. <u>drawing</u> (together with his blueprints) <u>was submitted</u>
8. <u>charts</u> <u>were</u>
9. <u>nurses</u> <u>record</u>
10. <u>reporter</u> (because of training and experience) <u>reports</u>

**Feedback 4-K**

1. <u>Each</u> (of the managers) <u>grades</u>
2. <u>One</u> (of the experiments) <u>was</u>
3. <u>All</u> (of our repair work) <u>is</u>
4. <u>one</u> (of my drawings) <u>is</u>
5. <u>Some</u> (of these errors) <u>are</u>
6. <u>few</u> (of the books) <u>were</u>
7. <u>Everybody</u> (in these cities) <u>pays</u>
8. <u>None</u> (of the supervisors) <u>approves</u>
9. <u>Everyone</u> <u>is</u>
10. <u>Neither</u> (of us) <u>works</u>

**Feedback 4-L**

1. <u>Each</u> (of the secretaries) <u>types</u>
2. <u>Neither</u> (of the house plans) <u>has</u>
3. <u>Most</u> (of the information) <u>has</u>
4. <u>Everybody</u> (at the hotel) <u>likes</u>
5. <u>All</u> (of the work) <u>was</u>
6. <u>few</u> (of the pine trees) <u>have</u>
7. <u>Some</u> (of the switches) <u>need</u>
8. <u>Neither</u> (of the newspapers) <u>prints</u>
9. <u>One</u> (of the accounts) <u>shows</u>
10. <u>Each</u> (of the truck drivers) <u>owns</u>

**Feedback 4-M**

1. <u>Both</u> (of those supervisors) <u>advise</u>
2. <u>auditors</u> (at the state agency) <u>were</u>
3. <u>crate</u> (of strawberries) <u>is</u>
4. <u>trucks</u> (on our highways) <u>have</u>
5. <u>Each</u> (of the computer operators) <u>was</u>
6. <u>technicians</u> (in the lab) <u>recognize</u>
7. <u>One</u> (of the students) <u>is</u>
8. <u>Neither</u> (of the detectives) <u>chooses</u>

9. <u>doctor</u> (in addition to a nurse) <u>makes</u>
10. <u>roof</u> (along with the chimney) <u>needs</u>

## Feedback 4-O

1. box (nor) crates <u>were</u>
2. Sam (or) father <u>is</u>
3. supplies (nor) book <u>has</u>
4. proprietorship (and) trade <u>are</u>
5. Fred nor George <u>has</u> (or) <u>wants</u>
6. Engineering (and) architecture <u>involve</u>
7. Randy, his roommate, (and) brother <u>have</u>
8. employees (or) employer <u>is</u>
9. college nor school <u>has</u> (or) <u>hires</u>
10. Monday (or) Tuesday <u>appears</u>

## Feedback 4-P

1. rancher (nor) farmer <u>specializes</u> or <u>tries</u>
2. hammering (and) sawing <u>were</u>
3. green (or) blue <u>absorbs</u>
4. pick-up (nor) wagons <u>were</u>
5. Energy (and) empathy <u>help</u>
6. Land, sea (or) air <u>is</u>
7. secretary (nor) stenographer <u>accepts</u> and <u>takes</u>
8. Science (and) technology <u>help</u>
9. type (and) topography <u>are</u>
10. pension (and) security <u>offer</u>

## Feedback 4-R

1. <u>machines, calculators</u> <u>are</u> (On the table)
2. <u>blueprints</u> <u>are</u> (for the motel)
3. <u>burners</u> <u>were</u> (In the lab)
4. <u>forms</u> <u>are</u> (Near the filing cabinet)
5. <u>room</u> <u>is</u> (At the end) (of the hall) (for special meetings)
6. <u>reports</u> <u>were</u> (on the desk)
7. <u>reason</u> <u>is</u> (in written form) (for accepting the proposal)
8. <u>row</u> <u>is</u> (Beside the new lab) (of chairs)
9. <u>men</u> <u>are</u> (for the job)
10. <u>reports, results</u> <u>are</u>

## Feedback 4-S

1. <u>printouts</u> <u>were</u> (for the systems analyst)
2. <u>games</u> <u>are</u> (In the prison compound)
3. <u>styles</u> <u>are</u>
4. <u>display</u> <u>is</u> (on the table) (of portable typewriters)
5. <u>desk, center</u> <u>are</u> (Near the end) (of the hall)
6. <u>temperature, pressure</u> <u>were</u>

7. <u>specifications</u> <u><u>are</u></u> (for this transmission)
8. <u>styles</u> <u><u>are</u></u> (of business letters)
9. <u>architect, surveyor</u> <u>do research</u> (of this lot)
10. <u>switch</u> <u><u>is</u></u> (behind the door) (for all the lights)

# MODULE 5

# Clauses

OBJECTIVE: In this module you will learn to identify and write clauses correctly.

Upon completion of this module, you will be able:

To identify independent clauses.

To identify dependent clauses.

To recognize appropriate clause connectors.

To recognize and to punctuate clauses correctly.

Like a sentence, a clause is a group of words that has a subject and a verb. However, as you will soon see, not all clauses are full sentences.

In the following sentences the clauses are enclosed in parentheses. Notice that each group of words in parentheses has its own subject and verb. Therefore, each group is a clause.

EXAMPLES

S  V       S  V
(He is the man) (who saw the accident.)

S  V       S  V  V
(I called him) (but he did not return my call.)

There are two kinds of clauses: *independent* and *dependent.* We will look at each type separately.

## PART I: INDEPENDENT CLAUSES

An *independent clause* (also called a major or main clause) is a clause that expresses a complete thought and can stand alone as a sentence. In the following examples the independent clauses are underlined.

EXAMPLES

S     V
The jury will announce its verdict soon.

S    V    S   V
The directors objected, and the president resigned.

S    V    S  V
Our sales manager spends lavishly; she has an unlimited expense account.

S  V
After leaving the office, Cheryl was exhausted.

*Note:* The introductory phrase is part of the independent clause.

Two or more independent clauses can be connected within a sentence in several ways.

*Independent clauses can be connected by a* **COORDINATE CONJUNCTION.** A conjunction is a connecting word. Coordinate conjunctions join words or groups of words of the same order or rank—for instance, two subjects, two verbs, two prepositional phrases, two verbal phrases, or two independent clauses.

**69**

Here's a device to help you remember the seven coordinate conjunctions. The word FANBOYS: *for, and, nor, but, or, yet, so.* (**Note: FOR** can also be a preposition. For example: The inspectors came *for the meeting.*)

EXAMPLES

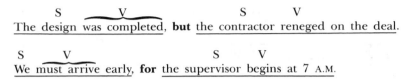

    S      V                  S      V

The design was completed, **but** the contractor reneged on the deal.

  S    V                 S     V

We must arrive early, **for** the supervisor begins at 7 A.M.

**Punctuation Pattern 1.** Two independent clauses (IC) joined by a coordinate conjunction (cc) usually (but not always) take a comma before the conjunction. Whenever a coordinate conjunction is used, the second clause is always independent if the first one is. The pattern looks like this:

---

*Punctuation Pattern 1*
**IC, cc IC.**

---

*Independent clauses can be joined by a **SEMICOLON**.*

EXAMPLE

S  V                       S    V

He gets the difficult assignments; he can handle them easily.

**Punctuation Pattern 2.** Use a semicolon to connect two *closely related* independent clauses. In this pattern the semicolon takes the place of a coordinating conjunction. (**Note:** If the clauses are not closely related, it is better to use a period and separate them into independent sentences.)

---

*Punctuation Pattern 2*
**IC; IC.**

---

*Independent clauses can be joined by a* **SEMICOLON AND A TRANSITIONAL EXPRESSION.** Transitional expressions are connectors that show some kind of relationship between the clauses. The most common ones are listed below. See pp. 78–79 for a more complete list.

EXAMPLES

S    V

We are expected to work overtime; **therefore,** we should get a higher salary.


The design was completed; **however,** the contractor reneged on the deal.

---

### TRANSITIONAL EXPRESSIONS

| | |
|---|---|
| accordingly | in fact |
| also | moreover |
| besides | namely |
| consequently | nevertheless |
| finally | next |
| for example | of course |
| for instance | on the other hand |
| furthermore | otherwise |
| however | still |
| in addition | then |
| in conclusion | therefore |
| | thus |

---

**Punctuation Pattern 3.** The transitional expression (trans) that joins two independent clauses should be preceded by a semicolon and followed by a comma. Note that the transitional expression is not a part of either independent clause.

---

*Punctuation Pattern 3*
**IC; trans, IC.**

---

Another correct way of punctuating these sentences would be to use a period at the end of the first independent clause and begin a new sentence with the transitional expression.

71

We are expected to work overtime. **Therefore,** we should get a higher salary.

The design was completed. **However,** the contractor reneged on the deal.

## PART II: DEPENDENT CLAUSES

A *dependent clause* (also called a subordinate or minor clause) does not express a complete thought and therefore cannot stand alone. The following clauses are dependent and incomplete:

after Jones took charge

because there are defects in its basic structure

that we submitted last week

A dependent clause, as its name implies, must be supported by an independent clause. Otherwise it is a fragment. A dependent clause usually qualifies the thought of the independent clause—that is, limits or affects it in some way—and it is related to some word in that clause.

In the following examples the dependent clauses are underlined twice. Note that dependent clauses can occur at the beginning, in the middle, or at the end of a sentence.

**Punctuation Pattern 4.** When a dependent clause (DC) is at the beginning of a sentence, a comma is placed after it.

---

*Punctuation Pattern 4*
**DC, IC.**

---

EXAMPLE

     S    V

After Jones took charge, he doubled sales.

**Punctuation Pattern 5.** When a dependent clause is at the end of a sentence, no comma is necessary between the independent and dependent clauses.

---

*Punctuation Pattern 5*
**IC  DC.**

---

V   S

The bridge is weak <u>because there are defects in its basic structure.</u>

**Punctuation Pattern 6.** When a dependent clause comes in the middle of an independent clause, sometimes commas precede and follow it and sometimes no commas are necessary. (This will be discussed in Module 12.)

---

*Punctuation Pattern 6*
**Part of IC   DC   rest of IC.**

---

EXAMPLE

S        V

The bid <u>that we submitted last week</u> has been returned.

It is important to be able to identify dependent clauses so that you do not make the error of writing fragments instead of full sentences.

Dependent clauses can be spotted easily because they are *always* introduced by a signal word such as the following:

---

### DEPENDENT CLAUSE SIGNALS

| | | | |
|---|---|---|---|
| after* | how | unless | which |
| although | if | until* | while |
| as* | once | what | who |
| as if | since* | whatever | whoever |
| as long as | so that | when | whom |
| as soon as | than | whenever | whomever |
| because | that | where | whose |
| before* | though | wherever | why |
| even though | | | |

---

*The starred words may be used as prepositions but only when followed by an object. When used as clause signals, the starred words are followed by a subject and a verb. Compare the examples below.

EXAMPLES

*Prepositional Phrase*
**after** the meeting
**until** noon

*Clause*
**after** the meeting was over
**until** the noon bell rings

Remember that these clause signals are *part of* the clause, not connectors between two independent clauses. The signals suggest that answers to certain questions must be included in the sentences. Look at the following examples.

EXAMPLES

**Because** John was overqualified for the job
**After** Jeanine asked a most insulting question
**Although** Mrs. Walsh was an expert in math

These fragments would lead you to ask: What happened because John was overqualified? What happened after Jeanine asked a most insulting question? What happened although Mrs. Walsh was an expert in math?

Note also that if you remove the signal words—**because, after,** and **although**—from the fragments, you have independent clauses:

EXAMPLES

John was overqualified for the job.
Jeanine asked a most insulting question.
Mrs. Walsh was an expert in math.

*Let these three items be your criteria for identifying a* **DEPENDENT CLAUSE**:

| |
|---|
| 1. Clause Signal |
| 2. Subject |
| 3. Verb |

If a group of words contains only a subject and verb but has no clause signal, it is considered an independent clause.

EXAMPLE

      S       V
The president knows <u>why the company went bankrupt</u>.

**The president knows** is an independent clause since it does not have a clause signal.

Sometimes what appears to be an independent clause does not make sense by itself. For example:

EXAMPLE:

<u>I heard</u> that you were in town.

**I heard** does not seem to make a complete thought by itself. However, grammatically, it is an independent clause: it has a subject and a verb, and it is not introduced by a clause signal.

Some clause signals can serve as the subjects of dependent clauses as well as the signal words. These are **who, which, that, whoever,** and **whatever.**

EXAMPLES

DEPENDENT CLAUSE
S            V
The man (**who** is discouraged easily) does not make a successful salesman.

clause signal as subject of dependent clause

DEPENDENT CLAUSE
S      V
The advertisement (**that** drew the greatest response) was designed by an intern.

clause signal as subject of dependent clause

---

**ACTIVITY 5-A: Clauses**

---

Circle each dependent clause signal and draw two lines under each dependent clause. If a sentence has no dependent clause, do not mark it.

1. Keyboarding is useful.
2. The draftsman who completes his drawing first will be excused.
3. He acted as if he knew the correct procedure.
4. The draftsmen conferred early this morning.
5. They decided to accept the plan that was less complicated.
6. She called us when she knew the proper procedure.
7. Because he was in Baton Rouge, he attended the seminar.
8. He studied so much that he became exhausted.
9. We stayed in the meeting until the final session ended.
10. The boy who is sitting in the lobby is my son.

Check your answers in Feedback 5-A at the end of this module. If your responses were correct, proceed to Activity 5-C. If you missed any, review Part II and then proceed to Activity 5-B.

---

**ACTIVITY 5-B: Clauses**

---

Circle the clause signals that introduce dependent clauses.

1. The problem that most technicians faced was lack of trained personnel.

2. A man is a good worker when he is willing to do his share.

3. As computers have become more widespread, many working hours have been saved.

4. Mr. Steel studied the instructions before he began the project.

5. Although Mrs. Brown had a quorum, she delayed the meeting.

6. The conclusions must be accepted and implemented.

7. Since he ran the cards through the computer, he could give Tom the information before noon.

8. The repairs that Mr. Marvel made have been added to the bill.

9. Mr. Barnidge sent the memo when the conference was cancelled.

10. She is very efficient, so she always meets the daily deadlines.

Check your answers in Feedback 5-B at the end of this module. If your responses were correct, proceed to Activity 5-C. If you missed any clause signals, review the list on page 73 and then proceed to Activity 5-C.

## ACTIVITY 5-C: Clauses

Draw one line under each independent clause and two lines under each dependent clause. Circle each dependent clause signal.

1. Because the interview was important, she planned carefully.

2. This is the building that the draftsmen designed.

3. When the job is finished, we shall return to our families.

4. We looked for an employee who needed a summer job.

5. If you do well, you will be promoted.

6. It was shown that she really was a dedicated doctor.

7. When you send the bill, the company will write you a check.

8. He knew that female engineers have excellent job opportunities.

9. He had the skill although he failed to use it.

10. As I started the machine, he walked out.

Check your answers in Feedback 5-C at the end of this module. If you missed any, review Parts I and II, especially the uses of coordinate conjunctions, transitional expressions, and dependent clause signals.

# PART III: APPROPRIATE CLAUSE CONNECTORS

Now that you can identify independent and dependent clauses, you will be presented with the three types of clause connectors that you worked with in Part II: *coordinate conjunctions, transitional expressions,* and *dependent clause signals.* Here you will learn how to choose the clause connector that is correct grammatically and that conveys the meaning you intend.

## Coordinate Conjunctions

First let's review what you already know about coordinate conjunctions. Coordinate conjunctions join two independent clauses. (They can also join two or more nouns, verbs, dependent clauses, etc. However, they do not connect an independent and a dependent clause.) The sentence pattern (IC, cc IC.) is used for joining two independent clauses by means of a coordinate conjunction. This is an important pattern for you to master in your own writing. To use it properly, you should memorize and distinguish the meanings of the seven coordinate conjunctions: **and, but, yet, or, nor, for,** and **so.**

Consider the meaning of each coordinate conjunction as it is used in a sentence.

1. **And** is used to show addition. It connects items of similar qualities.

EXAMPLE

The economy was good, **and** the new business thrived.

2. **But** and **yet** are used interchangeably to show contrast between ideas.

EXAMPLES

She could type rapidly, **but** she could not take dictation.
The wind was brisk, **yet** the day seemed mild.

3. **Or** and **nor** are used to show a choice.

EXAMPLE

The old beakers can be used in the experiment, **or** the lab can purchase new ones.

**Nor** indicates a negative choice between items. It means "not either one" is chosen. (Notice that using **nor** requires using a helping verb like **did** or **will** right after it.)

EXAMPLE

The architect did not draw the plans to scale, **nor** did he use correct symbols.

4. **For** introduces a reason or explanation. (Do not confuse it with the preposition *for,* which has a variety of other meanings.)

77

EXAMPLE

The architect did not draw the plans to scale, **for** he did not have the proper instruments.

**5. So** indicates a result.

EXAMPLE

The architect did not draw the plans to scale, **so** his drawings were rejected.

---

**ACTIVITY 5-D: Writing Sentences with Coordinate Conjunctions**

---

On your own paper, write seven sentences using each coordinate conjunction to join two independent clauses. Check your sentences with your instructor before going on.

**Transitional Expressions**

When a transitional expression is used to join two independent clauses, the transitional expression is preceded by a semicolon and followed by a comma (**IC; trans, IC.**). This pattern can add variety to your sentence structure: however, it is important to know the meaning of the various transitional expressions in order to use them effectively.

In Part I you were given a partial list of the more common transitional expressions. Here is a more complete list, grouped according to usage.

---

**TRANSITIONAL EXPRESSIONS**

| | | |
|---|---|---|
| *Indicating Result* | nearby | in truth |
| apparently | opposite | really |
| consequently | there | obviously |
| for this (that) reason | to the left (right) | of course |
| accordingly | *Indicating Concession* | *Indicating End* |
| therefore | at any rate | in conclusion |
| thus | at least | on the whole |
| hence | | to summarize |
| | *Indicating Examples* | |
| *Indicating Purpose* | for example | *Indicating Similarity* |
| for this purpose | for instance | likewise |
| in order to do this | to illustrate | similarly |
| to this end | | |
| with this in mind | *Indicating Emphasis* | *Indicating Addition* |
| with this in view | above all | again |
| | certainly | also |
| *Indicating Place* | indeed | besides |
| beyond | in fact | equally important |
| here | in short | finally |

| | | |
|---|---|---|
| first, second, etc. | specifically | in the meantime |
| further | *Indicating Contrast* | later |
| furthermore | however | meanwhile |
| in addition | in contrast | simultaneously |
| in the first place | in spite of this | soon |
| moreover | nevertheless | then |
| next | notwithstanding | first, second, next |
| then | on the contrary | *Indicating Order of* |
| too | on the other hand | *Importance* |
| *Indicating Details* | still | first, second, etc. |
| especially | | primarily |
| to enumerate | *Indicating Time* | most importantly |
| in particular | afterward | next |
| namely | earlier | finally |
| | at the same time | |

The following examples show how some of these bridging devices are used. Study them so that you will be able to incorporate these devices into your own writing, thereby adding more variety to your sentences.

EXAMPLES

The architect worked his way through college; **consequently,** he was very conservative with his money.
(*Since the second independent clause is a result of the first, the clauses are connected with a transitional expression that indicates result, such as* **consequently.**)

The architect worked his way through college; **for this purpose,** he had to give up many social activities.
(*Here the transitional expression* **for this purpose** *shows that the first clause has stated a purpose and the second cause tells what the architect did because of his purpose.*)

The architect worked his way through college; **likewise,** his sister had a job while in school.
(*The transitional expression* **likewise** *indicates an idea in the second clause that is similar to the first.*)

The architect worked his way through college; **however,** he never had a full-time job until after graduation.
(*The transitional expression* **however** *shows that the second clause is an idea that contrasts with the first.*)

The architect worked his way through college; **specifically,** he held jobs as a cook, a sales clerk, and a draftsman.
(*The transitional expression* **specifically** *indicates that details will follow.*)

The architect worked his way through college; **at least,** he was industrious if not brilliant.

*(The transitional expression* **at least** *indicates a concession that this architect had drive, which some might consider less important than genius.)*

These examples should give you an idea of how some of the transitional expressions on the list may be used to connect independent clauses. In most of the categories (except *time* and *place*), the expressions may be used interchangeably. Once you know what meaning you wish to convey, you can select the most appropriate word or phrase to use. (Of course you should use a dictionary if in doubt about any of the meanings!)

Notice how each transitional expression affects the meaning of the following series of sentences:

EXAMPLES

The company made proper guarantees; **therefore,** the contract was accepted.

The company made proper guarantees; **however,** the contract was not accepted.

The company made proper guarantees; **afterward,** the contract was accepted.

The company made proper guarantees; **in fact,** the contract was accepted.

The company made proper guarantees; **finally,** the contract was accepted.

The company made proper guarantees; **at any rate,** the contract was accepted.

---

### ACTIVITY 5-E: Writing Sentences with Transitional Expressions

---

Using any five transitional expressions from the list on pp. 78–79, connect two independent clauses of your own. Underline the transitional expressions. (If you are not sure of the meaning, use a dictionary.) Check your sentences with your instructor before proceeding.

### Dependent Clause Signals

You learned earlier that a dependent clause can come at the beginning, in the middle, or at the end of a sentence, and that it is introduced by a clause signal. Remember that a dependent clause signal, unlike a coordinating conjunction or a transitional expression, is actually a part of the clause and makes the clause an incomplete thought. You are already familiar with the dependent clause signals; here they are grouped according to use.

| DEPENDENT CLAUSE SIGNALS | | |
|---|---|---|
| *Indicating Time* | as long as | once |
| after | as soon as | since |
| as | before | until |

| | | |
|---|---|---|
| when | *Indicating Comparison* | unless |
| whenever | as | why |
| while | than | |
| | | *Adjective Clause Signals (referring to specific nouns)* |
| *Indicating Place* | *Indicating Result* | |
| where | as | that |
| wherever | because | what |
| | how | whatever |
| *Indicating Contrast* | since | which |
| although | so that | who |
| even though | | whoever |
| though | *Indicating Condition* | whom |
| | as if | whomever |
| | if | whose |

Here are some sentences showing the correct use of clause signals. Study the sentences so that you will be able to use these clause signals properly in your own sentences.

### EXAMPLES

The nurse was qualified for a job in pediatrics **when** she graduated from nursing school.
(*The clause signal* **when** *indicates a time relationship.*)

The nurse was qualified for a job in pediatrics **wherever** she wanted to work.
(*The clause signal* **wherever** *indicates place.*)

The nurse was qualified for a job in pediatrics **although** she was placed in the geriatrics ward.
(*The clause signal* **although** *indicates a contrasting idea.*)

The nurse is better qualified for a job in pediatrics **than** she is in geriatrics.
(*The clause signal* **than** *indicates comparison.*)

**Because** the nurse was qualified for a job in pediatrics, she was hired immediately after graduation.
(*The clause signal* **because** *indicates result.*)

**If** the nurse is qualified for a job in pediatrics, she will be hired immediately after graduation.
(*The clause signal* **if** *indicates condition.*)

The nurse **who** is qualified for a job in pediatrics will be hired immediately after graduation.
(*The clause signal* **who** *introduces an adjective cause modifying the noun* nurse. *The entire clause acts as an adjective.* **Note:** *An adjective clause is always next to the noun it modifies.*)

The nurse was qualified for a job **which** was in pediatrics.
(The *clause signal* **which** *introduces an adjective cause which modifies the noun* job.)

These examples should give you an idea of how some of the clause signals on the list are used to introduce dependent clauses. Decide on the meaning that you want your dependent clause to convey; then select an appropriate word from the proper group to begin the dependent clause.

You can change the meaning or emphasis of the sentence by changing the clause signal. Notice how the clause signals below give different meanings to the following sentence: **The office manager made out the payroll; he paid the taxes.**

EXAMPLES

The office manager made out the payroll **after** he paid the taxes.
The office manager made out the payroll **before** he paid the taxes.
The officer manager made out the payroll **because** he wanted to pay the taxes.
The officer manager **who** made out the payroll also paid the taxes.
The office manager made out the payroll **as soon as** he paid the taxes.
**Although** the office manager made out the payroll, he did not pay the taxes.

---

## ACTIVITY 5-F: Writing Sentences with Dependent Clause Signals

---

On your own paper, write five sentences using correctly any of the dependent clause signals from the list on pp. 80–81. Check your sentences with your instructor before proceeding.

---

## ACTIVITY 5-G: Review of Clauses

---

Circle each dependent clause signal and underline the dependent clause twice. Underline each independent clause once.

1. When we drove into the parking lot, we were given a space near the building.
2. The window overlooked the construction site, and we could see the experienced workers in their hard hats.
3. He always chose to perform those tasks that were most interesting to him.
4. Taking six weeks of sick leave was helpful; the compensation that he received was fair.
5. The emphasis by employers on accuracy, neatness, and initiative is to be expected by job applicants.
6. The receptionist who sits next to the telephone is responsible for taking all messages.

7. Because modern machinery can function unattended, the unemployment rate may increase.

8. Of course, the union members and business people will have to agree on the proposal.

9. The DuPont Company runs three shifts; otherwise, it does not get the necessary work completed on time.

10. Modes of transportation that have proved to be cost-efficient should be subsidized by the federal government.

Check your answers in Feedback 5-G at the end of this module. If you missed any, check with your instructor before asking for Test A.

---

## FEEDBACK FOR MODULE 5

### Feedback 5-A

1. (*None*)
2. (who) completes his drawing first
3. (as if) he knew the correct procedure
4. (*None*)
5. (which) was less complicated
6. (when) she knew the proper procedure
7. (Because) he was in Baton Rouge
8. (that) he became exhausted
9. (until) the final session ended
10. (who) is sitting in the lobby

### Feedback 5-B

1. (that)
2. (when)
3. (As)
4. (before)
5. (Although)
6. (*None*)
7. (Since)
8. (that)
9. (when)
10. (*None*)

### Feedback 5-C

1. (Because) the interview was important, she planned carefully.
2. This is the building (that) the draftsmen designed.
3. (When) the job is finished, we shall return to our families.
4. We looked for an employee (who) needed a summer job.
5. (If) you do well, you will be promoted.
6. It was shown (that) she really was a dedicated doctor.
7. (When) you send the bill, the company will write you a check.
8. He knew (that) female engineers have excellent job opportunities.
9. He had the skill (although) he failed to use it.

10. (As) I started the machine, he walked out.

**Feedback 5-G**

1. (When) we drove into the parking lot, we were given a space near the building.
2. The window overlooked the construction site, and we could see the experienced workers in their hard hats.
3. He always chose to perform those tasks (that) were most interesting to him.
4. Taking six weeks of sick leave was helpful; the compensation (that) he received was fair.
5. The emphasis by employers on accuracy, neatness, and initiative is to be expected by job applicants.
6. The receptionist (who) sits next to the telephone is responsible for taking all messages.
7. (Because) modern machinery can function unattended, the unemployment rate may increase.
8. Of course, the union members and business people will have to agree on the proposal.
9. The DuPont Company runs three shifts; otherwise, it does not get the necessary work completed on time.
10. Modes of transportation (that) have proved to be cost-efficient should be subsidized by the federal government.

# MODULE 6

# Punctuation

OBJECTIVE: This module is designed to help you in the three main areas in which students have trouble with punctuation.

Upon completion of this module, you will be able:

To identify the five basic patterns of punctuation.

To write sentences using the five punctuation patterns correctly.

To apply five basic comma rules for correct sentence construction.

To apply two rules governing the apostrophe to show possession.

To use the five-step process to form possessives.

Review and memorize the basic sentence patterns listed below. Using them as models will help you to punctuate your own sentences. (Pattern 6 has special rules and will be discussed later.)

| PATTERN ABBREVIATIONS* | | EXAMPLES |
|---|---|---|
| Pattern 1 | IC, cc IC. | My boss warned me about being late, but he didn't fire me. |
| Pattern 2 | IC: IC. | My boss warned me about being late; he didn't fire me. |
| Pattern 3 | IC; trans, IC. | My boss warned me about being late; however, he didn't fire me. |
| Pattern 4 | DC, IC. | Although my boss warned me about being late, he didn't fire me. |
| Pattern 5 | IC DC. | My boss didn't fire me although he warned me about being late. |

*Note:* For a discussion of essential and nonessential clauses, see Module 12, pages 241–42.

*Key to Abbreviations
IC:     Independent Clause (has a subject and a verb and can stand alone).
DC:     Dependent Clause (is introduced by a signal word and followed by a subject–verb unit). See list of dependent clause signals following.
cc:     Coordinate Conjunction (all seven in list following).
trans: Transitional Expression (see list of the most common ones following; more complete list is on pp. 78–79).

Look at **Pattern 1** (IC, cc IC.). If you have two Independent Clauses joined by a *coordinating conjunction,* you should have a *comma* before the conjunction. Look at **Pattern 2** (IC; IC.). If you remove the conjunction, you need a stronger mark of punctuation, the semicolon. One way to check a semicolon is to see if a period works as well.

Look at **Pattern 3** (IC; trans, IC.). If you use a Transitional Expression to tie the two Independent Clauses together, you should use a *semicolon before and a comma after* the Transitional Expression. It would also be correct to use a period in place of the semicolon. (Exception: The transitional expression **then** does not need to be followed by a comma.)

EXAMPLE

The young man took an intensive course; **then** he became a real estate salesman.

Look at **Pattern 4** (DC, IC.). If you introduce the sentence with a Dependent Clause, it should be separated from the Independent Clause

| DEPENDENT CLAUSE SIGNALS | | | COORDINATE CONJUNCTIONS | COMMON TRANSITIONAL EXPRESSIONS | |
| --- | --- | --- | --- | --- | --- |
| after | once | whenever | and | accordingly | in conclusion |
| although | since | where | but | also | in fact |
| as | so that | wherever | for | besides | namely |
| as if | than | which | nor | consequently | nevertheless |
| as long as | that | while | or | finally | of course |
| as soon as | though | who | so | for example | on the other hand |
| because | unless | whoever | yet | for instance | then |
| before | until | whom | | furthermore | therefore |
| even though | what | whomever | | however | thus |
| how | whatever | whose | | | |
| if | when | why | | | |

by a *comma*. (Consult the list of dependent clause signals on p. 87.)

Look at **Pattern 5** (IC DC.). If the Dependent Clause comes at the end of the sentence, you need no comma between the clauses.

To help you remember these five punctuation patterns, here they are again with illustrations.

**Punctuation Patterns**

**Pattern 1:** IC, cc IC. (Two independent clauses joined by a coordinate conjunction)

```
MY BOSS TELEPHONED ME        ,        BUT        I WASN'T HOME.
```

**Pattern 2:** IC; IC. (Two independent clauses joined by a semicolon)

```
MY BOSS TELEPHONED ME        ;        I WASN'T HOME.
```

**Pattern 3:** IC; trans, IC. (Two independent clauses joined by a transitional expression)

```
MY BOSS TELEPHONED ME    ;    HOWEVER    ,    I WASN'T HOME.
```

**Pattern 4:** DC, IC. (A dependent clause followed by an independent clause)

```
WHEN    MY BOSS TELEPHONED ME    ,    I WASN'T HOME.
```

**Pattern 5:** IC DC. (An independent clause followed by a dependent clause)

```
MY BOSS TELEPHONED ME    WHEN    I WASN'T HOME.
```

---

**ACTIVITY 6-A: Punctuation Patterns**

Write the five basic sentence patterns *from memory*.

Pattern 1 _____

Pattern 2 _____

Pattern 3 _____

Pattern 4 _____

Pattern 5 _____

Check your answers in Feedback 6-A at the end of this module. If you missed any, continue studying until you can write the patterns from memory.

## ACTIVITY 6-B: Sentence Punctuation Patterns

Take the following paired sentences and run each pair through the five patterns.

A. It rained on Friday. The construction crew didn't work.

   Pattern 1 _____

   2 _____

   3 _____

   4 _____

   5 _____

B. The blueprint machine was broken. The building plans weren't ready for the client.

   Pattern 1 _____

   2 _____

   3 _____

   4 _____

   5 _____

C. I kept a good record of my expenses for the year. I was ready for the accountant to do my taxes.

   Pattern 1 _____

   2 _____

   3 _____

   4 _____

   5 _____

Check your answers in Feedback 6-B at the end of this module. If your responses were correct, proceed to Activity 6-C. If you missed any, check them with your instructor before proceeding.

## ACTIVITY 6-C: Sentence Punctuation Patterns

Identify the pattern in each of the following sentences. Write the pattern abbreviation to the left of the sentence.

_____ 1. If we advertise in newspapers, our business will certainly increase.

_____ 2. He became very nervous as he read the contract.

89

_____ 3. Mr. Nyton should support company policy, or he should resign.

_____ 4. Some policies pay on disability; others pay on death.

_____ 5. She tried to improve sales; to illustrate, she called on more customers.

_____ 6. Mr. Wook showed his disapproval when he heard the bad report.

_____ 7. The money was allocated by the legislature, but the hospital received none of it.

_____ 8. The bridge is located in this country; in fact, it is only six miles from here.

_____ 9. Employment did not increase; the company experienced a slump.

_____ 10. He put his valuables into the office safe; however, the building burned down.

Check your answers in Feedback 6-C at the end of this module. If your responses were correct, proceed to Activity 6-D. If you missed any, review them with your instructor before proceeding.

### ACTIVITY 6-D: Writing Sentences with Punctuation Patterns

Write two original sentences for each pattern. Use separate paper.

Pattern IC, cc IC.
Pattern IC; IC.
Pattern IC; trans, IC.
Pattern DC, IC.
Pattern IC DC.

Check your sentences with your instructor before proceeding. When your sentences are acceptable to the instructor, proceed to Part II.

## PART II: BASIC COMMA RULES

You saw where the comma is required in sentence patterns 1, 3, and 4. In addition, there are several other rules to remember about where and when not to use a comma. These rules will help you avoid punctuation errors in your writing. The comma is a handy tool to help you make your sentences read clearly.

**Rule 1.** *Use a comma to separate words, phrases, or clauses in a series* (more than two items).

EXAMPLES

*Words in a series*
The hotel manager required her employees to be *neat, clean,* and *efficient.*

*Phrases in a series*
The hotel agreed *to host the conference, to provide for all meals,* and *to plan the closing banquet.*

*Clauses in a series*
The manager gave instructions on *how a bed is made, how a bathroom is cleaned,* and *how the heating system is regulated.*

In some publications you may see items in a series without a comma before the **and** preceding the last item. This can sometimes cause confusion.

EXAMPLE

The City Council elected a president, vice-president, secretary and treasurer.

Were three or four officers elected? Without the comma after the word *secretary,* it is not clear whether one person holds the combined office of secretary and treasurer or whether there are four officeholders. You need to place the comma after *secretary* to indicate clearly that there are four officers. To be sure your sentences are clear, it is wise always to use the comma before the **and** in a series.

The City Council elected a president, vice-president, secretary, and treasurer.

Probably if there were only three officers, *secretary-treasurer* would be hyphenated:

The County Council elected a president, vice-president, and secretary-treasurer.

Sometimes each item in a series is joined by **and.** In this case the commas are unnecessary.

The sisters spent the afternoon *cooking* and *laundering* and *sewing.*

**Rule 2.** *Use a comma to separate items in dates and addresses.*
*Dates.*
*Use a comma between the day of the week, the day of the month, and the year,*

*and also after the year when it is not the end of the sentence. Do not use a comma between the month and the day.*

### EXAMPLES

The first meeting will be held on Tuesday, May 5, at the high school.
The financial statement was mailed on March 13, 1991, in the late afternoon.
It rained on Monday, August 20, 1991, before the crop was harvested.
The tropical storms of July 1988 were very severe.

**Note:** No commas are needed when only the month and the year are used.

*Addresses.*

*Consider the street number and street name as one item and the state and zip code as one item. Each additional item is followed by a comma.*

### EXAMPLES

The branch office address is Route 1, Box 775, Topeka, KS 66603, a location which is near the home office.
His new business address is 958 Ridge Road, Hayes, KS, which is in the northern part of the state.
Portland, Oregon, is the site of the new factory.
Deliver the package to John Newton, Room 602, Holiday Inn, Ocean City, MD 21842.

Note that no comma is used between the state and the zip code.

**Rule 3.** *Use a comma to separate coordinate adjectives;* that is, adjectives equal in rank that modify the same noun or pronoun.

### EXAMPLE

The **long, involved** court case cost the company $200,000 in fees and fines.

In this example, *long* and *involved* are coordinate adjectives because they both describe the *court case.* Compare the sentence above with the following:

The **dull gray** building was an architectural nightmare.

In this sentence *dull* and *gray* do not both describe *building. Dull* describes *gray.* Thus the meaning is *dull gray,* not *dull building.* In this case, do not use a comma.

There are two tests you can apply to tell if adjectives are coordinate:

> 1. *Coordinate adjectives sound correct when joined by* **and**.
>
>    the long **and** involved court case  (*Right*)
>    the dull **and** gray building  (*Wrong*)
>
> 2. *Coordinate adjectives can be reversed and still sound right.*
>
>    the **involved, long** court case  (*Right*)
>    the **gray dull** building  (*Wrong*)

See how these tests apply:

> the **quick, efficient** secretary (*Use comma—quick and* efficient secretary)
>
> a **bright red** tractor (*No comma—not* bright *and* red tractor)
>
> a **scorching, sarcastic** book review (*Use comma—scorching and. . .*)
>
> a **tan shirtwaist** dress (*No comma—not* tan *and* shirtwaist dress)

## ACTIVITY 6-E: Comma Rules

Insert commas where necessary.

1. The Society for the Advancement of Management elected a chairman historian secretary and treasurer.
2. The journalist expects to interview the celebrity to take pictures and to write the feature article by Monday.
3. The next conference will be held on Friday January 12 1993 in Room 100.
4. The police officers will send condolence cards to Mrs. Jerome Gray 201 Olympia Drive Seattle Washington 90105 preferably by noon Friday.
5. The patient considerate nurse listened to the sick man's problems.
6. The brand new computer will soon be in operation.
7. The social worker spoke to the group on alcoholic services educational opportunities and job seminars.
8. The supervisors and the assembly line worker and the secretaries were all impressed with the presentation.
9. The technician reported that the television had been struck by lightning that the main tube was ruined and that it would cost $50 to fix it.
10. Contributions are being accepted at the main headquarters in Peoria Illinois 90555.

Check your answers in Feedback 6-E at the end of this module. If your responses were correct, proceed to Rule 4. If you missed any, review Rules 1, 2, and 3 and then do Activity 6-F.

Insert commas where necessary.

1. The law office hired a secretary a bookkeeper and an accountant. (3 employees)
2. A community college enables a student to get an education to qualify for a good job and to be a contributing member of society.
3. The last meeting was held on Monday June 12 1988 at 2 p.m.
4. The new office building will be located at 4123 First Avenue Salisbury MD 21801 behind the old factory.
5. The skillful clever architect designed an interesting building.
6. A dull gray building is an eyesore.
7. The architect and the builder and the interior decorator planned the facility.
8. Seminars were held in the conference room in the gym and in the theater.
9. The student nurses received instructions in how to administer artificial respiration how to use the CPR technique and how to take blood pressure.
10. The new supplies will arrive on January 2 1989 on the afternoon train.

Check your responses in Feedback 6-F at the end of this module. If your responses were correct, proceed to Rule 4. If you missed any, check with your instructor before proceeding.

**Rule 4.** *Use commas to set off the four types of interrupters described below.*
*Parenthetic elements.* Words and expressions that are not essential to the main idea of the sentence but that do add to its meaning (**nevertheless, however, moreover, therefore, on the other hand,** etc.) must be set off by commas.

You will notice that some of these words were listed earlier among the *transitional expressions.* They are transitional expressions when they connect two independent clauses, but they are *interrupters* when they come at the beginning, middle, or end of *one* independent clause.

EXAMPLES

*Transitional Expression:*
The bid for the construction job was submitted late; **consequently,** the local company did not get the job.

*Interrupters of one independent clause:*
**Consequently,** the local company did not get the job.
The local company, **consequently,** did not get the job.
The local company did not get the job, **consequently.**

One helpful way to check for a parenthetic element is to see if you can change its position in the sentence. If you can, it is an interrupter.

Another way to tell if a word or phrase is a transitional expression or a parenthetic element is to see if there is one sentence or two sentences. If there is one sentence, the expression is a parenthetic element interrupting the sentence. If there are two sentences, the phrase is a transition between the two.

*Note:* A phrase beginning with **such as** is punctuated like an interrupter.

EXAMPLES

Computer supplies, **such as** printer papers, are located on the shelf.
The advantages of solar heat, **such as** economy, efficiency, and cleanliness, are reasons for considering it for a home.

*Direct address.*
Use commas to separate the name of the person spoken to in direct address.

EXAMPLES

We know, *Mr. Lord,* that your data processing course is the best in the state. (Note two commas here.)
*Mary,* would you retype this letter?
Mail it today, *John.*

*Negative expressions* at the end of a sentence are set off by a comma.

EXAMPLES

The balance sheet was correct, *wasn't it?*
He took an exemption test, *not a diagnostic test.*

Be sure to use a question mark if the expression itself is a question.
*Appositives.*
Words, phrases, or clauses that rename or give added information about a noun or pronoun should be set apart with commas.

EXAMPLES

Ms. Smith, *the Agri-Business adviser,* has an extensive background in agriculture.
The company president, *a graduate in accounting,* spoke about the company's assets.

You do not need to set off an appositive that is closely associated with what it renames.

EXAMPLES

The class used Prentice-Hall's text *Handbook for Writers.*
His sister Cindy is a secretary.

**Rule 5.** *Use commas to set off certain introductory words and phrases.*
*One word expressions* at the beginning of a sentence should be set off.

> EXAMPLES
>
> *Oh,* did the report come in?
> *Yes,* I read it yesterday.

*Introductory verbal phrases* must be set off by a comma.

> EXAMPLES
>
> *Hearing his name called,* he turned around.
> *Hurt by the fall,* the lineman sat stunned.

*Preventing misreading.*
Use a comma to set off introductory words or phrases that might be misread.

> EXAMPLES
>
> *After smoking,* the nurse returned to the patient.
> *To John,* Henry was a good friend.
> *By 1992,* 450 students were enrolled.

---

### ACTIVITY 6-G: Comma Rules

Supply commas where necessary. Circle transitional expressions/interrupters and see if there are two sentences or one.

1. Mr. Jones meets with his class accordingly three times a week.
2. The journalism student writes well doesn't she?
3. Yes Ms. Winter will speak to the secretaries.
4. Tom seldom however answers the instructor's question in class.
5. Seeing her employer June asked for a raise.
6. Giving the receptionist her paycheck the lawyer said that it was time for her to go to the bank.
7. The employer said that the memo however was hard to read.
8. Taking his time he writes letters well.
9. Most of the time however he is late for class.
10. The student a chemistry major wrote the lab report.

Check your responses in Feedback 6-G at the end of this module. If your responses were correct, proceed to Activity 6-I. If you missed any, do Activity 6-H.

## ACTIVITY 6-H: Comma Rules

Supply commas where necessary.

1. Miss Jones will you please send a memo to all departments about the meeting.
2. The new lab technician a graduate of the local community college is doing all the blood samples.
3. Many times however the computer is not being used.
4. The new nursing program is very popular with the students isn't it?
5. Graduating with a business degree they will all have jobs.
6. The representative from IBM therefore will interview the graduates on June 24.
7. The floor supervisor Elizabeth Fleming has posted the schedule for next week on the bulletin board.
8. According to the freight department our shipment should be here by June 1.
9. To begin with the cafeteria is very busy at that time.
10. Did you write the memo Miss Earlson?

Check your responses in Feedback 6-H at the end of this module. If your responses were correct, proceed to Activity 6-I. If you missed any, check them with your instructor.

## ACTIVITY 6-I: Writing Sentences Using Comma Rules

Demonstrate your ability to apply the rules of punctuation by writing sentences with the following requirements. Use separate paper.

1. A series of words or phrases.
2. A month, day, and year (not at the end of a sentence).
3. A street address, city, state, and zip code (not at the end of a sentence).
4. Coordinate adjectives.
5. A parenthetic element.
6. Direct address.
7. An appositive.
8. An introductory word.
9. An introductory verbal phrase.
10. An introductory phrase that needs a comma to prevent misreading.
11. A negative expression at end of sentence.
12. A transitional expression.

Check your sentences with your instructor. If your work is satisfactory, you may proceed to Activity 6-J.

---

**ACTIVITY 6-J: Review of Punctuation Patterns and Rules**

---

Punctuate the following sentences correctly. In the space provided, identify the patterns or rules used.
*Patterns:* IC, cc IC. IC; IC. IC; trans, IC. DC, IC. IC DC.
*Rules:* series, date, address, coord. adj., interr., intro. word or phrase (specify one-word, verbal, or misreading).

_____ 1. The students took their texts and notebooks to class apparently they expected a review before the test.

_____ 2. However we are not requiring the civil engineers to participate in the experiment.

_____ 3. Arriving late for the meeting the reporter had to sit in the back of the room.

_____ 4. The famous murder trial in Emporia Virginia on March 28 1952 drew a large crowd.

_____ 5. Agri-Business is an interesting technology isn't it?

_____ 6. Yes Mrs. Grant it was an informative field trip.

_____ 7. Many students in data processing have information that they have to feed into the computer.

_____ 8. Accounting a technology dealing with keeping accurate financial records is necessary for anyone who wants to become a CPA.

_____ 9. The tall slender student was interested only in his technology and his job.

_____ 10. The biology instructor too gave a difficult assignment.

_____ 11. When we asked for a motel room the manager said that there were no vacancies.

_____ 12. To succeed in sales in 1991 500 new people must increase their accounts.

_____ 13. He told his supervisor the correct answer apparently to the question.

_____ 14. His address is 214 College Avenue Philadelphia PA 21069 a prosperous business area.

_____ 15. He spoke to the construction builders there was a flaw in the weatherstripping.

Check your responses in Feedback 6-J at the end of this module. If your responses were correct, proceed to Part III. If you missed any sentences, check them with your instructor.

## PART III: THE APOSTROPHE (Possession)

The apostrophe is a punctuation mark used to show possession in nouns and indefinite pronouns. Here is the basic rule: *If the word you wish to make possessive ends in* **s,** *add an apostrophe after the* **s;** *if the noun does not end in* **s,** *add an apostrophe and an* **s.**

**Rule 1.** *Don't worry about whether the noun is singular or plural. Just concern yourself with whether or not it ends in* **s.**

EXAMPLES

| NOUN | SINGULAR POSSESSIVE | PLURAL POSSESSIVE |
|------|---------------------|-------------------|
| man | man's | men's |
| woman | woman's | women's |
| supervisor | supervisor's | supervisors' |

| INDEFINITE PRONOUN | | |
|--------------------|--------|--|
| everyone | everyone's | |
| anybody | anybody's | |

**Rule 2.** *If the noun ends in* **s** *and you hear an extra* **s** *when you make it possessive, add an apostrophe* **s.**

| NOUN | SINGULAR POSSESSIVE | PLURAL POSSESSIVE |
|------|---------------------|-------------------|
| boss | boss's | bosses' |
| Jones | Jones's | Joneses' |
| waitress | waitress's | waitresses' |

There is a simple five-step process to help you locate and form a possessive.

Here is a sentence to use as an example:

> The news in the Student Center is about students grades.

**Step 1.** Locate nouns or indefinite pronouns ending in **s.**

> The **news** in the Student Center is about **students grades.**

**Step 2.** Check to see if there is a noun to the right.

> The **news** in the Student Center is about **students grades.**

There is no noun to the right of **news.**
There is no noun to the right of **grades.**
There is a noun to the right of **students.**

**Step 3.** Substitute the phrase *belonging to* or *of* to determine if possession is being shown.

> grades of students

*Note:* There is nothing belonging to **news** or **grades;** therefore, possession is not being shown. Be sure to check all nouns ending in **s** to see if they are possessive or if they are merely plural. **News** is a singular noun ending in **s** (an exception to the rule of the way most nouns form their plurals); **grades** is a plural noun showing no possession.

**Step 4.** Determine if the possessive noun or indefinite pronoun is singular or plural.

> **Students** is plural because the sentence is talking about the grades of more than one student.

**Step 5.** Turn the *belonging to* phrase around again, this time using the apostrophe to show that the noun is possessive. If the possessive noun ends in **s,** add only an apostrophe. If the noun does not end in **s,** add an apostrophe and an **s.**

> students' grades

Corrected sentence:

> The news in the Student Center is about students' grades.

Now, apply the five-step approach to a slightly different sentence:

> The news in the Student Center is about a students grades.

**Step 1.** Locate the nouns or indefinite pronouns ending in **s.**

> news, students, grades

**Step 2.** Check to see if there is a noun to the right.
*Note:* Be sure to check for words that qualify whether the noun is singular or plural, such as **a, an, each, every.**

> a students grades

**Step 3.** Substitute the phrase *belonging to* or *of* to determine if possession is being shown.
*Note:* Include any qualifying words that indicate whether the noun is singular or plural.

> the grades of a student

**Step 4.** Determine if the possessive noun or indefinite pronoun is singular or plural.

> *A student* is singular.

**Step 5.** Turn the *belonging to* phrase around again, this time using the apostrophe to show that the noun is possessive. If the possessive noun ends in **s,** add only an apostrophe. If the noun does not end in **s,** add an apostrophe and an **s.**

> a student's grades

Corrected sentence:

> The news in the Student Center is about a student's grades.

Now, do one more example before you try to use the five-step method for using the apostrophe to show possession. This time, the example will have a possessive indefinite pronoun instead of a noun.

**101**

> The cafeteria tables should be free of anyones books.

**Step 1.** Locate the noun or indefinite pronoun ending in **s.**

> tables, anyones, books

**Step 2.** Check to see if there is a noun to the right of it.

> The cafeteria tables should be free of anyones books.

**Step 3.** Substitute the phrase *belonging to* or *of* to determine if possession is being shown.

> books belonging to anyone

**Step 4.** Determine if the possessive noun or indefinite pronoun is singular or plural.

> **Anyone** is singular.

**Step 5.** Turn the *belonging to* phrase around again, this time using the apostrophe to show that the noun or pronoun is possessive.

> anyone's books

Corrected sentence:

> The tables in the cafeteria should be free of anyone's books.

Now it is time for you to try your hand at applying the five-step approach to solving possessive problems.

## ACTIVITY 6-K: Apostrophe

Sample sentence:

> The retailers meetings are held on Wednesdays and Fridays.

**Step 1.** Locate the nouns or indefinite pronouns ending in **s.**

**Step 2.** Check to see if there is a noun to the right.

> The retailers meetings are held on Wednesdays and Fridays.

**Step 3.** Substitute the *belonging to* or *of* phrase to determine if possession is being shown. _____

**Step 4.** Determine if the possessive noun or indefinite pronoun is singular or plural. _____

**Step 5.** Turn the *belonging to* phrase around, using the apostrophe to show possession. _____

Corrected sentence:

_____

Sample sentence:

> A computers keys need repair because of careless operators.

Step 1. _____
Step 2. _____
Step 3. _____
Step 4. _____
Step 5. _____

Corrected sentence:

_____

Sample sentence:

> Everybodys printouts are on the shelves.

Step 1. _____

Step 2. _____

Step 3. _____

Step 4. _____

Step 5. _____

Corrected sentence: _____

Check your responses in Feedback 6-K. If you missed any, see your instructor before proceeding.

## ACTIVITY 6-L: Apostrophe

Provide the correct possessive form.

1.  everyone            _____

2.  foreman             _____

3.  Ross                _____

4.  Lindquists          _____

5.  accountants         _____

6.  child               _____

7.  retailers           _____

8.  women               _____

9.  Davises             _____

10. waitress            _____

11. company             _____

12. companies           _____

Check your responses in Feedback 6-L at the end of this module. If you missed any, review Rules 1 and 2 and then go on.

**Rule 3.** *Make sure that possession is being shown by seeing if there is something that belongs to the noun. To do this, reverse the possessive phrase (such as* **the dog's bone**) *and use a prepositional phrase (***bone of the dog**).

### EXAMPLES

the book's pages  *becomes*  the pages of the book
the man's hat  *becomes*  the hat of the man

The policeman's badge  *becomes*  the badge of the policeman (*Singular*)
the policewomen's badges  *becomes*  the badges of the policewomen (*Plural*)

the boats in the harbor (*Can't turn phrase around—not possessive—no apostrophe needed*)

Note that in some situations there is no "belonging." Certain nouns may be possessive in form only.

EXAMPLES

a day's wages
a nickel's worth

---

## ACTIVITY 6-M: Apostrophe

Show possession with an apostrophe instead of the prepositional phrase. *Example:* the trial of Alger Hiss → Alger Hiss's trial.

1. the efficiency of the reporter _____

2. the work of the women _____

3. the duties of tomorrow _____

4. the manual of the student _____

5. the automobile of the company _____

6. the hat of the manager _____

7. the safety shoes of the workers _____

8. the hard hat of the electrician _____

9. the saw of the carpenter _____

10. the yellow shoes of Mrs. David _____

Check your responses in Feedback 6-M at the end of this module. If your responses were correct, proceed to Rule 4. If you missed any, review the five-step process on pp. 99–100 and then do Activity 6-N.

---

## ACTIVITY 6-N: Apostrophe

Show possession with an apostrophe instead of the prepositional phrase.

1. the drawing board of the architect _____

2. the syringes of the nurses _____

3. the ledger of the company _____

4. a vacation of two weeks _____

5. the work of one day _____

6. the secretaries of the boss _____

7. the secretary of the boss _____

8. the secretary of the bosses     _____

9. the secretary of Mr. Jones     _____

10. the paychecks of the women     _____

Check your responses in Feedback 6-N at the end of this module. If your responses were correct, proceed to Rule 4. If you missed any, check with your instructor before proceeding.

**Rule 4.** *Use an apostrophe after the last noun in a series to show joint possession.*

EXAMPLES

Bill, Henry, and **Fred's** project.
My aunt and **uncle's** anniversary
Mother and **Dad's** car

**Rule 5.** *Use an apostrophe with each name when two or more persons possess something individually.*

EXAMPLES

Hemingway's and Steinbeck's novels
my sister's and my brother's salaries

## ACTIVITY 6-O: Apostrophe

Provide the correct possessive form.

1. the cars of Pat and Mike (different cars)

   _____

2. the room of Eileen and Gail (same room)

   _____

3. the tools of Dan and Fred (same tools)

   _____

4. the tools of Dan and Fred (different tools)

   _____

5. the lunch of Ann and Sherry (same lunch)

   _____

Check your responses in Feedback 6-O at the end of this module. If your responses were correct, proceed to Rule 6. If you missed any, review Rules 4 and 5 and do Activity 6-P.

**ACTIVITY 6-P: Apostrophe**

Provide the correct possessive form.

1. the offices of Griffin and Kelly (same offices)

_____

2. the offices of Griffin and Kelly (different offices)

_____

3. the ears of Joe and Carl

_____

4. the boat of Dave and Wayne (same boat)

_____

5. the apartments of Marston and Santana (different apartments)

_____

Check your responses in Feedback 6-P at the end of this module. If you missed any, check with your instructor before proceeding.

**Rule 6.** *A company name is singular. Even though it may be composed of several names, it is one unit. In order to make a company name possessive, you need to add only one apostrophe (or apostrophe **s**) to the last name.*

EXAMPLES

| | |
|---|---|
| the lumber of Smart and Jordon | Smart and Jordan's lumber |
| the Band-Aids of Johnson and Johnson | Johnson and Johnson's Band-Aids |
| the toothpaste of Procter and Gamble | Procter and Gamble's toothpaste |
| the cigarettes of Benson and Hedges | Benson and Hedges' cigarettes |
| the rating of Standard and Poor | Standard and Poor's rating |

**ACTIVITY 6-Q: Apostrophe**

Provide the correct possessive form.

1. the law offices of Morgan and Anderson

_____

2. the cameras of Bell and Howell

_____

3. the cafeteria of Townsend and Baker

_____

4. the firm of Jones and Jones

_____

5. the equipment of Mead and Johnson

_____

Check your answers in Feedback 6-Q at the end of this module. If your responses were correct, proceed to Rule 7. If you missed any, review Rule 6 and do Activity 6-R.

## ACTIVITY 6-R: Apostrophe

Provide the correct possessive form.

1. the machinery of Smith, Jones & Brown

_____

2. the acreage of Ayres and Hull Farms

_____

3. the hospital facilities of Scott and White

_____

4. the catalog of Montgomery Ward

_____

5. the merchandise of Sears and Roebuck

_____

Check your answers in Feedback 6-R at the end of this module. If you missed any, check with your instructor before proceeding.

**Rule 7.** _Never use an apostrophe with the possessive pronouns._

### POSSESSIVE PRONOUNS

|  |
|---|
| yours   ours   theirs   its   his   whose   hers |

When you speak, there is no distinction in sound between **its** and **it's,** between **theirs** and **there's,** between **whose** and **who's.** When you write, however, it's important to make a distinction. None of the possessive pronouns ever takes an apostrophe.

**It's** is a contraction for **it is.**

**Who's** is a contraction for **who is.**

**There's** is a contraction for **there is.**

Fix clearly in your mind that **its** (*no apostrophe*) is the possessive form of **it.** When you write **it's** (*with apostrophe*), you mean **it is.**

**It's** time for the secretarial staff to take **its** coffee break.

*Note:* In business and technical writing, contractions are inappropriate. Do not use them, and you will not have any problems in this area.

## ACTIVITY 6-S: Apostrophe

Underline the correct pronoun.

1. The new lab reports are (your's/yours).
2. (Whose/Who's) printouts were left in the computer room?
3. (It's/Its) results will show on the graph.
4. (There's/Theirs/Their's) are the best.
5. The syringe is (her's/hers).
6. (Ours/Our's) is in the filing cabinet.
7. (Whose/Who's) going to proofread the letter?
8. (It's/Its) time for a salary increase.
9. (Theirs/There's/Their's) no more fuel in the gas tank.
10. (Yours/Your's) are in the office.

Check your responses in Feedback 6-S at the end of this module. If your responses were correct, proceed to the Apostrophe Review. If you missed any, review Rule 7 and do Activity 6-T.

## ACTIVITY 6-T: Apostrophe

Underline the correct pronoun.

1. The book lost (it's/its) cover.
2. (Your's/Yours) are in the desk.
3. He brought us (our's/ours).
4. (Whose/Who's) typewriter is unplugged?
5. (Whose/Who's) typing now?
6. (Theirs/There's/Their's) no way to check the records.
7. (Theirs/There's/Their's) are in the file folder.

8. The briefcase is (her's/hers).
9. (It's/Its) pages are torn.
10. (It's/Its) in the wrong place.

Check your responses in Feedback 6-T at the end of this module. If you missed any, check with your instructor before proceeding.

**Apostrophe Review**

Before your last practice using possessives, let's review the basic rule:

*If possessive noun ends in* **s** → *add* '
*If possessive noun does not end in* **s** → *add* **'s**
*If possessive noun ends in* **s** *and you hear an extra* **s** → *add* **'s**

---

**ACTIVITY 6-U: Apostrophe Review**

---

Provide the correct possessive form.

> The architects drawing revealed a large square building with an open courtyard in its center. Staff members offices opened onto the courtyard. Everyones desk had a view of a lovely colored fountain. Each employees chair was positioned to make the most of the restful fountain. Harris and Farmers design firm was credited with the imaginative layout. People from miles around came to observe the buildings design features.

Check your responses in Feedback 6-U at the end of this module. If your answers were correct, ask your instructor for Test A. If you missed any, ask your instructor for extra practice.

---

***FEEDBACK FOR MODULE 6***

**Feedback 6-A**

Pattern 1:  IC, cc IC.
Pattern 2:  IC; IC.
Pattern 3:  IC; trans, IC.
Pattern 4:  DC, IC.
Pattern 5:  IC DC.

**Feedback 6-B**

A.  1.  It rained on Friday, and (so) the construction crew didn't work.
    2.  It rained on Friday; the construction crew didn't work.

3. It rained on Friday; therefore (as a result), the construction crew didn't work.
4. Because (Since) it rained on Friday, the construction crew didn't work.
5. The construction crew didn't work on Friday because (since) it rained.

B. 1. The blueprint machine was broken, and (so) the building plans weren't ready for the client.
2. The blueprint machine was broken; the building plans weren't ready for the client.
3. The blueprint machine was broken; consequently (therefore), the building plans weren't ready for the client.
4. Because (since) the blueprint machine was broken, the building plans weren't ready for the client.
5. The building plans weren't ready for the client because (since) the blueprint machine was broken.

C. 1. I kept a good record of my expenses for the year, and (so) I was ready for the accountant to do my taxes.
2. I kept a good record of my expenses for the year; I was ready for the accountant to do my taxes.
3. I kept a good record of my expenses for the year; thus (therefore, consequently), I was ready for the accountant to do my taxes.
4. Since (because) I kept a good record of my expenses for the year, I was ready for the accountant to do my taxes.
5. I was ready for the accountant to do my taxes since (because) I kept a good record of my expenses for the year.

## Feedback 6-C

1. DC, IC.
2. IC DC.
3. IC, cc IC.
4. IC; IC.
5. IC; trans, IC.
6. IC DC.
7. IC, cc IC.
8. IC; trans, IC.
9. IC; IC.
10. IC; trans, IC.

## Feedback 6-E

1. chairman, historian, secretary, and treasurer.
2. to interview the celebrity, to take pictures, and to write the feature article by Monday.
3. Friday, January 12, 1993, in Room 100.
4. Mrs. Jerome Gray, 201 Olympia Drive, Seattle, Washington 90105, preferably by noon Friday.
5. patient, considerate
6. (No commas)
7. on alcoholic services, educational opportunities, and job seminars.
8. (No commas)
9. that the television had been struck by lightning, that the main tube was ruined, and that it would cost $50 to fix it.
10. Peoria, Illinois 90555.

## Feedback 6-F

1. secretary, bookkeeper, and accountant.
2. education, to qualify. . .job, and to be . . .

111

3. Monday, June 12, 1988, at 2 p.m.
4. 4123 First Avenue, Salisbury, MD 21801, behind. . .
5. skillful, clever architect
6. (No commas)
7. (No commas)
8. room, . . . gym,
9. respiration, . . . technique,
10. January 2, 1989, on the afternoon train.

### Feedback 6-G

1. class, (accordingly,) (one sentence)
2. well, doesn't she?
3. Yes, Ms. Winter
4. seldom, (however,) (one sentence)
5. employer,
6. paycheck,
7. memo, (however,) (one sentence)
8. time,
9. time, (however,) (one sentence)
10. student, a chemistry major,

### Feedback 6-H

1. Miss Jones, will
2. technician, . . . college,
3. times, however,
4. students, isn't it?
5. degree, they
6. IBM, therefore,
7. supervisor, Elizabeth Fleming,
8. According to the freight department, our
9. To begin with,
10. memo, Miss Earlson?

### Feedback 6-J

1. class; apparently,  *IC; trans, IC*
2. However,  *intro. word or interr.*
3. Arriving late for the meeting,  *intro. phrase (verbal)*
4. Emporia, Virginia, on March 28, 1952,  *address, date*
5. technology, isn't it?  *interr. (neg. expr.)*
6. Yes, Mrs. Grant,  *interr. (dir. add.)*
7. (no comma)  *IC DC*
8. Accounting, a technology dealing with keeping accurate financial records,  *interr. (appos.)*
9. tall, slender  *coord. adj.*
10. instructor, too,  *interr. (paren. elem.)*
11. room,  *DC, IC*
12. To succeed in sales in 1991,  *intro. phrase (verbal, misreading)*
13. answer, apparently,  *interr. (paren. elem.)*
14. College Avenue, Philadelphia, PA 21069,  *address*
15. builders;  *IC; IC*

**Feedback 6-K**

Sample sentence 1:
Step 1. retailers, meetings, Wednesdays, Fridays
Step 2. retailers meetings
Step 3. meetings of retailers
Step 4. **Retailers** is plural.
Step 5. retailers' meetings.
Corrected sentence: The retailers' meetings are held on Wednesdays and Fridays.

Sample sentence 2:
Step 1. computers, keys, operators
Step 2. computers keys
Step 3. keys belonging to a computer
Step 4. **A computer** is singular. Note the qualifying word *a*.
Step 5. computer's keys.
Corrected sentence: A computer's keys need repair because of careless operators.

Sample sentence 3:
Step 1. everybodys, printouts, shelves
Step 2. everybodys printouts
Step 3. printouts belonging to everybody
Step 4. **Everybody** is a singular indefinite pronoun.
Step 5. everybody's printouts
Corrected sentence: Everybody's printouts are on the shelves.

**Feedback 6-L**

| | | |
|---|---|---|
| 1. everyone's | 5. accountants' | 9. Davises' |
| 2. foreman's | 6. child's | 10. waitress's |
| 3. Ross's | 7. retailers' | 11. Company's |
| 4. Lindquists' | 8. women's | 12. Companies' |

**Feedback 6-M**

| | |
|---|---|
| 1. the reporter's efficiency | 6. the manager's hat |
| 2. the women's work | 7. the workers' safety shoes |
| 3. tomorrow's duties | 8. the electrician's hard hat |
| 4. the student's manual | 9. the carpenter's saw |
| 5. the company's automobile | 10. Mrs. David's yellow shoes |

**Feedback 6-N**

| | |
|---|---|
| 1. the architect's drawing board | 6. the boss's secretaries |
| 2. the nurses' syringes | 7. the boss's secretary |
| 3. the company's ledger | 8. the bosses' secretary |
| 4. a two weeks' vacation | 9. Mr. Jones's secretary |
| 5. one day's work | 10. the women's paychecks |

**Feedback 6-O**

1. Pat's and Mike's cars
2. Eileen and Gail's room
3. Dan and Fred's tools
4. Dan's and Fred's tools
5. Ann and Sherry's lunch

**Feedback 6-P**

1. Griffin and Kelly's offices
2. Griffin's and Kelly's offices
3. Joe's and Carl's ears
4. Dave and Wayne's boat
5. Marston's and Santana's apartments

**Feedback 6-Q**

1. Morgan and Anderson's law offices
2. Bell and Howell's cameras
3. Townsend and Baker's cafeteria
4. Jones and Jones's firm
5. Mead and Johnson's equipment

**Feedback 6-R**

1. Smith, Jones & Brown's machinery
2. Ayres and Hull Farms' acreage
3. Scott and White's hospital facilities
4. Montgomery Ward's catalog
5. Sears and Roebuck's merchandise

**Feedback 6-S**

1. yours
2. Whose
3. Its
4. Theirs
5. hers
6. Ours
7. Who's
8. Its
9. There's
10. Yours

**Feedback 6-T**

1. its
2. Yours
3. ours
4. Whose
5. Who's
6. There's
7. Theirs
8. hers
9. Its
10. It's

**Feedback 6-U**

architect's
members'
Everyone's

employee's
Farmer's
building's

114

# Fragments and Run-Ons

OBJECTIVE: This module is devoted to a punctuation problem that deserves special attention. It will help you to identify and correct two types of errors.

Upon completion of this module, you will be able:

To identify and to correct fragments of sentences.

To identify run-on sentences and to punctuate them for clarity.

In conversation, fragments and run-ons go unnoticed and are quite acceptable. In writing, however, fragments and run-ons must be avoided because they are incorrect and can result in misinterpretation of your intended meaning. So it is important to be able to recognize these errors and learn how to correct them.

A *fragment* is an incomplete sentence. *Run-ons* are two or more sentence units that have been run together as one sentence. Before we take up each of these types of errors, we need to define *sentence*.

A *sentence* is a group of words that has a subject and a verb and usually expresses a complete thought. An independent clause (as shown in Module 5) is a whole sentence. A sentence contains at least one independent clause. It can be very brief, consisting only of the S–V unit, or it can be amplified with modifiers. In an imperative sentence (command), only the verb is stated; the subject *you* is understood but not stated. For example, in the sentence *Close the file,* the understood subject is *you*.

EXAMPLES

| Subject | Verb |
| --- | --- |
| Draftsmen | design. |
| Secretaries | type. |
| Technicians | test. |
| He | spoke. |
| (You—*understood*) | Run! |

A sentence may be very short, containing only a subject and a verb, or it may be longer, with many modifiers and clauses. Whether long or short, a sentence must have the two requirements mentioned: subject and verb in an independent clause. Remember, a sentence contains at least one independent clause (**IC**), which is not introduced by a clause signal. It may, of course, also contain a dependent clause (**DC**), which is introduced by a clause signal.

EXAMPLE

As I came to work, I saw the accident.
      DC            IC

EXAMPLE: IC SENTENCES WITH MODIFIERS

Our draftsmen are designing many new products.
An efficient secretary types with speed and accuracy.
The technicians have tested all the specimens carefully.
He spoke with me for about an hour.
Run to the window quickly.

116

After having learned to recognize a complete sentence, you will be able to identify a fragment (which is only a part of a sentence) and not fall into the trap of punctuating a fragment as though it were a sentence. Here are the six types of fragments that are likely to cause problems. As you can see, there are several ways of turning fragments into sentences.

### FRAGMENT 1: A Dependent Clause

PROBLEM:    after the farmer cleared his field

SOLUTION:    *Add an independent cause.*
After the farmer cleared his field, he planted corn.

### FRAGMENT 2: A Prepositional Phrase

PROBLEM:    throughout his report

SOLUTION:    *Add an independent cause*
There were numerous errors throughout his report.

### FRAGMENT 3: A Verbal Phrase

PROBLEM:    typing the letter for the saleswoman

SOLUTION:

    A.    *Change the verbal into a verb and add a subject.*
Jane was typing the letter for the saleswoman.

    B.    *Add an independent cause.*
Typing the letter for the saleswoman, Jane was quick and efficient.

### FRAGMENT 4: A Subject

PROBLEM:    the engineers at the chemical plant

SOLUTION:    *Add a verb.*
The engineers at the chemical plant were on strike. (*or*) The engineers were at the chemical plant.

### FRAGMENT 5: A Verb

PROBLEM:    took his temperature

SOLUTION:    *Add a subject.*
The nurse took his temperature.

## FRAGMENT 6: Other Phrases

PROBLEM: such as memos and reports

SOLUTION: *Add an independent cause.*
The assistant typed business correspondence, such as memos and reports.

*Note:* One good way to spot fragments is to read from the bottom up in your paper; that is, read the last sentence, then the next to last sentence, and so on.

## ACTIVITY 7-A: Fragments

On your own paper, rewrite any fragments in 1 to 10 to make sentences; if the sentence is complete, write OK.

1. The car stopping too quickly.
2. The financial statement indicated a profit.
3. The farmer in the barn with the cows.
4. Cleaned and adjusted by the mechanic.
5. Ambulances raced toward the accident.
6. Thundering and lightning in the west.
7. On the blueprint an octagonal window.
8. Several college students surveying the field.
9. The typewriter clicked.
10. Seeming more concerned about his reactions than his answers.

Check your responses in Feedback 7-A at the end of this module. If your responses were correct, proceed to Part II. If you missed any, do Activity 7-B.

## ACTIVITY 7-B: Fragments

On your own paper, rewrite any fragments below to make sentences. If the sentence is complete, write OK.

1. Entered into the computer.
2. Sally's first patient in the recovery room.
3. Lime spreads evenly on a calm day.
4. While the engine was running rapidly.
5. During the investigation on Tuesday.
6. Drew an alternative plan that met specifications.
7. Smiling pleasantly, the receptionist, Miss Harrington.
8. Reestablished an obscure benchmark after researching the boundaries of adjoining lands.

9. Somewhere between the motor and the transmitter.

10. It is good business to be considerate.

Check your responses in Feedback 7-B at the end of this module. If your responses were correct, proceed to Part II. If you missed any, review Part I.

## PART II: RUN-ONS

*Run-on sentences* are two or more independent clauses written together as one sentence. All run-ons result from errors in punctuation.

Below are five ways to punctuate two or more independent clauses that will prevent them from becoming a run-on sentence.

| | | |
|---|---|---|
| (a) Sentence_____ | . Sentence_____ | . IC. IC. |
| (b) Sentence_____ | ; sentence_____ | . IC; IC. |
| (c) Sentence_____ | , conjunction sentence | . IC, cc IC. |
| (d) Sentence_____ | ; transition, sentence__ | . IC; trans, IC. |
| (e) One sentence___ | with a compound verb__ | . IC (cv). |

There are five common types of punctuation errors that result in run-on sentences. The following list shows you how to turn each of these run-ons into one of the correct patterns indicated above.

**Run-on 1:  Two independent clauses with no punctuation between them**

PROBLEM:    The foreman made up the payroll he issued the work orders for the crew.

SOLUTION:

A.  *Make two sentences* (IC. IC.):
The foreman made up the payroll. He issued the work orders for the crew.

B.  *Use a semicolon when the ideas are closely related* (IC; IC):
The foreman made up the payroll; he issued the work orders for the crew.

**Run-on 2:  Two independent clauses separated only by a comma**

PROBLEM:    The foreman made up the payroll, he issued the work orders for the crew.

SOLUTION:

A.  *Make two sentences* (IC. IC.):
The foreman made up the payroll. He issued the work orders for the crew.

**119**

B. *Use a semicolon when the ideas are closely related* (IC; IC.):
The foreman made up the payroll; he issued the work orders for the crew.

## Run-on 3: Two independent clauses and a conjunction without a comma

PROBLEM: The foreman made up the payroll and he issued the work orders for the crew.

SOLUTION:

A. *Use a comma before the conjunction* (IC, cc, IC.):
The foreman made up the payroll, and he issued the work orders for the crew.

B. *Rewrite with a compound verb* (IC with cv). For a discussion of compound verbs, see Module 4, Part V.
The foreman made up the payroll and issued the work orders for the crew.

**Note:** If the independent clauses are very short, the comma may be omitted:

EXAMPLE

The secretaries typed and they took dictation.

## Run-on 4: Two independent clauses joined by a transitional expression with no punctuation

PROBLEM: The foreman made up the payroll furthermore he issued the work orders for the crew.

SOLUTION:

A. *Use a semicolon and a comma* (IC; trans, IC.):
The foreman made up the payroll; furthermore, he issued the work orders for the crew.

B. *Make two sentences* (IC. IC.):
The foreman made up the payroll. Furthermore, he issued the work orders for the crew.

Note that words such as **however, therefore,** and **furthermore** are sometimes interrupters appearing in the middle of *one* sentence rather than transitional words appearing between two independent clauses. The following are two separate sentences, each with an interrupter in the middle. These are punctuated correctly. For a review of interrupters, see Module 6, Part II, Rule 4.

EXAMPLES

The foreman, however, made up the payroll.
He issued, furthermore, the work orders for the crew.

**Run-on 5:**  **Two independent clauses joined by a transitional expression with only commas**

PROBLEM:    The foreman made up the payroll, furthermore, he issued the work orders for the crew.

SOLUTION:

A.   *Use a semicolon and comma* (IC; trans, IC.):
The foreman made up the payroll; furthermore, he issued the work orders for the crew.

B.   *Make two sentences* (IC. IC.):
The foreman made up the payroll. Furthermore, he issued the work orders for the crew.

The word **then** is a possible signal of a run-on. Usually, it is a transitional expression and therefore should be preceded by a semicolon or a period. Note also that you do not need to use a comma after **then.**

EXAMPLES

PROBLEM:    The foreman made up the payroll, **then** he issued the work orders for the crew. (*Run-on*)

SOLUTIONS:   The foreman made up the payroll; **then** he issued the work orders for the crew. (IC; trans. IC.)
The foreman made up the payroll. **Then** he issued the work orders for the crew. (IC. IC.)

---

**ACTIVITY 7-C: Run-ons**

For numbers 1 to 10, punctuate any run-on sentences correctly in one of the five ways: *IC.IC.   IC;IC.   IC,ccIC.   IC;trans,IC.   or IC(cv)*. If a sentence is correctly punctuated, write OK after it.

1. The speaker on the subject of soil chemistry was famous, there was a large audience.

2. Contractors arrived early for the bid opening, they stayed late to ask about quotations.

3. The power source was a factor; established industries planned expansion of facilities.

4. The strike created a financial crisis, and the company applied for bankruptcy.

5. No clues were evident, a detective was assigned to the case.

6. Alcoholism is treated as a disease however it is not necessarily fatal.

7. You can save money by learning to rebuild your own engine, of course, you can always buy a rebuilt one.

8. Many students learn to interpret blueprints others learn to draw them.

9. Under a heavy workload, an efficient secretary learns to assign priorities; then she can complete the urgent tasks sooner.

10. In nearly every community, some people suffer from poverty their needs usually vary.

Check your responses in Feedback 7-C at the end of this module. If your responses were correct, proceed to Activity 7-E. If you missed any, review Part II; then do Activity 7-D.

## ACTIVITY 7-D: Run-ons

Correct any run-ons. If a sentence is correctly punctuated, mark it OK.

1. Most fertilizer companies employ truck drivers and warehouseworkers on a part-time basis, moreover a few companies maintain these employees on a full-time schedule.

2. Years ago, trees were often used as benchmarks; today, more lasting objects are preferred.

3. Donna is a legal secretary, she makes an excellent salary.

4. Most managers in large corporations prepare financial statements they are seldom involved in detailed accounting procedures.

5. Designing the building to specifications requires more consultation with the client than constructing the building on its site.

6. Servicing electrical motors and appliances is his vocation, designing electrical equipment is his hobby.

7. Many laborers develop low blood pressure, nevertheless they are able to continue working.

8. As an undercover agent, she was outstanding; as a traffic regulator, she was incompetent.

9. He works as an automobile mechanic during the week, and he rebuilds antique cars on weekends.

10. Some restaurants are exclusive, most cater to a wider clientele.

Check your responses in Feedback 7-D at the end of this module. If your responses were correct, proceed to Activity 7-E. If you missed any, review Part II again before proceeding.

## ACTIVITY 7-E: Fragments and Run-ons

In the space provided, identify the following items as F (fragment), R (run-on), or S (sentence). Correct each item that is not a sentence.

_____ 1. The conference speaker was famous, there was a large audience.

_____ 2. The executive having received the memo.

_____ 3. She was invited to be a guest speaker at the safety meeting, the main topic was fire prevention.

_____ 4. Of course, you can always find employees in the coffee shop you can also meet them in the lounge.

_____ 5. Coming in for a cup of coffee between appointments.

_____ 6. In the late evening the building is deserted, however in the morning it is alive with activity.

_____ 7. Only technicians who have served an apprenticeship will be hired.

_____ 8. Working in an air-conditioned office which has plush carpeting.

_____ 9. His strong point being his skill in electronics.

_____ 10. Architecture is an exciting field you can use your creative talents fully.

Check your responses in Feedback 7-E at the end of this module. If you missed any, check with your instructor and then do Activity 7-F.

## ACTIVITY 7-F: Fragments and Run-ons

In the space provided, identify the following items as F (fragment), R (run-on), or S (sentence). Correct each item that is not a sentence.

_____ 1. The hospital was large, it had a new south wing added last year.

_____ 2. The secretary having taken a coffee break.

_____ 3. The electronics specialist was called in to look at the spectrophotometer, it was not registering properly.

_____ 4. In my opinion, the nurses should ask for a higher salary; furthermore, they deserve added benefits.

_____ 5. The contractor building the new airport facility.

_____ 6. After the meeting, the group went to the new restaurant it had a reputation for good food.

_____ 7. Lab assistants who have experience are being hired.

_____ 8. The architect who won the award for his design.

_____ 9. Such as her desire to get a better job.

_____ 10. Nursing is a rewarding career one can help many people as a nurse.

Check your responses in Feedback 7-F at the end of this module. If your responses were correct, proceed to Activity 7-G. If you missed any, check with your instructor before proceeding.

## ACTIVITY 7-G: Fragments and Run-ons

Correct all fragments and run-ons.

Nursing is a very special career. Nurses being in great demand. A nurse can find an area of specialty in many fields for instance one can choose pediatrics or geriatrics. As well as looking into obstetrics or surgery. After receiving proper training. A nurse is easily able to get a job that would be fulfilling and rewarding. The career of nursing offering many opportunities.

Check your responses with your instructor. If your responses were correct, proceed to Activity 7-I. If you missed any, review Part II and do Activity 7-H.

## ACTIVITY 7-H: Fragments and Run-ons

Correct all fragments and run-ons.

A tax cut would be very beneficial to the American economy it would be a boost that is much needed. Retail sales and business profits going up. While the rate of unemployment would go down. Our foreign trade expanding. Consequently, a reduction in taxes would have a positive effect on American economics.

Check your responses with your instructor. If your responses were correct, proceed to Activity 7-I. If you missed any, your instructor will review your errors and give you extra practice.

## ACTIVITY 7-I: Fragments and Run-ons

On your own paper, write sentences as specified below.

1.  Write a compound sentence joining two independent clauses with a semicolon. (A compound sentence contains at least two independent clauses.)
2.  Write a compound sentence joining two independent clauses with a comma and a conjunction.
3.  Write a compound sentence using the transitional expression **therefore.**
4.  Write a compound sentence using the conjunction **but.**
5.  Write a sentence with a compound verb.
6.  Write a compound sentence using the transitional expression **then.**

Check your sentences with your instructor. Then ask for Test A.

**Feedback 7-A**

There is more than one possible correct answer. If your answers differ from the feedback, check them with your instructor.

1. The car was stopping too quickly; (*or*) stopped.
2. OK
3. The farmer in the barn with his cows is my brother. (*or*) The farmer was in the barn with his cows.
4. The engine was cleaned and adjusted by the mechanic.
5. OK
6. We noticed thundering and lightning in the west. (*or*) It was thundering and lightning in the west.
7. On the blueprint, an octagonal window is drawn near the corner.
8. Several college students were surveying the field.
9. OK
10. The supervisor seemed more concerned about his reactions than his answers.

**Feedback 7-B**

There is more than one possible correct answer. If your answers differ from the feedback, check them with your instructor.

1. The account was entered into the computer.
2. Sally's first patient in the recovery room had a kidney removed.
3. OK
4. While the engine was running rapidly, he shifted into third gear.
5. A fingerprint expert was summoned during the investigation on Tuesday.
6. The architect drew an alternative plan that met specifications.
7. Smiling pleasantly, the receptionist, Miss Harrington, guided us to our destination.
8. The surveyors reestablished an obscure benchmark after researching the boundaries of adjoining lands.
9. The problem was located somewhere between the motor and the transmitter.
10. OK

**Feedback 7-C**

There is more than one possible correct answer. If your answers differ from the feedback, check them with your instructor.

1. famous; (*or*) famous. There
2. opening; (*or*) opening. They (*or*) contractors arrived early . . . and stayed late . . .
3. OK

4. OK (*or*) crisis. The
5. evident; (*or*) evident. A
6. disease; however, (*or*) disease, However,
7. engine; (*or*) engine. Of course,
8. blueprints; (*or*) blueprints. Others
9. OK
10. poverty; (*or*) poverty. Their

## Feedback 7-D

There is more than one possible correct answer. If your answers differ from the feedback, check them with your instructor.

1. basis; moreover, (*or*) basis. Moreover,
2. OK
3. secretary; (*or*) secretary. She (*or*) Donna is . . . and makes . . .
4. statements; (*or*) statements. They
5. OK
6. vocation; (*or*) vocation. Designing
7. pressure; nevertheless, (*or*) pressure. Nevertheless,
8. OK
9. OK
10. exclusive; (*or*) exclusive. Most

## Feedback 7-E

There is more than one possible correct answer. If your answers differ from the feedback, check them with your instructor.

1. R   famous; (*or*) famous. There
2. F   The executive, having received the memo, wrote a response. (*or*) The executive received the memo.
3. R   meeting; (*or*) meeting. The
4. R   Of course, you can always find . . . and also meet . . . (*or*) . . . shop. You . . .
5. F   The boss came in for a cup . . . (*or*) Coming in . . . appointments, the boss relaxed.
6. R   deserted; however, (*or*) deserted. However
7. S
8. F   She was working . . . (*or*) Working . . . carpeting, she was happy with her job.
9. F   His strong point was his skill in electronics. (*or*) His strong point being his skill in electronics, he was hired immediately.
10. R   field; (*or*) field. You (*or*) field, and

## Feedback 7-F

There is more than one possible correct answer. If your answers differ from the feedback, check them with your instructor.

1. R   large; (*or*) large. It (*or*) large and had . . .

2. F The secretary, having taken a coffee break, went back to work. (*or*) The secretary took a coffee break.
3. R spectrophotometer; (*or*) spectrophotometer. It
4. S
5. F The contractor was building the new airport facility.
6. R restaurant; it (*or*) restaurant. It
7. S
8. F The architect won the award for his design. (*or*) The architect who won the award for the design was trained at the technical college.
9. F She held many hopes for the future, such as her desire to get a better job.
10. R career; one (*or*) career. One

# MODULE 8

# Pronouns

**OBJECTIVE:** In this module you will learn how to avoid the misuse of pronouns. The module consists of seven parts.

Upon completion of this module, you will be able:

To identify correct forms of personal pronouns for various uses in the sentence.

To apply six rules governing pronoun–antecedent agreement in number.

A pronoun is a word used in the place of a noun. In other words, a pronoun is a substitute for a noun. This module deals with what are called *personal* pronouns. You will study the forms and uses of the three types listed on this page: subject pronouns, object pronouns, and possessive pronouns.

## SUBJECT PRONOUNS
### Used as subjects or subject complements

|  | SINGULAR | PLURAL |
|---|---|---|
| 1st person (speaking) | I | we |
| 2nd person (spoken to) | you | you |
| 3rd person (spoken of) | he | they |
|  | she |  |
|  | it |  |

## OBJECT PRONOUNS
### Used as direct objects of action verbs or of prepositions

|  | SINGULAR | PLURAL |
|---|---|---|
| 1st person (speaking) | me | us |
| 2nd person (spoken to) | you | you |
| 3rd person (spoken of) | him | them |
|  | her |  |
|  | it |  |

## POSSESSIVE PRONOUNS
### Used to show ownership

|  | SINGULAR | PLURAL |
|---|---|---|
| 1st person (speaking) | my (mine) | our (ours) |
| 2nd person (spoken to) | your (yours) | your (yours) |
| 3rd person (spoken of) | his (his) | their (theirs) |
|  | her (hers) |  |
|  | its (its) |  |

Note that no apostrophe is used with a possessive pronoun. **It's** is a contraction for **it is. Who's** is a contraction for **who is. There's** is a contraction for **there is.** Remember that in business and technical writing, you should not use contractions.

## PART I: PRONOUNS AS SUBJECTS

When the subject of a sentence is a pronoun, use the subject form of the pronoun. You already know how to identify the subject of a sentence. In the sentences below, the subject is in bold type. For a review of locating the subject and verb, see Module 4, Part I (p. 49).

EXAMPLES

**I** applied for the job.
**You** are in line for promotion.
**He** got a raise.
**She** uses good judgment.
**It** was put in the file.

**We** drive to work together.
**He and I** were assigned to the project.
**Don and she** planned the program.
**They** attended a sales meeting.

In addition to being used as the subject of an independent clause (a sentence), the subject pronoun is also used as the subject of a dependent clause. You will remember from Module 5 that a clause (independent or dependent) has a subject and a verb. The dependent clause signals are in italics, and the subjects of the dependent clauses are in bold type.

EXAMPLES

*After* **I** applied for the job, I was called for an interview.
The letter was retyped *before* **it** was put in the file.
The banker *who* handles our account is ill today.

Note that the clause signal *who* in the last sentence is also the subject of the dependent clause. *Which* and *that* are frequently used in the same manner.

## ACTIVITY 8-A: Subject Pronouns

Underline the subject pronoun that is correct for the sentence.

1. (He/Him) arrived early for his interview.
2. Mary and (he/him) came together.
3. Have you and (she/her) had a vacation?
4. David and (me/I) usually work together.
5. In my opinion, (we/us) gave the best answers.

6. (They/Them) have made good progress.

7. To tell the truth, (she/her) made too many mistakes.

8. (We/Us), the consumers, will test the new product.

9. (She and I) (Her and me) are the advisers.

10. Are you and (him/he) going to the convention?

Check your responses in Feedback 8-A at the end of this module. If your responses were correct, proceed to Part II. If you missed any, review the subject pronouns and then do Activity 8-B.

---

**ACTIVITY 8-B: Subject Pronouns**

---

Underline the correct pronoun form.

1. Mr. Newton and (she/her) worked late at the office.

2. After Julia and (she/her) left, the office was closed.

3. What are you and (he/him) going to do about the deficit?

4. Kate and (I/me) attended the conference.

5. On the other hand, (he/him) and Brett did not attend.

6. For our benefit, Michael and (he/him) will explain the new product.

7. (She and I) (Her and me) took the patient to the operating room.

8. Are you and (they/them) writing the report together?

9. How are you and (he/him) getting to the meeting?

10. Did Jimmy and (she/her) leave early?

Check your responses in Feedback 8-B at the end of this module. If your responses were correct, proceed to Part II. If you missed any, check them with your instructor before proceeding.

---

## PART II: PRONOUNS AS SUBJECT COMPLEMENTS

In Module 1 you learned that the verb **to be** is a linking verb. Some of its forms are **am, is, are, was, were, has been, have been, may be, might be, can be, could be, want to be,** and **like to be.** When the word following the **be** verb is a noun or pronoun, it is called the *subject complement*. The subject complement renames the subject; therefore, if it is a pronoun, it must be a subject pronoun.

> Subject–Linking Verb–Subject Complement
> S–LV–SC

EXAMPLE

Jane is she. (**she** stands for Jane; **she** = Jane)

Treat the linking verb as an equal sign (see Module 1, page 4.) In mathematics, what is on one side of the equal sign must equal what is on the other side of the equal sign. You can reverse the order without changing the meaning.

---

Subject = Subject Complement

---

In the examples below, the subject complement is in bold type.

EXAMPLES

The caller was **I**. I was the caller. (**I** = caller)
Was the chairman **he**? The chairman was he. (**he** = chairman)
The girl who took the message was **she**. She was the girl who took the message. (**she** = girl)
The new supervisors are **she** and **I**. She and I are the new supervisors. (**she** and **I** = supervisors)
The graduates were **they**. They were the graduates. (**they** = graduates)
The judges should have been **we**. We should have been the judges. (**we** = judges)

The subject complement may also be part of a dependent clause.

EXAMPLES

He thought that the *caller* was **I**. (**I** was the caller.)
The committee will not be effective unless the *chairman* is **he**. (**He** is the chairman.)

---

## ACTIVITY 8-C: Subject Complement Pronouns

---

Underline the correct pronoun form.

1. The new boss is (he/him).
2. The one who called was (me/I).
3. I don't think that it was (her/she).
4. Could it have been (him/he)?
5. It was probably Dan or (me/I).
6. It was (I/me) who saw the accident.
7. The consumers are you and (me/I).
8. Was it (him/he) who took first prize?

9. The winner should have been (she/her).

10. The candidates were John and (I/me).

Check your answers in Feedback 8-C at the end of this module. If your responses were correct, proceed to Part III. If you missed any, review Part II; then do Activity 8-D.

## ACTIVITY 8-D: Subject Complement Pronouns

Underline the correct pronoun form.

1. The winner of the award was (he/him).
2. The person who called for an appointment was (she/her).
3. I don't know if it was (he/him).
4. Do you suppose it could have been (they/them)?
5. It was probably (I/me) who made the error.
6. It was (we/us) who solved the problem.
7. The best customers are you and (I/me).
8. Was it (he/him) who designed the house?
9. The new secretary we hired yesterday was (she/her).
10. The applicants for the job were you and (he/him).

Check your responses in Feedback 8-D at the end of this module. If your responses were correct, proceed to Part III. If you missed any, check with your instructor before proceeding.

## PART III: PRONOUNS AS DIRECT OBJECTS

An action verb, you will remember from Module 1, shows what the subject is doing—it shows an action. The noun or pronoun that receives that action is called the *direct object*. In other words, the direct object answers the question "what?" or "whom?" after an action verb. When a direct object is a pronoun, it must be the *object pronoun* form. (See the box at the beginning of this module.)

> Subject–Action Verb–Direct Object
> S–AV–DO

EXAMPLES

She hastily called **me**. Called whom? Answer: **me** (*object pronoun*)
I know **him**. Know whom? Answer: **him** (*object pronoun*)

I thanked **her** and **him**. Thanked whom? Answer: **her** and **him** (*object pronouns*)

Maureen invited **us**. Invited whom? Answer: **us** (*object pronoun*)

Janelle missed **them**. Missed whom? Answer: **them** (*object pronoun*)

Randy hit **it**. Hit what? Answer: **it** (*object pronoun*)

## ACTIVITY 8-E: Object Pronouns

Underline the correct pronoun form.

1. Tell the supervisor and (him/he) what your job is.
2. Do not bother the technician and (me/I).
3. Do you remember (him and me) (he and I) from the conference?
4. Peggy will take (she and I) (her and me) to the meeting.
5. They will send you and (me/I) to the interview.
6. Tell (him/he) to finish the report by Thursday.
7. Do you know (her/she) from work?
8. Mr. Clark asked (me/I) to speak at the next seminar.
9. He will send (him/he) the dimensions of the rooms.
10. Have you told (they/them) about the project?

Check your responses in Feedback 8-E at the end of this module. If your responses were correct, you may proceed to Part IV. If you missed any, review Part III and do Activity 8-F.

## ACTIVITY 8-F: Object Pronouns

Underline the correct pronoun form.

1. Call the receptionist and (I/me) when you have finished.
2. Did you ask the doctor and (she/her) to give you the report?
3. You should remember (he and she) (him and her) from last year's meeting.
4. Matthew will drive Paula and (she/her) to the appointment.
5. The company will call Betsy and (I/me) for an interview.
6. Tell Mr. Watson and (he/him) about the audit.
7. Do you know Ellen and (she/her) through your business?
8. Mrs. Delano required Collins and (I/me) to write an agenda.
9. Dr. Insley sent Harry and (she/her) the X-ray report.
10. We will see Innis and (they/them) at the board meeting.

Check your responses in Feedback 8-F at the end of this module. If your responses were correct, proceed to Part IV. If you missed any, check with your instructor before proceeding.

## PART IV: PRONOUNS AS OBJECTS OF PREPOSITIONS

You will recall that a prepositional phrase consists of a preposition, its object, and any modifier of the object. If the object of the preposition is a pronoun, it must be in the *object* form. (You may wish to review the list of prepositions in Part I of Module 3.)

EXAMPLES

from me
with him
beside her
around us
among them
above it
for you
between you and me
to him and her

The ticket agent took the money **from me**.
Jack sat down **beside her**.
Here is a package **for you**.

When there is more than one object of a preposition, *each pronoun is in the object form*. It would be incorrect to say **between you and I** or **to he and she**. Repeat the preposition in your mind as a test (see Rule 1, page 139):

between you and me (between you and between me)

to him and her (to him and to her)

for John and him (for John and for him)

## ACTIVITY 8-G: Object Pronouns

Underline the correct pronoun form.

1. How long did you talk to (they/them)?
2. I sent the memo to (she/her).
3. She left her estate to (us/we).
4. He stood between you and (I/me).
5. Bill worked for Mr. Handy and (him/he) for ten years.
6. Give the report to (he and I) (him and me).
7. Between (you and I) (you and me), we can finish the work by tomorrow.
8. The yearly bonus was shared among Tom and (they/them).

9. Tell the boss about the secretary and (he/him).

10. At the conference, I sat beside (he and she) (him and her).

Check your responses in Feedback 8-G at the end of this module. If your responses were correct, proceed to Part V. If you missed any, review Part IV and then do Activity 8-H.

---

### ACTIVITY 8-H: Object Pronouns
---

Underline the correct pronoun form.

1. How long have you been employed by Mr. Brown and (he/him)?
2. The letter was written to (he and I) (him and me).
3. The government awarded the contract to (she and I) (her and me).
4. The nurse waited in line between (you and I) (you and me).
5. Joseph worked for (he and I) (him and me) for the summer.
6. Give the blood pressure gauge to (she and I) (her and me).
7. Between (you and I) (you and me), this is a difficult job.
8. The company profits were shared by (they and I) (them and me).
9. Ask the doctor about (she and they) (her and them).
10. In the workshop, she sat beside (him and me) (he and I).

Check your responses in Feedback 8-H at the end of this module. If your responses were correct, proceed to Part V. If you missed any, check with your instructor before proceeding.

---

## PART V: POSSESSIVE PRONOUNS
---

### Used as Adjectives Modifying Nouns

The possessive form of a noun is used as an adjective to modify a noun; for example, *Mary's book*, the *city's streets*, a *day's work*. (See Module 6, Part III, on the apostrophe.) When a pronoun is substituted for a possessive noun, the possessive form of the pronoun must be used. Refer to the list of possessive pronouns at the beginning of this module.

EXAMPLES

John's report                          His report
The workers' lunch hour                Their lunch hour

Possessive nouns have apostrophes. *However, possessive pronouns never have apostrophes.*

EXAMPLES

| | |
|---|---|
| **Its** (possessive of **it**): | **Its** tail was caught in the door. |
| **It's** (contraction of **it is**): | **It's** cold in the building. |

Like all adjectives, possessive pronouns modify specific nouns.

EXAMPLES

| | |
|---|---|
| Howard took **my** paper. | **Its** fur is warm. |
| **Your** uniform is torn. | **Our** building is brick. |
| **His** calculator is new. | **Their** plane runs well. |
| **Her** report was lost. | |

## Used as Adjectives Modifying Gerunds

*A gerund* is a verb form end in **-ing** used as a noun. Examples: *playing, walking, running, swimming, working.*

In the sentences below, each gerund is in bold type. Do you see that each one functions as a noun in that particular sentence?

EXAMPLES

**Walking** is good exercise. (*Subject*)
My favorite sport is **swimming**. (*Subject complement*)
Today is a good day for **sleeping**. (*Object of preposition*)
Of all the leisure activities, I prefer **fishing**. (*Direct object*)

Now consider the sentences below. In front of each gerund there is a possessive pronoun used as an adjective modifying the gerund.

EXAMPLES

**His playing** has improved. (*Not* Him playing)
We always enjoy **his playing.** (*Not* him playing)
**His passing** is incredibly smooth. (*Not* Him passing)
We love to watch **his passing.** (*Not* him passing)
The doctor objected to **my eating** *candy.* (*Not* me eating)
**Your speaking** to them aroused concern. (*Not* You speaking)
**His arriving** late became a problem. (*Not* Him arriving)

## Used as Subjects, Objects, and Complements

Sometimes a pronoun is used *alone* to replace both the possessive pronoun and the noun that it modifies. This can be done when it is clear what noun is being referred to. In this case a special form of the possessive pronoun is used: **mine, yours, theirs,** etc. (These forms are shown in parentheses in the list of possessive pronouns at the beginning of this module.) ***Reminder:*** *No apostrophe is ever used with the possessive pronouns.*

EXAMPLES

The tractor with the new battery is **mine. Yours** has no oil.
That folder was **hers. Ours** is on the desk.
My typewriter is broken, so I used **theirs.**

Notice in the examples above that these possessive pronouns can function as subjects, as subject complements, and as direct objects.

## ACTIVITY 8-I: Possessive Pronouns

Underline the form that is correct for the sentence.

1. No one could understand (him/his) forgetting to write the report.
2. After (their/them) talking to us, we decided to test the product again.
3. Did he approve of (you/your) writing the report?
4. The new calculator is (hers/her's).
5. Do you object to (my/me) being at the meeting?
6. (Its/It's) keys make the typewriter easy to use.
7. My desk is located opposite (your's/yours).
8. The foreman agreed to (us/our) taking the early shift.
9. (Him/His) leaving the room caused much concern.
10. (Theirs/Their's/There's) is in the drawer.

Check your responses in Feedback 8-I at the end of this module. If your responses were correct, proceed to Part VI. If you missed any, review Part V and then do Activity 8-J.

## ACTIVITY 8-J: Possessive Pronouns

Underline the form that is correct for the sentence.

1. Everyone approved of (him/his) being hired for the job.
2. Before (them/their) coming into the building, the meeting began.
3. The boss did not approve of (me/my) recording the telephone conversation.
4. (His/Him) being late was annoying.
5. The old thermometer is (hers/her's).
6. (It's/Its) motor was running smoothly.
7. (Theirs/Their's/There's) fell off the desk.
8. The memo was not mailed because (it's/its) not legible.
9. (Theirs/Their's/There's) no reason for this error.
10. The new office is (yours/your's).

Check your responses in Feedback 8-J at the end of this module. If your responses were correct, proceed to Part VI. If you missed any, check with your instructor before proceeding.

## PART VI: PRONOUN RULES

Here are some additional guides that will help you to choose the correct pronoun.

**Rule 1.** *When two pronouns are joined by a conjunction, take each pronoun separately to determine the correct one to use.* In the following sentences, which forms are correct?

Mail the portfolio to (him or I) (him or me).

(She and I) (Her and I) will be out of town.

The personnel manager selected (them and her) (them and she).

The boss talked to (you and me) (you and I).

To help you choose, try each pronoun by itself. You would not say, "Mail the portfolio to *I*," for example. Here is how to decide in the above sentences.

EXAMPLES

Mail the portfolio to **him.** Mail the portfolio to **me.** (Mail the portfolio to **him or me.**)
**She** will be out of town. I will be out of town. (**She and I** will be out of town.)
The personnel manager selected **them.** The personnel manager selected **her.** (The personnel manager selected **them and her.**)
The boss talked to **you.** The boss talked to **me.** (The boss talked to **you and me.**)

**Rule 2.** *When a pronoun and a noun are joined by a conjunction, try dropping the noun to determine which pronoun to use.* Which of the following sets are correct?

(He and the boss) (Him and the boss) planned the presentation.

The receptionist directed (the guests and her) (the guests and she) to the exhibit.

The foreman had a talk with (the supervisor and I) (the supervisor and me).

When you try the pronoun without the noun, it becomes easy to select the right pronoun for the sentence:

139

**He** [and the boss] planned the presentation.
The receptionist directed [the guests and] **her**.
The foreman had a talk with [the supervisor and] **me**.

**Rule 3.** *When using* **than** *or* **as** *in a comparison, complete the sentence in your mind to determine which pronoun to use.*

EXAMPLES

The captain played better than **he**. (than he played)
Are you as tall as **she**? (as she is)
He is nicer to Jan than **me**. (than he is to me)
He is nicer to Jan than **I**. (than I am)

**Rule 4.** *When a pronoun is next to the noun it refers to in apposition, omit the noun to decide on the correct pronoun.* (Remember that an appositive renames a noun or pronoun.) How would you choose the correct form in the following sentences?

(We mechanics) (Us mechanics) service our own vehicles.

The instructor greeted (us new students) (we new students).

Give the cards to (us members) (we members).

To help you determine which form to use, omit the noun. You would not say. "Us service our vehicles," or "The instructor greeted we," or "Give the cards to we." Here are the correct responses:

EXAMPLES

**We** [mechanics] service our own vehicles.
The instructor greeted **us** [new students].
Give the cards to **us** [members].

**Rule 5.** *Avoid using reflexive pronouns (* **myself**, **himself**, **yourself**, *etc.*) *if another pronoun form* (without **-self**) *is suitable.*

EXAMPLES

POOR: Mr. Samson gave the two best tractors to my good friend and **myself**.

BETTER: Mr. Samson gave the two best tractors to my good friend and **me**.

WRONG: My boss, my secretary, and **myself** will go.

CORRECT: My boss, my secretary, and **I** will go.

The reflexive pronouns are used for emphasis and with so-called reflexive verbs; that is, where the action of the verb is done by and to the same subject. They must be used in conjunction with another noun or pronoun to be reflexive.

| EMPHASIS | REFLEXIVE ACTION |
|---|---|
| I **myself** intend to join. | She cut **herself** accidentally. |
| He did the job **himself.** | I dusted **myself** off. |
| You **yourself** are to blame. | Ask **yourselves** the same question. |
| We wrote the report ourselves. | The lights burned **themselves** out. |

*Note:* Never use "hisself" or "theirselves"; they are not standard English words, although you may sometimes hear them spoken.

## ACTIVITY 8-K: Pronoun Rules

Underline the correct pronoun form.

1. Mail the report to (him and I) (him and me).
2. (Her and I) (She and I) will be late for our interview.
3. The secretary asked (them and her) (they and she) for the letters.
4. (Him and the nurse) (He and the nurse) filled in the patient's chart.
5. The receptionist showed (the speaker and her) (the speaker and she) to the main office.
6. He types better than (she/her).
7. (Us nurses) (We nurses) registered early for the seminar.
8. The new building pleased (us employees) (we employees).
9. She gave instructions to my colleague and (myself/me).
10. He accidentally hit (himself/hisself) with the hammer.

Check your responses in Feedback 8-K at the end of this module. If your responses were correct, proceed to Part VII. If you missed any, review Part VI and then do Activity 8-L.

## ACTIVITY 8-L: Pronoun Rules

Underline the correct pronoun form.

1. Send the report to (she and I) (her and me).
2. (He and I) (Him and me) will look at the account books tonight.
3. The radiologist asked (them and her) (they and she) to do the test again.
4. (Her and the supervisor) (She and the supervisor) felt the conference was profitable.

5. The receptionist showed the (patient and I) (patient and me) to the private room.

6. He programs a computer faster than (I/me).

7. (Us secretaries) (We secretaries) take a break at noon.

8. The design was sent to (we architects) (us architects).

9. The directions were given by the foreman and (myself/me/I).

10. The worker cut (himself/hisself) on the sharp metal.

Check your responses in Feedback 8-L at the end of this module. If your responses were correct, proceed to Part VII. If you missed any, check with your instructor before proceeding.

## PART VII: PRONOUN–ANTECEDENT AGREEMENT

The noun a pronoun stands for is called its *antecedent*. When you use a pronoun, you must make sure it agrees with its antecedent. The following six rules will help you.

**Rule 1.** *A pronoun must agree in number with its antecedent.* If the antecedent is singular (meaning one), the pronoun also is singular. If the antecedent is plural (more than one), the pronoun must be plural.

EXAMPLES

A **secretary** should write **his** (or **her**) own letters. (*Singular*)
**Secretaries** should write **their** own letters. (*Plural*)

**Rule 2.** *Use a plural pronoun to refer to two singular antecedents joined by* **and**.

EXAMPLE

**Cathy** and her **friend** bought **their** train tickets.

**Rule 3.** *When the antecedent consists of two words in a* **neither** . . . **nor** *or* **either** . . . **or** *construction, the pronoun agrees in number with the second word; that is, the word closer to the pronoun.*

EXAMPLES

*Neither* the **nurse** *nor* the **doctor** wore **his** surgical mask.
*Either* **Mrs. Moore** *or* the **assistants** have performed **their** jobs.
*Neither* the **nurses** *nor* the **doctors** wore **their** surgical masks.
*Either* the **assistants** *or* **Mrs. Moore** has performed **her** job.

**Rule 4.** *The following indefinite pronouns are singular. They require a singular personal pronoun and a singular verb.* (See Module 4, Part IV.)

```
┌─────────────────────────────────────────────────────────────────────────┐
│                              SINGULAR                                     │
│                                                                           │
│   each          one           everybody          someone                 │
│   anyone        everyone       nobody             either                  │
│   anybody       no one         somebody           neither                 │
└─────────────────────────────────────────────────────────────────────────┘
```

EXAMPLES

**Everyone** is working at **his** desk.
**Each** of the waiters is at **his** station.
**Neither** of the applicants brought **her** resume.

**Rule 5.** *The following indefinite pronouns are plural; when used as antecedents, they take a plural pronoun.*

```
┌─────────────────────────────────────────────────────────────────────────┐
│                               PLURAL                                      │
│                                                                           │
│                  both     few     many     several                        │
└─────────────────────────────────────────────────────────────────────────┘
```

EXAMPLES

**Both** of the engineers brought **their** lunches.
**Few** of the bullets found **their** target.
**Many** of the students forgot **their** rulers.

**Rule 6.** *The following indefinite pronouns may be singular or plural.* The object of the preposition that usually follows them determines whether they are to be treated as singular or plural. (See Module 4, Part IV, for a fuller discussion of these pronouns.)

```
┌─────────────────────────────────────────────────────────────────────────┐
│                        SINGULAR OR PLURAL                                 │
│   all           none           half                     most             │
│   any           some           part                                      │
└─────────────────────────────────────────────────────────────────────────┘
```

EXAMPLES

| Plural | Singular |
|---|---|
| **All** of the patients liked **their** rooms. | **All** of the equipment is in **its** last year of usefulness. |
| **None** of the books had **their** pages torn. | **None** of the appreciation was relayed to **its** recipient. |

143

| **Half** of the soybeans rotted in **their** bins. | **Half** of the crop lost **its** leaves to worms. |
|---|---|

*Note:* Avoid sexist language in your writing by choosing plural pronouns when possible, by eliminating gender reference, or by using a specific gender when there is no question of the composition of the group.

EXAMPLES

**All** employees were instructed to give **their** permits at the gate.
The administration ordered all employees to display parking permits on vehicles.
**Each** of the waitresses picked up **her** orders for the shift.

## ACTIVITY 8-M: Pronoun Agreement

Underline the correct pronoun.

1. Workers should perform (his/their) own duties.
2. All of the secretaries wished (she/they) could type as fast as Marcia.
3. The foreman is good at (his/their) jobs.
4. Neither Ted nor Tom received (his/their) bonus.
5. Neither the foreman nor the supervisors took (his/their) vacation.
6. Everybody was happy when (he/they) saw the bonus check.
7. Part of the letters need (its/their) headings reprinted.
8. Several of the technicians brought (his/their) instruments.
9. Either the ledger or the account book lost (its/their) cover.
10. The Dilly Dally company likes (their/its) employees to be punctual.

Check your responses in Feedback 8-M at the end of this module. If your responses were correct, proceed to Activity 8-O. If you missed any, review Part VII and then do Activity 8-N.

## ACTIVITY 8-N: Pronoun Agreement

Underline the correct pronoun.

1. Accountants should do (his/their) own calculations.
2. Everyone wants (her/their) job to be exciting.
3. Neither debit nor credit was posted in (its/their) proper column.
4. Either the accountant or the bookkeepers left (her/their) books in the office.
5. Everyone brought (his/their) own sets of figures.
6. Neither of the accountants did (her/their) share of the work.
7. Some of the bookkeepers brought (his/their) books to the session.

8. None of the accounts were in (its/their) original folder.

9. Few accountants could give (his/their) explanation of the deficit.

10. No one believed in (his/their) own responsibility.

Check your responses in Feedback 8-N at the end of this module. If your responses were correct, proceed to Activity 8-O. If you missed any, check with your instructor before proceeding.

## ACTIVITY 8-O: Pronoun Review

Choose the correct pronoun.

1. Everybody should know (his, their) own special skills.
2. Most of the account showed (its, their) profits clearly.
3. The company president and (she, her) made the policy decision.
4. (He and I, Him and me) will check with the radiology department.
5. Are you and (she, her) going to attend the conference?
6. The newly hired radiology technician is (she, her).
7. The best draftsmen are (he and I, him and me).
8. Call the nurse and (he, him) about the meeting.
9. Did you ask (he and she, him and her) to go to the conference?
10. Between you and (I, me), a raise would be preferable to increased benefits.
11. Give the award to (he and she, him and her).
12. The reaction was caused by (him, his) giving the shot too soon after other medication.
13. (You, Your) driving to work in snow could be dangerous.
14. (We, Us) computer programmers have a monthly staff meeting.
15. Everyone filled out (his, their) request for reimbursement.

Check your responses in Feedback 8-O at the end of this module. If your responses were correct, proceed to Activity 8-P. If you missed any, check with your instructor before proceeding.

## ACTIVITY 8-P: Writing Sentences with Pronouns

Follow the directions for each item. Write your sentences on separate paper.

1. Write a sentence using a pronoun as a subject complement.
2. Write a sentence using a pronoun as the direct object of an action verb.
3. Write a sentence using a pronoun as object of a preposition.
4. Write a sentence using a pronoun following **than** or **as** in a comparison.
5. Write a sentence using a possessive pronoun before a gerund.

6. Write sentences using:

   a. we engineers

   b. us nurses

7. Write a sentence using correctly the **-self** form of a pronoun.

8. Complete the following, using a pronoun to refer to the subject given.

   a. Everyone in the office

   b. All of the secretaries

   c. Neither of the nurses

   d. Each of the architects

Check your sentences with your instructor. If you feel you have mastered all the parts of this module, ask for Test A. If not, ask your instructor for extra help.

---

### *FEEDBACK FOR MODULE 8*

**Feedback 8-A**

1. He (He arrived)
2. he (he came)
3. she (she had)
4. I (I work)
5. we (we gave)
6. They (They have)
7. she (she made)
8. We (We will test)
9. She and I (She and I are)
10. he (you and he are going)

**Feedback 8-B**

1. she (she worked)
2. she (she left)
3. he (you are going, he is going)
4. I (I attended)
5. he (he did not attend)
6. he (he will explain)
7. She and I (She took, I took)
8. they (are you and they writing)
9. he (you and he are getting)
10. she (Jimmy and she did leave)

**Feedback 8-C**

1. he (The boss = he. He = the boss.)
2. I (The one . . . = I. I = the one . . .)
3. she (. . . it = she. She = it.)
4. he (. . . it = he. He = it.)
5. I (It = I. I = it.)
6. I (It = I. I = it.)
7. I (Consumers = you and I. You and I = consumers.)
8. he (It = he. He = it.)
9. she (Winner = she. She = winner.)
10. I (Candidates = John and I. John and I = candidates.)

**Feedback 8-D**

1. he (Winner = he. He = winner.)
2. she (person = she. She = person.)
3. he (It = he. He = it.)
4. they (It = they. They = it.)
5. I (It = I. I = it.)
6. we (It = we. We = it.)
7. I (customers = you and I. You and I = customers.)
8. he (It = he. He = it.)
9. she (Secretary = she. She = secretary.)
10. he (Applicants = you and he. You and he = applicants.)

**Feedback 8-E**

1. him (tell him)
2. me (bother me)
3. him and me (remember him, remember me)
4. her and me (take her, take me)
5. me (send me)
6. him (tell him)
7. her (know her)
8. me (asked me)
9. him (send him)
10. them (told them)

**Feedback 8-F**

1. me (call me)
2. her (ask her)
3. him and her (remember him, remember her)
4. her (drive her)
5. me (call me)
6. him (tell him)
7. her (know her)
8. me (required me)
9. her (sent her)
10. them (see them)

**Feedback 8-G**

1. them (to them)
2. her (to her)
3. us (to us)
4. me (between you, between me)
5. him (for Mr. Handy, for him)
6. him and me (to him, to me)
7. you and me (between you, between me)
8. them (among Tom, among them)

9. him (about secretary, about him)
10. him and her (beside him, beside her)

## Feedback 8-H

1. him (by Mr. Brown, by him)
2. him and me (to him, to me)
3. her and me (to her, to me)
4. you and me (between you, between me)
5. him and me (for him, for me)
6. her and me (to her, to me)
7. you and me (between you, between me)
8. them and me (by them, by me)
9. her and them (about her, about them)
10. him and me (beside him, beside me)

## Feedback 8-I

1. his (his *forgetting*)
2. their (their *talking*)
3. your (your *writing*)
4. hers (possessive pronoun)
5. my (my *being*)
6. Its (its *keys*)
7. yours (possessive pronoun)
8. our (our *taking*)
9. His (His *leaving*)
10. Theirs (possessive pronoun)

## Feedback 8-J

1. his (his *being* hired)
2. their (their *coming*)
3. my (my *recording*)
4. His (His *being*)
5. hers (possessive pronoun never has an apostrophe)
6. Its (Its *motor*)
7. Theirs (possessive pronoun)
8. it's (it is)
9. There's (There is)
10. yours (possessive pronoun)

## Feedback 8-K

1. him and me (*to him, to me*)
2. She and I (*She will be late, I will be late*)
3. them and her (*asked them, asked her*)
4. He and the nurse (*He filled in, the nurse filled in*)
5. the speaker and her (*showed the speaker, showed her*)
6. she (*than she types*)

7. We nurses (*We registered*)
8. us employees (*pleased us*)
9. me (*to me*)
10. himself ("hisself" is not a word)

## Feedback 8-L

1. her and me (*to her, to me*)
2. He and I (*He will look, I will look*)
3. them and her (*asked them, asked her*)
4. She and the supervisor (*She felt, the supervisor felt*)
5. patient and me (*showed the patient, showed me*)
6. I (*than I do*)
7. We secretaries (*we take*)
8. us architects (*to us*)
9. me (*by me*)
10. himself ("hisself" is not a word)

## Feedback 8-M

1. their (*Workers,* plural)
2. they (*all,* plural)
3. his (*foreman,* singular)
4. his (Ted nor *Tom,* singular)
5. their (*supervisors,* plural)
6. he (*everybody,* singular)
7. their (part of the *letters,* plural)
8. their (*several,* plural)
9. its (*account book,* singular)
10. its (*company,* singular)

## Feedback 8-N

1. their (*accountants,* plural)
2. her (*everyone,* singular)
3. its (debit nor *credit,* singular)
4. their (accountant or *bookkeepers,* plural)
5. his (*everyone,* singular)
6. her (*neither,* singular)
7. their (*bookkeepers,* plural)
8. their (*accounts,* plural)
9. their (*few accountants,* plural)
10. his (*no one,* singular)

## Feedback 8-O

1. his
2. its
3. she
4. He and I
5. she
6. she
7. he and I
8. him
9. him and her
10. me
11. him and her
12. his
13. your
14. We
15. his

# MODULE 9

# Paragraph Writing

OBJECTIVE: This module provides the fundamentals of paragraph writing.

Upon completion of this module, you will be able:

To choose an appropriate topic for a paragraph.

To construct a topic sentence with a controlling idea.

To outline a coherent paragraph.

To write a cohesive reasons paragraph.

To write a cohesive reasons and examples paragraph.

To write a cohesive pro and con paragraph.

To write a cohesive process paragraph.

## PART I: INTRODUCTION

Writing is not just a matter of correct grammar. Good writing results from careful planning, thoughtful revising, and precise proofreading. Look at some of these techniques as they apply to composing a paragraph.

Writing an effective paragraph—one that is completely developed and within the right range of development—takes planning. Most paragraphs are too short and therefore do not cover a topic well enough. Some paragraphs are too long, because of repetition or wordiness. Other paragraphs are oversimplified and do not really say anything. It is not an easy job to create a detailed, well-developed paragraph.

Of greater importance, the paragraph is an effective writing technique used in business and desired by managers who must deal with great amounts of written correspondence. Writing on the job must therefore be as precise and as clear and concise as possible. The important thing to remember is that you should never sacrifice clarity for brevity. By learning methods of planning, designing, and developing paragraphs, you can be an asset on the job when you must deal with written correspondence.

The paragraph format can be found in many areas of business and technical writing. Often, a memo (memorandum) is paragraph length. You will frequently be asked to summarize or to prepare abstracts of lengthier correspondence. In cases of multiparagraph formats, such as business letters and reports, a well-constructed paragraph can be very useful in helping focus thoughts and ideas so that they can be easily and readily absorbed by the reader. Proposals and requests are often limited to paragraph length. So you can see that the paragraph is not only a good way to learn writing techniques but also a most effective tool on the job.

## PART II: The Paragraph

What is a paragraph? You will probably remember being taught that a *paragraph* is a group of related sentences about one idea. Structurally, a paragraph is a group of sentences consisting of a topic sentence, sentences of development (called the body), and a concluding sentence. The paragraph can exist alone in many cases, but it is commonly used to separate longer papers into shorter segments of thought. Whether the paragraph exists as a unit on its own or is part of a larger whole depends on the amount of detail that is needed to explain your purpose. In report and letter writing, you will use sequences of paragraphs to form reports and business letters.

One of the most frequent questions writing students ask is, "How long should the paragraph be?" Obviously, there is no one correct answer, but there are certain guidelines for length and development. Certainly, you will want to choose a subject you know something about. The more you know about the subject, the more you can select and share with your readers. Another consideration is to avoid repetition. Sometimes a paragraph looks lengthy but is actually saying the same thing over and over. Some writers combine all their ideas into one or two longer sentences. Others use a series of short sentences, each containing one idea. Since sentence formation will have a definite effect on length, you should separate all your ideas in the planning process and then make choices about whether to combine them as you write a rough draft. At a minimum, a paragraph should contain one topic sentence, at least three sentences of development, and a concluding sentence. The content and length of these will be determined by your own writing style. Your aim in writing is to think through your idea and say as much as you can without repeating yourself. In this way, your writing will be more interesting because of the development, more persuasive because of the support you include for your opinion, and more successful in achieving its goal because it provides a thorough explanation instead of a superficial overview.

Here is a sample paragraph:

| | |
|---|---|
| Topic sentence | There are several advantages to fast food restaurants. First of all, their big draw is the time saved. Customers can walk in the door, walk up to the counter, place an order, and have their lunch in a matter of minutes. If |
| Body | customers prefer to remain in their car, they can go through the drive-in window and eat in the automobile. The quality of the food is consistent; people can learn which items on the menu suit them and which ones they can count on. Best of all, the prices are usually |
| Concluding sentence | unbeatable. Consequently, fast food restaurants are attracting more and more customers. |

Now that you have an overview of the paragraph, let's examine its elements carefully.

## PART III: CONSTRUCTING THE TOPIC SENTENCE

Perhaps the most important sentence in the paragraph, and therefore the one that deserves a lot of attention, is the topic sentence. The *topic sentence* establishes the purpose of the paragraph by stating the main or controlling idea about a certain subject. The topic sentence consists of two parts: the *subject* and the *controlling idea*. Both must be carefully chosen if your paragraph is to be successful.

> *Subject* (S)—what you are talking about (not necessarily the grammatical subject of the sentence)
>
> *Controlling Idea* (CI)—what you say about the subject (often with an opinion)

For example, note the subjects and controlling ideas marked in the following topic sentences.

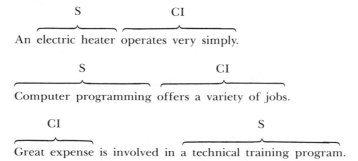

As you can see from these examples, the *subject* indicates generally what the paragraph will deal with, whereas the *controlling idea* indicates specifically the direction the supporting sentences will take.

Because of its importance to your reader in establishing your purpose, the topic sentence works best as the first sentence in the paragraph. Thoughtfully composed, the topic sentence will be the key to your selection of supporting ideas in the body of the paragraph. Finally, the topic sentence will help you decide how to conclude the paragraph when you have presented all the details.

## PART IV: CHOOSING A SUBJECT

Because the paragraph is a relatively short piece of writing, it should deal with only one subject. Even so, you must be careful to select a subject that will be narrow enough to be covered in 8 to 10 sentences at most. Not all subjects will lend themselves for discussion at that length. *Proper Telephone Techniques in Business* is one subject that you could develop in a single paragraph. However, *The History of the Telephone* would probably be better suited to a longer paper because of the extensive detail needed. When you choose a subject for a paragraph, one of the first steps is to narrow the scope to paragraph length. Look at the following examples:

| Broad Subject | Multiparagraph Length | Paragraph Length |
|---|---|---|
| Beach | Employment Opportunities at the Beach | Problems of Working at a Resort Hotel |
| Working | Getting a Job | Self-employment |
| Public Speaking | Oral Communication Course | Benefits of Being Videotaped in a Speaking Course |

In essence, what you should strive for in selecting your subject is to choose one you know a lot about so that you can narrow it to a number of precise areas. Visualize slicing a pie:

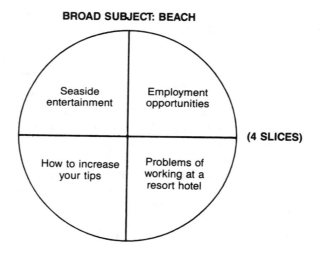

**BROAD SUBJECT: BEACH**

Seaside entertainment

Employment opportunities

How to increase your tips

Problems of working at a resort hotel

**(4 SLICES)**

From your final topics you can choose the slice you feel comfortable with or have the ideas to support. Surprisingly enough, sometimes the points you want to stress in the body of a paper will fall into place once you have narrowed the topic. Writers often reveal that once this decision is made, the rest of the paragraph is easy.

You can see why this very first step in selecting the subject of your paragraph is so critical. When you write, take the time to think before you actually write. Examine and explore options. Instead of jumping right in and writing a paragraph, try jotting down different approaches toward a subject. With some careful planning, the final product can be much more effective and appealing. Why not make the final product one you are proud of because of the thought and consideration you have put into it? Now complete Activity 9-A.

Narrow the following broad subjects, making them suitable for a paragraph.

| Broad Subject | Paragraph Length |
|---|---|
| 1. Technical Training | _____ |
| 2. Jobs | _____ |
| 3. Business | _____ |
| 4. Books | _____ |
| 5. Data Processing | _____ |
| 6. College | _____ |
| 7. Automobiles | _____ |
| 8. Newspapers | _____ |
| 9. Communication | _____ |
| 10. Politics | _____ |

Check your responses with your instructor; then proceed to Part V.

## PART V: CHOOSING A CONTROLLING IDEA

Once you have decided on a subject (for example, the Peer Counseling Program), you are ready to convert your *topic* into a *topic sentence* by choosing the controlling idea. The controlling idea is the main statement you wish to make about your subject.

---

The Peer Counseling Program at Delaware Technical and Community College *has many advantages.*

---

By adding the second half to the original subject, you can make a statement about the subject. Now you can select information that will support the idea of "advantages." These ideas will become the body of your paragraph. Practice identifying the subject and controlling idea by completing Activity 9-B.

### ACTIVITY 9-B: Subject and Controlling Idea

Bracket and label the subject (S) and controlling idea (CI) in the following topic sentences.

1. A gasoline carburetor functions better at night.

2. The coastal area offers many recreational activities.
3. What is engineering?
4. Architecture interests me.
5. Shortages of materials today have seriously affected many companies.

Check Feedback 9-B at the end of this module. If your responses were correct, proceed to "Focusing on the Topic Sentence." If you missed any, do Activity 9-C.

## ACTIVITY 9-C: Subject and Controlling Idea

Bracket and label the subject (S) and controlling idea (CI).

1. Most homeowners need a well-equipped toolbox for repair jobs.
2. Courtesy pays off in improved job relations.
3. Assembling parts without first reading instructions promises disaster.
4. Safety rules are established for a purpose.
5. Certain qualities of an applicant are observed in a job interview.

Check your answers in Feedback 9-C at the end of this module. If your responses were correct, you may proceed. If you missed any, check with your instructor before going on.

### Focusing the Topic Sentence

The next step in constructing a paragraph is to determine whether the topic sentence is well focused, too broad, or too narrow. In writing a topic sentence, you must take into consideration whether it is for a paragraph or a longer paper. In this module, confine your thinking to writing topic sentences that are logical in scope—neither too broad nor too narrow—for a paragraph.

Examine the following sentences:

EXAMPLE A

The computer has a color monitor. (*Too narrow*)
Computers have changed greatly over the last two decades. (*Too broad*)
A home computer can perform several helpful functions. (*Well focused*)

EXAMPLE B

CPR stands for cardiopulmonary resuscitation. (*Too narrow*)
Scientists and doctors have developed many life-saving techniques. (*Too broad*)
CPR (cardiopulmonary resuscitation) involves several basic steps. (*Well focused*)

Remember that a paragraph is a relatively small unit of writing. Therefore, you should have a controlling idea that is narrow enough to be supported well in a few sentences. If your CI is too broad it may take many, many paragraphs, maybe pages and pages, to develop it adequately. Say your assignment is to write a paragraph on the broad subject of social security. Here are two possible topic sentences that would narrow the subject properly. The CI is underlined.

1. At the current rate, social security payments are not <u>sufficient to meet the needs of the elderly.</u> (*This TS could be supported by giving examples of normal expenses the elderly face.*)

2. Some people are concerned that the social security fund <u>may go broke</u> before they draw retirement benefits. (*This TS could be supported by the questionable methods being used to administer the program today.*)

The controlling idea is the key to a unified paragraph. If your CI is too broad, as in "Social security is bad," or too narrow, as in "A radio station plays music," it will not help you develop a unified paragraph. One thing to consider at this point is choice of words for the controlling idea. Words such as "nice," "interesting," and "bad" are usually ineffective because they lack specific meaning. Words like "bad" can be confusing because they can also be slang. If you are at a loss for a good word to use as your controlling idea, you may want to consult a thesaurus or a dictionary of synonyms. But if it is a logical, well-focused CI, then the supporting statements will flow naturally, and your paragraph will be unified.

---

### ACTIVITY 9-D: Subject and Controlling Idea

In each group of sentences, one sentence is too broad (TB), one is too narrow (TN), and one is well focused (WF). Label them.

Group 1

_____ a. Poultry production is increasing.

_____ b. Poultry production is increasing in our area.

_____ c. Poultry production originated in our area.

Group 2

_____ a. The telephone is on the desk.

_____ b. The telephone provides a vehicle for good public relations.

_____ c. The telephone is convenient.

Group 3

_____ a. Data processing offers many career opportunities.

_____ b. Data processing is a technology.

_____ c. Many careers are available to today's graduate.

Group 4

_____ a. Compact automobiles are the most economical vehicles.

_____ b. Compact automobiles are more economical to operate than larger cars.

_____ c. Compact automobiles are small.

Check your responses in Feedback 9-D at the end of this module. If your responses were correct, proceed to Activity 9-F. If you missed any, do Activity 9-E.

## ACTIVITY 9-E: Subject and Controlling idea

In each group of sentences, one sentence is too broad (TB), one is too narrow (TN), and one is well focused (WF). Label them.

Group 1

_____ a. The engineer went to work.

_____ b. Engineering is an important field.

_____ c. An architectural engineer performs a variety of jobs.

Group 2

_____ a. A good nurse should possess certain specific qualities.

_____ b. Nursing is an art.

_____ c. The nurse took the patient's temperature.

Group 3

_____ a. There is going to be a great need for fuel in the future.

_____ b. A source of energy is oil.

_____ c. The use of nuclear energy has many dangerous aspects.

Group 4

_____ a. Nutrition is important.

_____ b.  A dietician uses nutritional guidelines to plan a well-balanced meal.

_____ c.  The dietician prepared the menu for the evening meal.

Check your responses in Feedback 9-E. If your responses were correct, proceed to Activity 9-F. If you missed any, check with your instructor before proceeding.

## ACTIVITY 9-F: Writing Topic Sentences

On your own paper, develop a well-focused sentence on each of these subjects. Underline your controlling idea.

1.  Computers
2.  Solar heat
3.  Drug abuse
4.  Nuclear power
5.  Compact laser disks
6.  Consumer loans
7.  Hazardous waste
8.  Word processing

Check your sentences with your instructor. Then do Activity 9-G.

## ACTIVITY 9-G: Writing Topic Sentences

On your own paper, write five topic sentences on subjects of your choice. Underline the S and CI and label each. Check your sentences with your instructor. Then proceed to Part VI.

## PART VI: WRITING THE CONCLUDING SENTENCE

A paragraph has three main parts—the topic sentence, the body, and the concluding sentence. For the paragraph to function as a unit, you must end it properly to let your reader know that you have finished your discussion. The best way to conclude your paragraph is to remind the reader of what you originally set out to do. You may want to restate the main idea of the topic sentence using different wording to avoid repetition. If the paragraph has at least three main points of discussion, you may want to use a summary technique to conclude.

Consider the following examples:

Topic sentence:        Exercise routines should be carefully planned for best results.

159

| Restatement type concluding sentence: | Therefore, exercise can be beneficial if some basic guidelines are followed. |
|---|---|
| Summary type concluding sentence: | As you can see, proper supervision, good eating habits, and strict routines can produce excellent outcomes for the exercise enthusiast. |

## ACTIVITY 9-H: Writing a Topic Sentence and a Concluding Sentence

Write a topic sentence and a concluding sentence for each of the following paragraphs.

---

*Topic Sentence:* _____

_____

Students can enroll in business or data processing. In addition, there are careers available in the medical areas, such as nursing and lab technology. Engineering is another broad field including electronics and architecture.

*Concluding Sentence:* _____

---

*Topic Sentence:* _____

_____

First, you must choose a subject. Next, you should narrow the subject so that you can deal with it in a paragraph. Then you need to construct a topic sentence that contains a controlling idea which tells the reader how you plan to deal with the subject. Following that, you must supply sufficient facts, details, and examples to develop the body of the paragraph. Finally, you write a concluding sentence that restates the idea expressed in the topic sentence.

*Concluding Sentence:* _____

---

*Topic Sentence:* _____

_____

Arrive for the interview early. Be certain that you are neatly and appropriately dressed. Take your cues from the interviewer. Give that person a firm handshake as you announce your name. Wait to be invited to have a seat. Answer questions completely yet briefly, always being honest in your replies. When the interviewer signals the close of the interview, be sure to thank the person for his or her time.

*Concluding Sentence:* _____

Check your responses with your instructor. Then proceed to Part VII.

## PART VII: DEVELOPING UNITY

Unity means oneness. In writing, it has to do with combining ideas—facts, details, examples—into an entity or a harmonious whole. You have been told that a paragraph is a group of *related* sentences. The word *related* is the key. Each sentence must contribute to the support or proof of the controlling idea. Note that a sentence can be related to the subject, but not to the controlling idea. It therefore destroys the unity of the paragraph.

To see how this happens, look at the sample paragraph on *page 152.* Its topic was *fast food restaurants.* Its controlling idea was *advantages.* A sentence such as the following would be related to the subject, but not to the controlling idea and thus should be eliminated.

> There are too many fast food restaurants in our town.

The main reason errors in unity occur is that many writers sit down and compose from their thoughts, without taking the time to organize their ideas through the use of a plan or an outline. If you compose without planning, you run the risk of wandering off the topic or, more precisely, your controlling idea. If you do not make a habit of planning, commit yourself to start right now. You will be delighted with the improvement you will see in your writing.

In your writing, check each fact, detail, or example you include to see that it supports the controlling idea. After you jot down supporting ideas, look at each one in relation to the controlling idea. It is much easier to spot material that does not belong in a paragraph at this stage than after you have proofread your final product.

Now it is your turn to practice focusing on paragraph unity by making sure that each sentence relates to the controlling idea. Complete Activity 9-I.

### ACTIVITY 9-I: Developing Unity

In the following paragraphs, circle the controlling idea in the topic sentence and cross out any sentences that do not support it.

There are several definite guidelines to use in writing a resumé. It must be typed and only one page long. The Job Objective should be clearly defined. It should be noted that a resumé is the same as a data sheet. The wording should be as brief as possible, using phrases rather than complete sentences. References should not be included. The letter of application is used to ask for the job interview. Previous salaries should not be included. Neatness and appearance are extremely important. An effective resumé will be the result of following these principles.

You should make every effort to apply the basic punctuation rules to your writing. Do not forget to separate words in a series by using commas. Also, use commas to separate items in dates and addresses. Make sure your subjects and verbs agree. Coordinate adjectives provide another occasion to use the comma. In addition, commas are needed with interrupters and introductory words or phrases. Avoid using fragments in your writing. A review of the fundamentals of punctuation will improve your writing.

Check your responses in Feedback 9-I. Then proceed with Activity 9-J.

**ACTIVITY 9-J: Paragraph Unity**

The following paragraph illustrates how sentences that do not support the controlling idea can destroy paragraph unity. See if you can spot the unrelated statements that should be eliminated. (In any paragraphs you write, be sure to avoid any statements that do not directly support the CI.) Read the paragraph and then fill in the blanks below it.

*Topic Sentence:* The county's technical colleges have a wide variety of curriculum offerings. (1) They are located in the county seat. (2) Students can find course offerings adapted to their aptitudes and interests. (3) For example, students who would like to own their own businesses can enroll in Business Administration. (4) In addition, they can play on the basketball team if they are sports-minded. (5) Another course offered is in the very popular field of Data Processing. (6) For those interested in engineering, there are such technologies as architecture, electronics, and electricity. (7) One student who took the Architectural Engineering course obtained a job as a lab technician. (8) Other students may wish to pursue a career as a secretary, a lab technician, a practical nurse, or a newspaper reporter. (9) They may also come to enjoy the social life. (10) As you can see from the wide variety of courses offered at technical colleges, there is something for everyone.

Subject: _____

CI: _____

Supporting Statements (give sentence numbers): _____

Unrelated Statements: _____

Concluding Statements: _____

Transitional Expressions: _____

_____

_____

_____

_____

Check your answers in Feedback 9-J at the end of this module. If your responses were correct, proceed to Part VIII.

## PART VIII: DEVELOPING COHERENCE

Coherence (pronounced cō-hēr-ĕnce) may look like a difficult concept because of its strange name. It is a crucial area in writing because it has to do with the logical connection between ideas. Unity is necessary because the sentences in the body of a paragraph must *relate* to the topic sentence. Coherence is directly related to the results you will achieve from your writing, for the overall impact will depend on the way you *order* or *sequence* ideas.

There are two basic approaches to coherence. The first one is called chronological and is used when *time element* helps with sequencing. For example, sets of directions follow a chronological sequence since steps must be done in a certain order to achieve the correct result. Paragraphs using details of time, such as historical development, will use a chronological approach. (See transitional expressions indicating time on page 79.)

The second type of sequencing ideas is a bit more complicated, for it is based on the order of importance. In paragraph development, your ideas should be sequenced from the most important to the least important or vice versa. In other words, put the most important ideas first *or* last. Whichever way you choose is up to you as long as you are aware of your plan and are able to explain your approach. This step in writing is best accomplished at the plan or outline stage. (See transitional expressions indicating order of importance on page 79.)

Coherence is especially important in business and technical writing. In persuasive writing, your arguments not only must relate to the issue at hand but also be properly ordered so that the reader is able to follow your logic. Writing is a precise exercise; readers cannot know what you intend unless you state your meaning clearly and completely. This same notion is true for writing sets of directions. Following directions is not that easy, especially if the directions are oversimplified or major steps are overlooked.

### Transitional Expressions

*Transitions* are linking words and phrases that show relationships between two or more ideas. They are the glue that holds the parts together. If you do not use enough, the parts will fall apart; if you use too much, you will see the glue instead of the parts. Your goal should be to move smoothly from one sentence to the next, so that the reader is unaware of the links that connect your ideas and unify the paragraph.

Transitional expressions can be used to emphasize organization and direction of thought. They may appear at the beginning, middle, or end of a sentence. Refer to page 78 for a list of transitional expressions you can use in writing paragraphs.

---

**ACTIVITY 9-K: Transition**

---

Supply appropriate transitional expressions in the blanks. (*Note:* When writing actual paragraphs it is not necessary to use a transitional expression for every sentence.)

> A police officer has a thankless job. No one, whether right or wrong, appreciates being reprimanded. _____ very often in the process of breaking up an argument the officer winds up being injured.
>
> _____ even when the officer is simply doing his or her job, the officer is criticized. _____, it is rare that the public shows gratitude to a police officer.

Check your responses with your instructor. Then proceed to Part IX.

---

## PART IX: ORGANIZING AND WRITING A PARAGRAPH

---

You have mastered the first step in writing a unified paragraph by demonstrating your ability to write a topic sentence (TS) with a clear-cut *subject* (S) and *controlling idea* (CI). Your next step is to organize your paragraph by constructing an outline.

Making an outline need not be a complicated procedure. Simply jot down, in grocery list fashion, all ideas you can think of to give solid support to the controlling idea. It is preferable *not* to use complete sentences. Then write the *concluding sentence* (CS), which restates the topic sentence in different words. Here is how to construct an outline for a TS.

### SAMPLE PARAGRAPH OUTLINE

| | |
|---|---|
| TS | Using a word processor for writing saves time. |
| Outline of ideas | 1. Setting margins and tabs simply.<br>2. Typing faster with no carriage returns.<br>3. Using helpful features such as underlining or highlighting.<br>4. Revising easily.<br>5. Checking spelling.<br>6. Saving work on diskette (more efficient storage). |
| CS | It is easy to see that writing with a word processor has many advantages over a typewriter or a pad and pencil. |

The outline makes your job easier because you think out the paragraph before you begin writing it. If your ideas are out of order or one doesn't really support your CI, you can reorganize or eliminate at the beginning. (As your paragraphs become more complex, the outline will be even more helpful in organizing than in this simple topic.) Constructing the outline is a critical step because it forces you to plan your paragraph from the beginning.

### ANOTHER SAMPLE PARAGRAPH OUTLINE

| | |
|---|---|
| TS | The use of cruise control in an automobile is beneficial on long trips for several reasons. |
| Outline | 1. Maintain regular speed<br>2. Save gasoline<br>3. Have no threat from highway patrol<br>4. Feel less tired and more alert during trip<br>5. Feel more rested at destination |
| CS | Consequently, it would be beneficial to use cruise control on a long trip. |

After writing a topic sentence and jotting down all the points you can think of to support it, you then write a concluding sentence. This skeleton provides the basis for your paragraph. To put flesh on the skeleton, you will need to expand the phrases listed as points in your outline. Each point may or may not be a separate sentence. You will want to use transitional expressions to tie the thoughts together. Also, you should try to vary your sentence patterns.

---

### ACTIVITY 9-L: Writing an Outline

---

On your own paper, construct a simple outline using one of the topic sentences in Activity 9-F. List five supporting ideas and then add a concluding sentence. Check your outline with your instructor. Then proceed to Part X.

---

## PART X: THE REASONS PARAGRAPH

---

There are many different types of paragraphs. Here are four that are most commonly used by technicians.

The first type of paragraph you will write is the paragraph supported by *reasons*. In a reasons paragraph, the controlling idea of the TS is usually a statement of opinion. The supporting statements must give reasons to verify that opinion.

Look back at the outline for "Cruise Control." What follows is a reasons paragraph developed from that outline. Note that the following paragraph is more expansive than its outline. Your writing should reflect college-level thinking with varied sentence structure.

Note the transitional words and phrases (in italics) that link the sentences smoothly.

---

The use of cruise control is beneficial on a long trip for several reasons. *First,* once cruising speed is reached, that speed is maintained; *as a result,* less gasoline is used. Assuming the cruise control is set on or below the legal speed limit, the highway patrol should pose no threat to the driver. Because drivers do not have to keep a foot on the gas pedal constantly, the leg and foot muscles are more relaxed, leaving drivers less tired and more alert during a trip. This *also* means drivers are more rested when they reach their destination. *Consequently,* it would be beneficial to use cruise control on a long trip.

---

In this paragraph, each sentence goes directly back to support the CI, *beneficial for several reasons.* There are no irrelevant sentences to destroy the unity of the paragraph. Also, transitional expressions tie the sentences together nicely.

Choose one of the topics listed and write a unified reasons paragraph with at least four supporting statements and a concluding sentence. Follow the procedures given below; write an outline and then the paragraph. If you are not inspired by any of these topic sentences, write one on a subject to your liking.

**Topics**

1. Reduced speed limits on highways have many benefits.
2. There is a great demand for electronics technicians.
3. Compulsory seat belt laws are necessary (or unnecessary).
4. Getting a technical education provides for a sound future.
5. Credit cards are beneficial (or harmful).

**Procedures for Paragraph Writing**

1. Construct outline as follows:
   Topic sentence
   (1) Reason
   (2) Reason
   (3) Reason
   (4) Reason
   Concluding sentence

2. Write a rough draft from the outline.

3. Proofread, using the following checklist:
   a. Spelling (Spelling Aids).
   b. Punctuation (Module 6).
   c. Pronoun agreement (Module 8).
   d. Subject–verb agreement (Module 4).
   e. Fragments (See note on p. 118, Module 7).
   f. Apostrophe for possession (no contractions, no apostrophe for possessive pronouns; Module 6).
   g. Read your paragraph aloud to hear any omissions, incorrect verb endings, or awkward phrases.

4. Revise to improve unity through the use of transitional expressions (see list on page 78).

5. Write final copy on $8\frac{1}{2}'' \times 11''$ notebook paper in ink on one side of paper. Do not use paper torn from a spiral notebook. Write neatly. Crossouts are unacceptable.

6. Assemble in this order: outline (on top), final copy, and rough draft.

7. Put your name and type of paragraph in upper right-hand corner of first sheet.

8. Hand it in to your instructor.

Upon achieving a passing grade on the reasons paragraph, proceed to Part XI.

## PART XI: THE REASONS AND EXAMPLES PARAGRAPH

A more advanced method of expanding a topic sentence is to use both *reasons* (major support) and *examples* (minor support). It is basically the same as the reasons paragraph, except that each reason is further developed or clarified by one or more examples.

Every *reason or major supporting statement* should be a direct and definite explanation of the controlling idea stated in the topic sentence. In other words, you should be able to draw a line from the major support to the CI.

### SAMPLE OUTLINE FOR REASONS AND EXAMPLES PARAGRAPH

| | | |
|---|---|---|
| TS | | A career in business administration appeals to me. |
| | (Reason) | It has a wide variety of available jobs. |
| | (Example) | I can work in real estate, in retail stores, in hotel-motel management for large or small companies, indoors or outdoors. |
| | (Reason) | Business careers often have good fringe benefits. |
| | (Example) | An employee often receives dental, medical, and optical care. |
| | (Reason) | I can meet many business and community leaders. |
| | (Example) | Businessmen deal constantly with politicians, lawyers, public officials, and many other prominent figures. |
| CS | | Thus, you can see why I am interested in a business career. |

Every *example or minor supporting statement* should explain its major statement in terms of the CI. You should be able to draw a line from the minor support to the major support.

Thus, you have a way to check yourself to see if every sentence supports the CI either directly or indirectly. If a sentence doesn't refer to the CI, you should eliminate it or it will destroy your paragraph unity.

Notice how the major and minor supports work in the paragraph on business administration (above). Here is another sample outline for a reasons and examples paragraph.

| | |
|---|---|
| TS | The addition of organic matter improves soil in several ways. |
| | (Reason)    Improves soil structure. |
| | (Example)   a. Loosens hard soil. |
| |               b. Gives sandy soil holding ability. |
| | (Reason)    Increases ability to retain moisture. |
| | (Example)   a. Acts as sponge. |
| |               b. Reduces erosion. |
| | (Reason)    Raises level of fertility. |
| | (Example)   a. Breaks organic matter down. |
| |               b. Builds up humus. |
| CS | In conclusion, the best way to improve soil is by the incorporation of organic matter into the soil. |

---

**ACTIVITY 9-N: Reasons and Examples Paragraph**

Analyze the following paragraph by underlining the subject and the CI in the TS. Next underline the CI in each sentence and draw arrows, as in the model paragraph on page 168.

---

The addition of organic matter improves soil in several ways. One of the benefits of adding organic matter is improved soil structure. Organic matter loosens hard-packed clay soil. It enables sandy soil to hold more water and nutrients. Another benefit of a high level of organic matter in soil is an increased ability to retain water. Organic matter acts as a sponge, soaking up rainwater and storing it. As a result, erosion is reduced because water is absorbed by the soil and does not run off. As organic matter is broken down by soil organisms, the level of fertility is raised. Humus, the residue of decay, is built up in the soil, providing plants with the nutrients for growth. In conclusion, the best way to improve soil is by the incorporation of organic matter into the soil.

---

Check your answers in Feedback 9-N. Then proceed to Activity 9-O.

---

**ACTIVITY 9-O: Reasons and Examples Paragraph**

Analyze this paragraph according to the criteria following the paragraph. For reasons, examples, and conclusion, give the numbers of the appropriate sentences.

(TS) The split-level house design offers many advantages. (1) First of all, it gives more freedom with floor plan arrangements. (2) The greater expanse of living space on two levels allows rooms to be moved about to suit the owner. (3) Another positive feature is that there are at least two main floors. (4) The living quarters can be separated from the sleeping and eating quarters. (5) Also, with two floors, areas can be closed off to conserve heat in winter. (6) Equally important, this house is adaptable to varying land contours. (7) The lower level is usually set into a hill while the upper level can be above ground in the lowest part of the lot. (8) Needless to say, these benefits can contribute to a very comfortable home.

Subject _____

CI _____

Reasons _____ Examples _____ Conclusion _____

Transitional Expressions _____

_____

_____

_____

Check your responses in Feedback 9-O at the end of this module. Then proceed to Activity 9-P.

## ACTIVITY 9-P: Writing a Reasons and Examples Paragraph

Using one of your own topic sentences, write a paragraph supported by reasons and examples. Construct your outline similarly:

Topic Sentence
(1)  Reason (major)
    a.  Example (minor)
    b.  Example (minor)
(2)  Reason (major)
    a.  Example (minor)
    b.  Example (minor)
(3)  Reason (major)
    a.  Example (minor)
    b.  Example (minor)
Concluding Sentence

*Note:* There is no magic number for the major reasons and their supporting examples. The important thing is to cover the subject thoroughly and accurately.

After outlining your paragraph, follow procedures given in Activity 9-M. Upon achieving a passing grade on the reasons and examples paragraph, proceed to Part XII.

## PART XII: THE PRO AND CON PARAGRAPH

The third type of paragraph in this module is the pro and con. In this type of paragraph you develop two (or more) opposing ideas. You must mention both controlling ideas in the topic sentence, and you will need to use a compound CI to express the ideas. The central thought of the paragraph has two parts, and each part contrasts with the other. The contrasting idea may be stated, as in the first example, or implied, as in the second example.

EXAMPLES

1. A student may find that a weekend job has its advantages as well as its
                               S                       CI

   disadvantages. (*stated*)

2. In our society, there are many arguments concerning legalized abortion.
   tion.                                CI                S

   (*implied*)

The concluding sentence of a pro and con paragraph does not take a stand but merely restates both sides of the issue.

The following paragraph illustrates the development of a compound CI. Note that the TS indicates divided opinion on an issue. Notice the italicized transitional expression of contrast which notifies the reader when the writer shifts from explaining the desirable aspects of a job (pro) to the less desirable (con). Also, notice that in the conclusion the writer remains objective, letting the reader make up his or her own mind. You should not take a stand in the conclusion.

SAMPLE OUTLINE

> TS   Solar energy as a heat source for homes has potential,
>            S                                        CI
>      but there are some problems that need to be resolved.
>                              CI

                    Pro
                    1. Unlimited resource
                    2. Nonpolluting energy
                    3. Resource not controlled by humans for profit
                    Con
                    1. High construction cost of collection devices
                    2. Collection and storage not perfected
                    3. Collectors somewhat unsightly
          CS        To sum up, using the sun's energy for home heating is
                    an option that must be carefully considered.

## SAMPLE PARAGRAPH

Solar energy as a heat source for homes has potential, but there are some problems that need to be resolved. Compared to other sources of energy, the sun is an unlimited, largely untapped reserve. Millions of nonpolluting units of energy are released every day. Also, the sun is a source of energy that no corporation or nation can gain control of and sell for profit. On the other hand, the high construction costs of solar collection devices can be an obstacle for many. In addition, collection and storage of that energy has not been perfected. A further drawback is that many people object to collectors perched on rooftops and clinging to the sides of buildings. To sum up, using the sun's energy for home heating is an option that must be carefully considered.

## ACTIVITY 9-Q: Pro and Con Paragraph

Study the following pro and con paragraph and then answer the questions following it.

In our society, there is little agreement on the merits of incarcerating (putting in prison) those who have committed crimes. One of the main arguments used by those who favor incarceration is that criminals must pay for their crimes; in other words, "an eye for an eye." They also feel that removing these offenders from society eliminates possible criminal activities by them for that period. In addition, these people believe that offenders should be exposed to a good rehabilitation program before they are released. Another argument advanced favoring imprisonment is that it curbs others when they see the possible consequences for similar acts. On the other hand, those with opposing viewpoints have strongly voiced arguments that some crimes, such as crimes of passion, are likely one-time offenses, and they question what imprisonment accomplishes. These same people also contend that the chances these crimes would be repeated are negligible. They further stress that rehabilitation programs are not only ineffective but also practically nonexistent in most institutions. Besides this, opponents fear that so-called correctional institutions can be teaching grounds for crime. Just as strongly, they challenge the idea that incarceration serves to deter others from crime. All in all, a meeting of the minds on this issue is yet to come.

What is the subject? _____

What are the two CIs? _____

What expression signals transition to opposing arguments?

_____

List the supporting ideas briefly:

|  *Pros*  |  *Cons*  |
| --- | --- |
| a. _____ | a. _____ |
| b. _____ | b. _____ |
| c. _____ | c. _____ |
| d. _____ | d. _____ |
|  | e. _____ |

Check your responses in Feedback 9-Q at the end of this module. If you have any questions, check with your instructor. Then proceed to Activity 9-R.

---

### ACTIVITY 9-R: Writing a Pro and Con Paragraph

---

Write a paragraph supported by the pro and con method. Construct your outline as follows:

Topic Sentence (with compound CI)

(1) Pro reasons:
    a.
    b.
    c.

(2) Con reasons:
    a.
    b.
    c.

Concluding Sentence

After writing an outline for your paragraph, follow the procedures given in Activity 9-M. Upon achieving a passing grade on the Pro and Con Paragraph, proceed to Part XIII.

The final type of paragraph you will learn to write is probably the most significant to you as a technician. This is the *process* paragraph, which explains how to do something or how something is done. The topic sentence is a statement of what process is to be explained. Supporting statements take the reader through the process, step by step. The concluding sentence restates the topic sentence in different words.

Following is one example of a process paragraph. Notice especially that numbers are used here to show transition from one point to another.

### SAMPLE OUTLINE

TS  The following procedure will greatly improve your ability to assist in artificial respiration during a respiratory arrest.

Preparation
1. Position victim
2. Loosen clothing
3. Check mouth for objects
4. Pull tongue forward

Procedure
1. Tilt head
2. Lift chin
3. Open jaw
4. Keep head back
5. Pinch nostrils
6. Take deep breath
7. Place mouth over victim's
8. Blow
9. Repeat
10. Watch for normal breathing

CS  In conclusion, the knowledge and ability to perform the technique of artificial respiration properly could mean the difference between life and death.

### SAMPLE PARAGRAPH

The following procedure will greatly improve your ability to assist in artificial respiration during a respiratory arrest.

Preparation
1. Lay the victim on his or her back.
2. Prepare the victim for artificial respiration by helping loosen clothing around the neck, chest, and waist.

3. Be sure to check the mouth for false teeth, gum, or other objects that could block the flow of air.
4. Make certain that the victim's tongue is pulled forward before starting artificial respiration.

Procedure
1. Tilt the head back as far as possible.
2. Make sure the chin is up so that the neck is stretched tight.
3. Insert your thumb between the victim's teeth; at the same time, pull victim's lower jaw open.
4. Keep victim's head pushed back.
5. Pinch the nostrils shut.
6. Open your mouth, and take a deep breath.
7. Place your mouth firmly over the victim's mouth.
8. Blow forcefully into the victim's mouth until you can see the chest rise.
9. Repeat this method every three or four seconds.
10. Normal breathing should start after not more than fifteen minutes.

In conclusion, the knowledge and ability to perform artificial respiration properly could mean the difference between life and death.

Note how the process paragraph can be enumerated, as in the previous example, or developed in conventional paragraph form, as follows. Choose the one that best suits your purpose.

### SAMPLE PROCESS PARAGRAPH OUTLINE

TS    Calculating the percent increase or decrease between this year's sales figures and last year's sales figures can be accomplished with a series of computations on an electronic calculator.

Preparation
1. Turn machine on.
2. Turn grand total key off.
3. Clear memory.
4. Set decimal at 2.

Procedure
1. Enter this year's sales.
2. Press plus key.
3. Enter last year's sales.
4. Press memory plus key.
5. Press minus key.
6. Press subtotal key.
7. Press divide key.
8. Press memory recall key.
9. Press percent key.

In conclusion, using an electronic calculator to find the percent increase or decrease can be quite simple if you follow the correct procedure.

## ACTIVITY 9-S: Identifying S, CI, and Transitions

In the spaces provided, list the S, the CI, and ten transitional expressions in the paragraph on calculating sales increases.

### SAMPLE (CONVENTIONAL FORMAT)

Calculating the percent of increase or decrease between this year's sales figures and last year's sales figures can be accomplished with a series of computations on an electronic calculator. Initially, make sure the machine is turned on. Also, be sure the grand total key is off and the memory key is cleared. Set the decimal indicator at two. The primary step in calculating the percent increase or decrease is to find the actual increase or decrease between this year's sales and last year's sales. First, enter this year's sales into the calculator; press the plus key. Then enter last year's sales into the calculator; press the memory key. Next, press the minus key, and then the subtotal key. This figure is the actual increase or decrease between this year's and last year's sales. After that, press the divide key followed by the memory recall key. Finally, press the percent key. This figure is the percent of increase or decrease between this year's and last year's sales. In conclusion, using an electronic calculator to find the percent of increase or decrease can be quite simple if you follow the correct procedure.

*Subject:* _____

*CI:* _____

*List transitions:* _____

_____

_____

_____

Check your responses in Feedback 9-S at the end of this module. If you have any questions, check with your instructor. Then proceed to Activity 9-T.

## ACTIVITY 9-T: Writing a Process Paragraph

Write a process paragraph supported by one of the illustrated types. Construct your outline as follows:

Topic Sentence

Preparation (if applicable)

(1)

(2)

(3)

Procedure

(1)

(2)

(3)

Concluding Sentence

After constructing your outline, follow the procedures given in Activity 9-M. Upon achieving a passing grade on the process paragraph, ask your instructor for the Final In-class Paragraph.

**Feedback 9-B**

⌐————S————⌐ ⌐————CI————⌐
1. A gasoline carburetor functions better at night.

⌐———S———⌐ ⌐————CI————⌐
2. The coastal area offers many recreational activities.

⌐—CI—⌐ ⌐——S——⌐
3. What is engineering?

⌐———S———⌐ ⌐——CI——⌐
4. Architecture interests me.

⌐——————S——————⌐ ⌐—————CI—————⌐
5. Shortages of materials today have seriously affected many companies.

**Feedback 9-C**

⌐———S———⌐ ⌐————CI————⌐
1. Most homeowners need a well equipped toolbox for repair jobs.

⌐———S———⌐ ⌐————CI————⌐
2. Courtesy pays off in improved job relations.

⌐——————————S——————————⌐ ⌐———CI———⌐
3. Assembling parts without first reading instructions promises disaster.

⌐———S———⌐ ⌐—————CI—————⌐
4. Safety rules are established for a purpose.

⌐—————CI—————⌐ ⌐———S———⌐
5. Certain qualities of an applicant are observed in a job interview.

**Feedback 9-D**

| Group 1 | Group 2 | Group 3 | Group 4 |
|---------|---------|---------|---------|
| (a) TB | (a) TN | (a) WF | (a) TB |
| (b) WF | (b) WF | (b) TN | (b) WF |
| (c) TN | (c) TB | (c) TB | (c) TN |

**Feedback 9-E**

| Group 1 | Group 2 | Group 3 | Group 4 |
|---|---|---|---|
| (a) TN | (a) WF | (a) TB | (a) TB |
| (b) TB | (b) TB | (b) TN | (b) WF |
| (c) WF | (c) TN | (c) WF | (c) TN |

**Feedback 9-I:**

There are (several definite guidelines) to use in writing a resumé. It must be typed and only one page long. The Job Objective should be clearly defined. ~~It should be noted that a resumé is the same as a data sheet.~~ The wording should be as brief as possible, using phrases rather than complete sentences. References should not be included. ~~The letter of application is used to ask for the job interview.~~ Previous salaries should not be included. Neatness and appearance are extremely important. An effective resumé will be the result of following these principles.

You should make every effort to apply the (basic punctuation rules) to your writing. Do not forget to separate words in a series by using commas. Also, use commas to separate items in dates and addresses. ~~Make sure your subjects and verbs agree.~~ Coordinate adjectives provide another occasion to use the comma. In addition, commas are needed with interrupters and introductory words or phrases. ~~Avoid using fragments in your writing.~~ A review of the fundamentals of punctuation will improve your writing.

**Feedback 9-J**

*Subject:* Technical colleges
*CI:* wide variety of curriculum offerings
*Supporting:* 2, 3, 5, 6, 8
*Unrelated:* 1, 4, 7, 9
*Concluding Sentence:* 10
*Transitions:* For example, In addition, Another, also

**Feedback 9-N**

The addition of organic matter (S) improves soil in (CI) several ways. One of the benefits of adding organic matter is improved soil structure. Organic matter loosens hard-packed clay soil. It enables sandy soil to hold more water and nutrients. Another benefit of a high level of organic matter in soil is an increased ability to retain water. Organic matter acts as a sponge, soaking up rainwater and storing it. As a result, erosion is reduced because water is absorbed by the soil and does not run off. As organic matter is broken down by soil organisms, the level of fertility is raised. Humus, the residue of decay, is built up in the soil, providing plants with the nutrients for growth. In conclusion, the best way to improve soil is by the incorporation of organic matter into the soil.

## Feedback 9-O

*Subject:* Split-level house design
*CI:* advantages
*Reasons:* 1, 3, 6
*Examples:* 2, 4, 5, 7
*Concluding Sentence:* 8
*Transitional Expressions:* first of all, another positive feature, also, equally important, needless to say

## Feedback 9-Q

*Subject:* Incarceration (imprisonment)
*CIs:* for and against (little agreement)
*Transition:* on the other hand

| *Pros* | *Cons* |
|---|---|
| a. Criminals must pay for crimes. | a. Some crimes are one-time offenses. |
| b. Imprisonment prevents further crimes. | b. Chances of repetition are negligible. |
| c. Criminals need rehabilitation. | c. Rehabilitation programs are ineffective. |
| d. Threat of prison curbs others. | d. Prisons teach crime. |
| | e. Incarceration does not deter others. |

## Feedback 9-S

(S)

Calculating the percent of increase or decrease between this year's sales figures and last year's sales figures can be accomplished with a series of computations (CI) on an electronic calculator. Initially, make sure the machine is turned on. Also, be sure the grand total key is off and the memory key is cleared. Set the decimal indicator at two. The primary step in calculating the percent of increase or decrease crease is to find the actual increase or decrease between this year's sales and last year's sales. First, enter this year's sales into the calculator; press the plus key. Then enter last year's sales into the calculator; press the memory plus key. Next, press the minus key, and then the subtotal key. This figure is the actual increase or decrease between this year's and last year's sales. After that, press the divide key followed by the memory recall key. Finally, press the percent key. This figure is the percent of increase or decrease between this year's and last year's sales. In conclusion, using an electronic calculator to find the percent of increase or decrease can be quite simple if you follow the correct procedure.

# 10

# Shifts

OBJECTIVE: This module will help you to recognize and to correct various shifts or inconsistencies so that you may attain smoothness and clearness in your writing.

Upon completion of this module, you will be able:

To identify and to correct inconsistencies in tense and voice of a verb.

To identify and to correct shifts in two pronoun forms: person and number.

Your writing goal should be to develop your thoughts clearly and concisely so that they move easily from one sentence to the next. If you begin a sentence in one way and then change its flow, the reader becomes confused. To achieve smoothness and clearness, you must pay careful attention to being consistent in the use of voice, tense, person, and number.

One of the basic guidelines governing good writing is the concept of unity. Unity implies a sense of oneness. A good paper has one basic idea to develop; it has one point of view; it should be presented in one tense. All of these factors support the idea of unity. In order to achieve unity, therefore, the writer must be familiar with the concept of *shifting,* for it is through shifting voice, tense, person, and number that unity is broken.

Shifts occur in verbs and pronouns. Shifts in voice and tense occur in verbs; shifts in person and number occur in pronouns. To check for shifts in your writing, you need only examine those two kinds of words: verbs (tense and voice) and pronouns (person and number).

Unity is important to good writing. Once shifts are identified, errors that contribute to breakdowns in unity can be avoided.

## PART I: SHIFTS IN VOICE

You will remember that every sentence must have a subject and a verb. The verb can be in *active voice* or *passive voice.* In the *active voice,* the subject is *doing* the action of the verb.

EXAMPLES

              V

ACTIVE:    **He read** the manual.

In the *passive voice,* the subject is *receiving* the action of the verb.

                   V

PASSIVE:    **The manual was read** by him.

Look at some more examples to see how the voice of the verb can be changed.

ACTIVE VOICE

He wrote his report. (*Subject* **he** *doing action of verb* **wrote**)
The board approved the new pension plan. (*Subject* **board** *doing action of verb* **approved**)
Mr. Jones programmed the computer. (*Subject* **Mr. Jones** *doing action of verb* **programmed**)

## PASSIVE VOICE

His report was written. (*Subject* **report** *receiving action of verb* **written**)
The new pension plan was approved by the board. (*Subject* **plan** *receiving action of verb* **approved**)
The computer was programmed by Mr. Jones. (*Subject* **computer** *receiving action of verb* **programmed**)

*Voice* is a concept that is rather new to most writers. Voice determines if the subject of the sentence is performing or receiving the action of the verb. In *active voice,* the subject performs the action; in *passive voice,* the subject receives the action. Passive voice usually includes a prepositional phrase beginning with *by* to indicate the doer of the action. Another signal of the passive voice is a form of the helping verb *be,* such as *is, am, are, was, were, been, being.*

### EXAMPLES

ACTIVE:     John drove the car for inspection.
PASSIVE:    The car was driven by John for inspection.

You probably have noticed that the *sentences written in the active voice* are more forceful than those written in the passive voice. Active verbs convey information with much more emphasis and vigor, and for that reason they are preferred. Sentences in the active voice are less wordy and therefore more practical in business writing. Unlike the vague and sometimes weak passive voice, the active voice catches the subject in action.

If the active voice is preferred, why use the passive voice at all? The answer is that there are a few instances in which the passive voice is useful. Consider the following example:

An error in the account was made.

Here the passive voice is more diplomatic than the active because it shifts the emphasis from *who* made the error (which is not mentioned) to the fact that an error was made, thereby blaming no particular person. However, in most cases you will want to use the active voice for emphasis and forcefulness. The passive voice can be used when the doer of the action is either not known or unimportant.

The most important thing to remember about voice is that you should keep it consistent. If you start out a sentence in the active voice, all verbs in that sentence should be in the active voice. If, on the other hand, you begin a sentence in the passive voice, all verbs in that sentence should be in the passive voice. The same is true for a paragraph or longer report. You should be consistent throughout.

In the following examples, the voice shifts from active to passive within one sentence. Notice how the shifts are corrected by changing the second verb from passive to active voice.

EXAMPLES

|         |  Active                 |    Passive       |
| SHIFT:  | **Jason liked** journalism, but **agriculture was preferred** by Keith. |

|           | Active                 | Active           |
| CORRECTED: | **Jason liked** journalism, but **Keith preferred** agriculture. |

|         | Active                 |                  |
| SHIFT:  | **Karen took** a course in nursing while a program in |
|         |             Passive              |
|         | **data processing was pursued** by Anita. |

|            | Active               | Active            |
| CORRECTED: | **Karen took** a course in nursing while **Anita pursued** a program in data processing. |

*Note that the passive voice always has a helping verb which is a form of the verb* **to be** (**is, am, are, was, were, been, being**). However, forms of the verb **to be** are not always signals for the passive voice.

When these verbs are used as linking verbs (as explained in Module 1, Part II), they are not in the passive voice. (Another signal of the passive voice is the *by* phrase, as in *by Keith* and *by Anita.*)

EXAMPLES

Pete **was given** a job in accounting.
**Was** *is a helper for the main verb* **given** (*past participle of* **give**). *The verb is in the passive voice.*
Pete **was** a good accountant.
**Was** *is the main verb; therefore, it is a linking verb—not in the passive voice.*

To change a sentence from passive to active voice, follow these three steps:

1.  Find the main verb (without the helper).
2.  Ask the question *who* or *what* does (or did) the action of the verb.
3.  Rewrite the sentence with the new subject doing the action of the verb. The old subject is now the direct object.

EXAMPLES

PASSIVE:   Directions **are given** to the drivers by the transportation chief.
    1.  Main verb? *given*
    2.  Who does the giving? *transportation chief*

3. New sentence:

ACTIVE: The transportation chief gives directions to the drivers.

PASSIVE: The ads **were prepared** by the journalism students.

    1. Main verb? *prepared*

    2. Who did the preparing? *journalism students*

    3. New sentence:

ACTIVE: The journalism students prepared the ads.

PASSIVE: The data **is selected** by computers.

    1. Main verb? *selected*

    2. What does the selecting? *computers*

    3. New sentence:

ACTIVE: Computers select the data.

---

## ACTIVITY 10-A: Voice

Underline the complete verbs in the following sentences. If the verb is in the active voice, write *active* in the blank; if the verb is in the passive voice, write *passive* in the blank. Change the sentences in passive voice to active voice.

1. The field trip was arranged by the supervisor. _____

2. The architectural engineer surveyed the lot. _____

3. The Chicago Police Department hired one of our criminal justice students. _____

4. Very often the lab results are written by the lab technicians. _____

5. A very accurate story was written by the reporter. _____

6. The lab technician completed the blood test. _____

7. A report was written by her. _____

8. The prints were drawn by the architectural engineer. _____

9. The company constructed the new plant. _____

10. The patient's temperature was taken by the nurse's aide. _____

Check your responses in Feedback 10-A at the end of this module. If your responses were correct, proceed to Activity 10-C. If you missed any, review and then do Activity 10-B.

---

## ACTIVITY 10-B: Voice

Underline the complete verbs in the following sentences. Identify the voice by writing *active* or *passive* in the blank. Change all passive voice sentences to active voice.

1. The nurse checked the patient's pulse. _____

2. The programs are written by the computer programmer. _____

3. Every morning the electrical engineer checks all the switches. _____

4. Faulty switches are repaired by the maintenance men. _____

5. The police investigated the murder. _____

6. The theft was reported by the shop owner. _____

7. The Criminalistics Unit was called in after the theft. _____

8. The supervisor scheduled the plant visitation. _____

9. The lot was surveyed by the civil engineer. _____

10. One of our graduates was hired by the Atlanta Police Department. _____

Check your responses in Feedback 10-B at the end of this module. If your responses were correct, proceed to Activity 10-C. If you missed any, check them with your instructor before proceeding.

## ACTIVITY 10-C: Voice

Correct any shift in voice by making sure both parts of the sentence are written in the same voice. Rewrite the sentences on separate paper.

1. The lab technician completed the blood test, and a report was written by her.

2. Plans were drawn by the architectural engineer, and his company constructed the new plant.

3. The nurse checked the patient's pulse, and his temperature was taken by the nurse's aide.

4. The programs are usually written by the personnel in the computer room, but we write our own program when they are too busy.

5. Every morning the electrical engineer checks all the switches, and any that are faulty are repaired by the maintenance men.

6. As we came in on the bus, the factory was seen on the right.

7. Not enough attention is devoted to quality-control instruction; the company conducts seminars only once a year.

8. An apology was made by him when he saw the evidence.

9. The transformer was checked because the engineer had discovered a current shortage.

10. Instructions were received by mail and I typed the report.

Check your responses in Feedback 10-C at the end of this module. If your responses were correct, proceed to Activity 10-D. If you missed any, check them with your instructor before proceeding.

**ACTIVITY 10-D: Voice**

Read the following paragraph and correct all shifts in voice.

> Forestry rangers have a wide variety of responsibilities. One of their duties is to watch for forest fires. Also, as a preventive measure trenches must be dug by them. In addition, trees must be marked for cutting. Sometimes, they have to supervise campgrounds. Diseased trees must be found. In short, forest rangers are kept busy by their many duties.

Check your responses in Feedback 10-D at the end of this module. If your responses were correct, proceed to Part II. If you missed any, check with your instructor before proceeding.

## PART II: SHIFTS IN TENSE

Probably the easiest shift to locate is one in tense. Once the verb tense is established in the introduction, you should be sure to keep that tense throughout the paper. In business writing, most reports will occur in the present, past, or future tense. You must be careful to establish the tense and keep it through the report. In fact, shifts in tense are rare, so this is not a critical problem for most writers.

*Tense* means *time*. When you change time in a sentence or within a report without justification, you make a shift in tense. You might be talking about a past event and suddenly, for no reason, switch to the present.

EXAMPLE
John **started** on his new job yesterday. He **checked** his equipment and **begins** to work. (*Shift in tense*)

The first two verbs in this example—**started** and **checked**—are *past* tense, but the third verb—**begins**—is *present* tense. There are two ways to correct this inconsistency: Change all the verbs to past tense, or change all the verbs to present tense:

EXAMPLES
Shift corrected (*past tense*):
   John **started** on his new job yesterday. He **checked** his equipment and **began** to work.
Shift corrected (*present tense*):
   John **starts** on his new job. He **checks** his equipment and **begins** to work.

Once you have set the time of the action, you should be consistent. This does not mean that you can never change tense. A shift in tense is logical if time words such as **today** (present), **yesterday** (past), **tomorrow** (future), and many other expressions of time are used. The verb tense must be consistent with the time expressed.

EXAMPLE

Yesterday, I **worked** on the computer. Today, I **am working** in the lab. Tomorrow, I **will take** the day off. (*Acceptable shifts*)

Here are some examples of inappropriate shifts in tense. Notice how the shifts are corrected by putting all verbs in the same tense.

EXAMPLES

SHIFT:
                Past
Kendall **noted** the drop in secretarial students while
        Present
Elizabeth **discusses** the increase in electronics students.

CORRECTED:
                Past
Kendall **noted** the drop in secretarial students while
        Past
Elizabeth **discussed** the increase in electronics students.

SHIFT:
              Present              Present
The architect **talks** to the prospective builder, **draws** the
                  Past
house plans, and then **consulted** the builder again.

SHIFT:
              Present              Present
The architect **talks** to the prospective builder, **draws** the
                Present
house plans, and then **consults** the builder again.

---

**ACTIVITY 10-E: Tense**

---

Underline any verb that is inconsistent in tense with the rest of the sentence. Write the correct form above the inconsistent verb.

1. The inspector will visit your plant Monday, and next week she visited my plant.
2. Finally, the salesman reaches his goal, and he won the award for being the top salesman.
3. We hurried to the board meeting, but nobody is there.
4. The arbitration board announced that it reaches agreement on the new contract.

5. The new secretary knows how to operate the word processor, but he did not know how to run the answering machine.

6. The carpenter began repairing the fence while the painter paints the walls.

7. The accountant checked the data, and then she writes the profit and loss statement.

8. The nurse checked the patient, and then she talks to the doctor.

9. After we ate lunch yesterday, the boss tells the employees about their new working hours.

10. When the weather gets better, I plan to have finished the job.

Check your responses in Feedback 10-E at the end of this module. If your responses were correct, proceed to Activity 10-G. If you missed any, review and then do Activity 10-F.

## ACTIVITY 10-F: Tense

Underline any verb that is inconsistent in tense with the rest of the sentence. Write the correct form above the inconsistent verb.

1. The doctor visits the patients early in the morning; at night he made rounds again.

2. Finally, the architect finishes the drawing, and she won an award for the design.

3. The reporter hurried to the scene of the accident, but no one is there.

4. The committee notified the board of trustees that it reaches its decision at noon yesterday.

5. The receptionist greeted the callers while the secretary starts the meeting.

6. Before the journalist writes a story, she carefully checked the facts.

7. After the nurse took the patient's blood pressure, the doctor checks his heart.

8. Yesterday afternoon, the computer breaks down in the middle of a program.

9. I wanted to interview him tomorrow, but he cancels the appointment.

10. When summer comes, the farmers looked forward to better weather.

Check your responses in Feedback 10-F at the end of this module. If your responses were correct, proceed to Activity 10-G. If you missed any, check them with your instructor before proceeding.

## ACTIVITY 10-G: Tense

Read the following paragraph and correct any shifts in tense.

> A field trip is a valuable experience for a student. For instance, a civil engineering student benefits from visiting various types of bridges. A nursing student learned a great deal from a trip to the hospital. In addition, a secretarial trainee gets helpful hints while he visited an office. On the whole, a relevant field trip enlightens a student.

Check your responses in Feedback 10-G at the end of this module. If your responses were correct, proceed to Part III. If you missed any, check with your instructor before proceeding.

## PART III: SHIFTS IN PERSON

The most troublesome shift for the writer is the shift in *person* or *point of view*. At the organizational state of writing, you should determine the point of view and keep it consistent throughout the paper. There are three persons or points of view: First person (**I, we, our, us, me,** etc.) is used only for very personal writing. It is used in business only in memos and letters. Second person (**you, your**) is used only with sets of directions or when a very informal approach is taken to a report. Most of the time, the report should be written in the third person (**he, she, it, one, they**, all nouns, and all indefinite pronouns).

Since most business writing is formal, third person is the preferred point of view. And point of view must be consistent throughout the paper. It is easy to maintain consistency within a sentence or even a single paragraph, but maintaining consistency throughout an entire report is rather difficult. Unless you are aware of what you are doing, shifts can creep in rather easily. Often they are easily overlooked because they do not sound awkward or incorrect while you are writing. The only way to avoid this error is to proofread for shifts in person or point of view. This should be one of the final steps in the revision process.

Your paragraph unity can be destroyed if you shift "person" without good reason. If you begin writing in the first person (**I**), do not shift to the second person (**you**) or the third person (**he, she, it, one,** or **they**).

Consult the chart below to make sure you remain consistent in person. That is, make certain the antecedent (the word the pronoun refers to) is in the same person form as the noun it refers to (see Module 8, Part VII on pronouns).

189

| | 1ST PERSON (*person speaking*) | 2ND PERSON (*person spoken to*) | 3RD PERSON (*person spoken about*) |
|---|---|---|---|
| Singular | I (my, mine, me) | You (your, yours) | He (his, him) She (her, hers) It (its) One (one's) All singular nouns |
| Plural | We (our, ours, us) | You (your, yours) | They (their, theirs, them) All plural nouns |

Here are some examples of shifts in person. Notice how the shifts are corrected.

EXAMPLES

                                3rd sing.                2nd

SHIFT: To be a good nurse, a **person** needs to be alert. **You** should continually be aware of what the patient is doing.

                                3rd sing.                3rd

CORRECTED: To be a good nurse, a **person** needs to be alert. **She** should continually be aware of what **her** patient is doing.

                   3rd sing.                              2nd

SHIFT: The **client** will find these stores very convenient; **you** cannot get the supplies **you** need by mail.

                   3rd sing.                              3rd

CORRECTED: The **client** will find these stores very convenient; **he** cannot get the supplies **he** needs by mail.

---

**ACTIVITY 10-H: Person**

---

Correct the shifts in person by writing the correct form above the inconsistent word. In some cases, the verb form may need to be changed as well.

1. Marty would like to know where you could find a good mechanic.
2. You prepared the bids that one must submit to get the contract.
3. The bookkeeper balanced out the account which you must total every day.

4. They reported for work early each morning to find a place to park your car.

5. I broke my microscope; you always hurry to finish the experiment on time.

6. If one is to finish the program for the computer on time, you probably will have to work overtime.

7. You will receive your check from the comptroller after one completes the job.

8. Anyone can fill in the application if you concentrate.

9. Everybody should develop a résumé, which you need when applying for a job.

10. When the contractors finished with the shopping center project, you moved on to the next assignment—building a high-rise apartment.

Check your responses in Feedback 10-H at the end of this module. If your responses were correct, proceed to Activity 10-J. If you missed any, review Part III and do Activity 10-I.

## ACTIVITY 10-I: Person

Correct the shifts in person by writing the correct form above the inconsistent word. In some cases, the verb form may need to be changed as well.

1. I asked the employment office where you could find an efficient secretary.

2. Mr. Blevins did the work you must do to qualify for the job promotion.

3. We checked the patients' charts, which you must look at every day.

4. His calculator was not working; therefore, you must check the warranty.

5. If one is to get paid for overtime, you first must work a 40-hour week.

6. You will get a raise as soon as one passes the competency examination.

7. Anyone can do the job correctly if you read the manual.

8. Everybody brought a stock portfolio, which you need to sit on the Stock Exchange.

9. When they completed the job assignment, you went on to the next task.

10. When a person goes for an interview, you should dress appropriately.

Check your responses in Feedback 10-I at the end of this module. If your responses were correct, proceed to Activity 10-J. If you missed any, check them with your instructor before proceeding.

## ACTIVITY 10-J: Person

Read the following paragraph and correct any shifts in person.

A personnel manager may try in several ways to upset a job applicant to see how you handle an awkward situation. You may offer the interviewee coffee but no cream or sugar. Another trick is for the interviewer to have the applicant stand awkwardly without offering a seat. It would be wise for a prospective employee to be aware of possible attempts to frustrate you.

Check your responses in Feedback 10-J at the end of this module. If your responses were correct, proceed to Part IV. If you missed any, check with your instructor before proceeding.

## PART IV: SHIFTS IN NUMBER

Pronouns always present a problem with shifts. Whenever a pronoun is used, the noun it refers to (called its *antecedent*) should be double-checked for agreement. One area to check is that of number. This simply means making sure a plural pronoun is used to refer to a plural noun; likewise, a singular pronoun must be used for a singular noun. The indefinite pronouns are particularly troublesome here, so it is necessary to know which are singular and which are plural. See Module 8 on Pronoun Agreement (Part VII, Rules 4–6) for a list of these indefinite pronouns. In addition, the collective nouns or group nouns, such as **committee** or **team,** take the singular pronoun **it** because they are usually used as singular nouns.

You can also confuse the meaning of your paragraph by making an unjustified shift in number. If you begin with a plural subject, every pronoun you subsequently use to refer to that subject should be plural; if you start with a singular noun, refer to it with a singular pronoun.

Here are some examples of shifts in number. Notice how the shifts are corrected.

EXAMPLES

                        Sing.

SHIFT:    Each **draftsman** has done a fine job designing the new
                               Pl.
          beachhouse. Not only have **they** worked well together, but
          Pl.
          **they've** also produced some good ideas. Furthermore, the
          Pl.                                 Pl.
          **men** seem to have enjoyed working on **their** project.
                        Pl.

CORRECTED:    All of the **draftsmen** have done a fine job designing the new
                               Pl.
          beachhouse. Not only have **they** worked well together, but

Pl.

**they've** also produced some good ideas. Furthermore, the
Pl.                         Pl.

**men** seem to have enjoyed working on **their** project.

                             Sing.                      Pl.

SHIFT:      Each electronics **student** was asked to bring in **their**
old television set to repair.

                             Sing.                   Sing.

CORRECTED:      Each electronics **student** was asked to bring in **his** (or **her**)
old television set to repair.

Collective nouns (such as **administration, association, club, committee, company, faculty, family, group, jury, organization, personnel,
staff, team,** etc.) are considered singular when the group is thought of
as a unit but are considered plural when the individual members of the
group are stressed. Usually, collective nouns are singular.

EXAMPLES

                        Coll.                                Pl.

SHIFT:      The **jury** deliberated three hours before **they** reached a
verdict. (*Emphasizes members*)

                        Coll.                            Sing.

BETTER:      The **jury** deliberated three hours before **it** reached a
verdict. (*Acts as a unit*)

                        Pl.

ALSO CORRECT:      The **members** of the jury deliberated three hours before
Pl.

**they** reached a verdict.

                                      Coll.

SHIFT:      The **Business and Professional Women's Club** are
Pl.

holding **their** annual meeting soon.

                                      Coll.

BETTER:      The **Business and Professional Women's Club** is hold-
Sing.

ing **its** annual meeting soon. (*Acts as a unit*)

                        Pl.

ALSO CORRECT:      The **ladies** of the Business and Professional Women's Club
Pl.

are holding **their** annual meeting soon.

You will recall from Module 8, Part VII (see pages 142–44) that
some indefinite pronouns, such as **all, any, some, part, most, none,** and
**half,** can be singular or plural. Certain other indefinite pronouns, such
as **anyone, everybody, each, either,** etc., are always singular. The indefinite pronouns **both, few, several,** and **many** are always plural.

**193**

## ACTIVITY 10-K: Number

Underline any shift in number, and write the correct form above it. Circle the antecedent. Consider all collective nouns as singular. Change verb forms if necessary.

1. Colleges should encourage teaching methods other than the lecture. It should promote consideration of individualized instruction.
2. The accounting club agreed to elect their officers at the next meeting.
3. Businessmen build goodwill through advertising. He should set aside money in the budget for sales promotion.
4. Every one of the secretaries was asked to retype their letters.
5. All of the nurses are wearing her new uniforms today.
6. The group discussed the problem and decided on their strategy.
7. The publishing company asked for the script. They wanted to publish the play.
8. We all know that my financial resources are devalued in time of depression.
9. A good accountant knows that neatness is important. In addition, they always strive for accuracy.
10. The archery team won the match yesterday. They were pleased at the victory.

Check your responses in Feedback 10-K at the end of this module. If your responses were correct, proceed to Activity 10-M. If you missed any, review and do Activity 10-L.

## ACTIVITY 10-L: Number

Correct the shifts in number by writing the correct form above the inconsistent word. Consider all collective nouns as singular. Change verb forms if necessary.

1. Employment agencies should advertise job openings; furthermore, it should help match people to jobs.
2. The board of trustees agreed to announce their findings at the July meeting.
3. Salespersons attend conventions regularly. One must be away from home a great deal as a salesperson.
4. Every one of the stewardesses checked their schedule before going home.
5. Both of the architects displayed his new design in the showcase.
6. The group met to review their news articles.
7. The manufacturing company discussed their sales promotion with the new employees.

8. We are all aware that my sales decrease in summer.

9. A good waitress is conscious of personal appearance. They know how important first impressions are.

10. The college staff met to discuss the issue; they made an important decision.

Check your responses in Feedback 10-L at the end of this module. If your responses were correct, proceed to Activity 10-M. If you missed any, check them with your instructor before proceeding.

## ACTIVITY 10-M: Number

Read the following paragraph and correct any shifts in number.

> Nurses have many jobs to perform during a typical day. He or she must check the patients' temperature and blood pressure at regular intervals. They should also ask patients if they are having any complications. Furthermore, a nurse must administer medication to their patients and enter the dosage on their charts. Truly, nurses have a busy schedule.

Check your responses in Feedback 10-M at the end of this module. If your responses were correct, proceed to Activity 10-N. If you missed any, check with your instructor before proceeding.

## ACTIVITY 10-N: Review

Rewrite these sentences on your own paper to correct any shifts in voice, tense, person, or number. Check verbs (voice and tense) and pronouns (person and number).

1. The tour of the industry was planned by the public relations officer, and the group of engineers arrived at 9:00 A.M.

2. The tour guide was a petroleum engineer, and she takes the group around the plant.

3. The public relations officer planned the industrial tour, and they set up an itinerary for the group.

4. Anyone could participate in the tour if you wanted to.

5. The group took the tour; then there is a question-and-answer period.

6. The engineers seemed to enjoy the tour; you got a complete view of the plant's operation.

7. The engineers enjoyed the tour; a complete view of the plant's operation was gotten.

8. As the members of the group entered the processing room, large vats were seen by them.

9. After the tour was completed, the guide invites the group to have lunch.

10. Everyone should take advantage of such a tour if they would like to learn more about a company.

Check your responses in Feedback 10-N at the end of this module. If your responses were correct, proceed to Activity 10-O. If you missed any, check with your instructor before proceeding.

## ACTIVITY 10-O: Review

Correct the unnecessary shifts in each of the following sentences. In the space provided, identify the type of shift (voice, tense, person, or number).

EXAMPLE:

*Tense*   The surveyor had remembered to bring his transit, but he forgets his clipboard.
*The surveyor had remembered to bring his transit, but he had forgotten his clipboard.*

_____   1. The salesman worked to meet his quota, and ten new accounts were opened in one week.

_____

_____

_____   2. Bradford will repair the television, and Stillman helped him.

_____

_____

_____   3. We transported the tire to Indianapolis, and it has been charged to the manufacturer.

_____

_____

_____   4. Sue totaled the daily receipts, but several errors were made.

_____

_____

_____   5. Since Ross will retire at the conclusion of this project, no suggestions will be offered by him.

_____

_____

_____ 6. The supervisor installed and tested the new equipment. Next month, it will be put into operation.

_____

_____

_____ 7. The hotel manager made arrangements for the convention, and his secretary requests the confirmations.

_____

_____

_____ 8. The computer has been programmed by Murphy, and he checked it for bugs yesterday.

_____

_____

_____ 9. A police officer holds a very important job in the community. Many people depend on them for help.

_____

_____

_____ 10. Because everyone works hard, you should take a midmorning break to relax.

_____

_____

_____ 11. When the boss saw that an employee was sick, she was sent home to rest.

_____

_____

_____ 12. Before I started to drive, my seat belt was fastened and the emergency brake released.

_____

_____

_____ 13. A tourist can stop frequently if they drive their own car.

_____

_____

_____ 14. A person does well in an interview if they prepare ahead of time.

_____

_____

_____   15. People should not trust rumors without checking for oneself.

_____

_____

Check your responses in Feedback 10-O at the end of this module. If your responses were correct, proceed to Activity 10-P. If you missed any, check with your instructor before proceeding.

## ACTIVITY 10-P: Writing Sentences for Review

Follow the directions for each item.

1. Construct a compound sentence (sentence with two independent clauses) showing consistency in *voice* from one independent clause to the other. Underline the verbs and identify them as active or passive.
   EXAMPLE: The newspaper reporter <u>arrived</u> at the scene of the crime, and she quickly <u>made</u> notes on the theft. (Active voice)

2. Construct a compound sentence showing consistency in *tense* from one independent clause to the other. Underline the verbs and identify their tense.

   EXAMPLE: The social worker <u>interviewed</u> the applicant for food stamps; then he <u>filled</u> out the forms. (Past tense)

3. Construct a compound sentence showing consistency in *person* from one independent clause to the other. Underline the noun or pronoun and its antecedent, and indicate whether it is first, second, or third person.

   EXAMPLE: <u>Jones and I</u> attended the meeting; <u>we</u> took notes on the speech. (1st person)

4. Construct a compound sentence showing consistency in *number* from one independent clause to the other. Underline the noun or pronoun and its antecedent. Identify the number as singular or plural.

   EXAMPLE: <u>All</u> of the secretaries took their coffee break at 10:00 A.M.; <u>they</u> liked to visit together in the lounge. (Plural)

Check your responses with your instructor; then ask for Test A.

## FEEDBACK FOR MODULE 10

### Feedback 10-A

1. was arranged (*passive*). The supervisor arranged the field trip.
2. surveyed (*active*)
3. hired (*active*)
4. are written (*passive*). Very often the lab technicians write the lab results.
5. was written (*passive*). The reporter wrote a very accurate story.
6. completed (*active*)
7. was written (*passive*). She wrote a report.
8. were drawn (*passive*). The architectural engineer drew the prints.

9. constructed (*active*)
10. was taken (*passive*). The nurse's aide took the patient's temperature.

1. checked (*active*)
2. are written (*passive*). The computer programmer writes the programs.
3. checks (*active*)
4. are repaired (*passive*). The maintenance men repair the faulty switches.
5. investigated (*active*)
6. was reported (*passive*). The shop owner reported the theft.
7. was called (*passive*). After the theft, the manager [or any suitable subject] called in the Criminalistics Unit.
8. scheduled (*active*)
9. was surveyed (*passive*). The civil engineer surveyed the lot.
10. was hired (*passive*). The Atlanta Police Department hired one of our graduates.

All sentences are written in the active voice. If your responses differ, check with your instructor since there is more than one possible correct answer.

1. The lab technician completed the blood test, and she wrote a report.
2. The architectural engineer drew the plans, and his company constructed the new plant.
3. The nurse checked the patient's pulse, and the nurse's aide took his temperature.
4. The personnel in the computer room usually write the programs, but we write our own program when they are too busy.
5. Every morning the electrical engineer checks all the switches, and the maintenance men repair any that are faulty.
6. As we came in on the bus, we saw the factory on the right.
7. The company does not devote enough attention to quality-control instruction; it conducts seminars only once a year.
8. He made an apology when he saw the evidence.
9. The engineer checked the transformer because he had discovered a current shortage.
10. I received instructions by mail and typed the report.

Forestry rangers have a wide variety of responsibilities. One of their duties is to watch for forest fires. Also, as a preventive measure *they must dig* trenches. In addition, *they must mark* trees for cutting. Sometimes, they have to supervise campgrounds. *They must find* diseased trees. In short, the many duties of forest rangers keep them busy.

Alternate answers are shown in parentheses, but you must be consistent! If your responses differ, check with your instructor.

1. The inspector *will visit* your plant Monday, and next week she *will visit* my plant.
2. Finally, the salesman *reached (reaches)* his goal, and he *won (wins)* the award for being the top salesman.
3. We *hurried (hurry)* to the board meeting, but nobody *was (is)* there.
4. The arbitration board *announced* that it *reached* agreement on the new contract.
5. The new secretary *knows* how to operate the word processor, but he *does not know* how to run the answering machine.
6. The carpenter *began* repairing the fence while the painter *painted* the walls.
7. The accountant *checked (checks)* the data, and then she *wrote (writes)* the profit and loss statement.
8. The nurse *checked (checks)* the patient, and then she *talked (talks)* to the doctor.
9. After we *ate* lunch yesterday, the boss *told* the employees about their new working hours.
10. When the weather gets better, I plan to *finish* the job.

## Feedback 10-F

**Alternate answers are shown in parentheses, but you must be consistent! If your responses differ, check with your instructor.**

1. The doctor *visits (visited)* the patients early in the morning; at night he *makes (made)* rounds again.
2. Finally, the architect finished *(finishes)* the drawing, and she *won (wins)* an award for the design.
3. The reporter *hurried (hurries)* to the scene of the accident, but no one *was (is)* there.
4. The committee *notified* the board of trustees that it *reached* its decision at noon yesterday.
5. The receptionist *greeted (greets)* the callers while the secretary *started (starts)* the meeting.
6. Before the journalist *writes (wrote)* a story, she carefully *checks (checked)* the facts.
7. After the nurse *took (takes)* the patient's blood pressure, the doctor *checked (checks)* his heart.
8. *Yesterday* afternoon, the computer *broke* down in the middle of a program.
9. I *wanted* to interview him tomorrow, but he *cancelled* the appointment.
10. When summer *comes (came)*, the farmers *look (looked)* forward to better weather.

## Feedback 10-G

**There may be more than one correct answer. If your responses differ, check with your instructor.**

A field trip is a valuable experience for a student. For instance, a civil engineering student benefits from visiting various types of bridges. A nursing student *learns* a great deal from a trip to the hospital. In addition, a secretarial trainee gets helpful hints while he *visits* an office. On the whole, a relevant field trip enlightens a student.

### Feedback 10-H

There may be more than one correct answer. If your responses differ, check with your instructor.

1. *Marty* would like to know where *he* could find a good mechanic.
2. *You* prepared the bids that *you* must submit to get the contract.
3. The *bookkeeper* balanced out the account which *she* must total every day.
4. *They* reported for work early each morning to find a place to park *their* car.
5. *I* broke my microscope; *I* always hurry to finish the experiment on time.
6. If *one* is to finish the program for the computer on time, *he* probably will have to work overtime. (or) If *you* (or *we*) are to finish the program for the computer on time, *you* (or *we*) probably will have to work overtime.
7. *You* will receive your check from the comptroller after *you* complete the job. (Note verb change.)
8. *Anyone* can fill in the application if *he* (or *she*) concentrates. (Verb change) (or) *You* can fill in the application if *you* concentrate.
9. *Everybody* should develop a résumé, which *he* needs when applying for a job. (Verb change) (or) *You* should develop a résumé, which *you* need when applying for a job.
10. When *the contractors* finished with the shopping center project, *they* moved on to the next assignment—building a high-rise apartment.

### Feedback 10-I

There may be more than one correct answer. If your responses differ, check with your instructor.

1. *I* asked the employment office where *I* could find an efficient secretary.
2. *Mr. Blevins* did the work *he* must do to qualify for the job promotion.
3. *We* checked the patients' charts, which *we* must look at every day.
4. *His* calculator was not working; therefore, *he* must check the warranty.
5. If *one* is to get paid for overtime, *he* first must work a 40-hour week. (or) If *you* are to get paid for overtime, *you* first must work a 40-hour week. (Note verb change.)
6. *You* will get a raise as soon as *you* pass the competency examination. (Verb change)
7. *Anyone* can do the job correctly if *he* (or *she*) reads the manual. (Verb change) (or) *You* can do the job correctly if *you* read the manual.
8. *Everybody* brought a stock portfolio, which *he* (or *she*) needs to sit on the Stock Exchange. (Verb change)
9. When *they* completed the job assignment, *they* went on to the next task. (or) When *you* completed the job assignment, *you* went on to the next task.
10. When a *person* goes for an interview, *he* (or *she*) should dress appropriately. (or) When *you* go for an interview, *you* should dress appropriately. (Verb change)

**Feedback 10-J**

There may be more than one correct answer. If your responses differ, check with your instructor.

A personnel manager may try in several ways to upset a job applicant to see how *he* handles an awkward situation. *He* may offer the interviewee coffee but no cream or sugar. Another trick is for the interviewer to have him stand awkwardly without offering him a seat. It would be wise for a prospective employee to be aware of possible attempts to frustrate *him*.

**Feedback 10-K**

There may be more than one correct answer. If your responses differ, check with your instructor.

1. Colleges . . . They
2. club . . . its
3. Businessmen . . . They
4. Every one . . . her
5. All . . . their
6. group . . . its
7. company . . . It
8. We . . . our
9. accountant . . . he (*or* she) *strives* (singular verb)
10. team . . . It *was* (singular verb)

**Feedback 10-L**

There may be more than one correct answer. If your responses differ, check with your instructor.

1. agencies . . . they
2. board . . . its
3. Salespersons . . . They . . . salesperson.
4. Every one . . . her
5. Both . . . their
6. group . . . its
7. company . . . its
8. We . . . our
9. waitress . . . She *knows* (singular verb)
10. staff . . . it

**Feedback 10-M**

Alternate possibilities appear in parentheses. To be correct, your paragraph must be consistent with either all of the italicized words or all of the words in parentheses. Other correct answers are possible. Check with your instructor if your responses differ.

*Nurses* (A nurse) *have* (has) many jobs to perform during a typical day. *They* (He or she) must check the patients' temperature and blood pressure at regular intervals. *They* (He or she) should also ask the patients if *they* (they) are having any complications. Furthermore, *nurses* (a nurse) must administer medication to *their* (his or her) patients and enter the dosage on *their* (their) charts. Truly, *nurses* (a nurse) *have* (has) a busy schedule.

### Feedback 10-N

1. *The public relations officer planned the tour of the industry,* and the group of engineers arrived at 9:00 A.M.. (Voice)
2. The tour guide was a petroleum engineer, and she *took* the group around the plant. (Tense)
3. The public relations officer planned the industrial tour, and *he* set up an itinerary for the group. (Number)
4. Anyone could participate in the tour if *he* wanted to. (Person)
5. The group took the tour; then there *was* a question-and-answer period. (Tense)
6. The engineers seemed to enjoy the tour; *they* got a complete view of the plant's operation. (Person and number)
7. The engineers enjoyed the tour; *they got* a complete view of the plant's operation. (Voice)
8. As the members of the group entered the processing room, *they saw large vats.* (Voice)
9. After the tour was completed, the guide *invited* the group to have lunch. (Tense)
10. Everyone should take advantage of such a tour if *he* (or *she*) would like to learn more about a company. (Number)

### Feedback 10-O

There may be more than one correct answer. If your responses differ, check with your instructor.

1. VOICE: The salesman worked to meet his quota, and *he opened ten new accounts* in one week.
2. TENSE: Bradford will repair the television, and Stillman *will help* him.
3. VOICE: We transported the tire to Indianapolis, and *(we) charged it* to the manufacturer.
4. VOICE: Sue totaled the daily receipts but *(she) made several errors.*
5. VOICE: Since Ross will retire at the conclusion of this project, *he offered no suggestions.*
6. VOICE: The supervisor installed and tested the new equipment. Next month, *he will put it* into operation.
7. TENSE: The hotel manager made arrangements for the convention, and his secretary *requested* the confirmations.
8. VOICE: *Murphy programmed the computer,* and he checked it for bugs yesterday.

9. NUMBER: A police officer holds a very important job in the community. Many people depend upon *him* (or *her*) for help.
10. PERSON: Because everyone works hard, *he* (or *she*) should take a midmorning break to relax.
11. VOICE: When the boss saw that an employee was sick, *he sent her* home to rest.
12. VOICE: Before I started to drive, *I fastened my seat belt and released the emergency brake.*
13. NUMBER: A tourist can stop frequently if *he* (or *she*) *drives his* (or *her*) own car.
14. NUMBER: A person does well in an interview if *he* (or *she*) *prepares* ahead of time.
15. NUMBER: People should not trust rumors without checking for *themselves.*

# MODULE 11

# Clarity

OBJECTIVE: This module covers four areas that will help you prevent any misunderstanding in your writing.

Upon completion of this module, you will be able:

To identify and to correct unclear pronoun reference.

To identify and to correct unclear or misplaced modifiers.

To define certain confusing pairs of words.

To identify and to correct problems in five areas of parallel construction.

One way to make sure your writing is clear is to shift your point of view from that of the writer to that of the reader. When you sit down to write, put yourself in the place of the person who is going to read what you write. The importance of this technique is illustrated by the following incident, which occurred in a chemical laboratory.

On going off duty one evening, the senior laboratory technician left the following note for his night relief man, who was new on the job: "The flasks on the table probably have some sodium residue in them. Discard residues into a beaker, but check for water. Keep an eye on the B.B. Better use a metal one."

The new night man asked himself, "What does 'check' mean? To add water? To remove water? What does the note mean by 'a metal one'? A metal B.B.? A metal beaker?"

Fortunately, the assistant guessed right. He chose a metal beaker. He removed all moisture from it, poured in the sodium residue, and kept the beaker away from the Bunsen burner, which burned with a hot gas flame. Had he done otherwise, the action of sodium on water could have released pure hydrogen. If heated by the burner, this highly volatile gas could have exploded and seriously injured him.

In another case, a technician in a big planing mill wrote the following instructions to the night shipping clerk, who was to send out a load of door frames and a load of window frames. "The door frames go by rail this time and the windows by motor express. Have them stacked on loading platform B for 6 A.M. pickup Tuesday. Put the others on the flats." The clerk wondered: "Were the doors or the windows to be stacked for a pickup?" He guessed wrong and shipped the windows to Miami and the doors to Alaska. Loss to the company in shipping charges and man-hours amounted to hundreds of dollars before the mess was straightened out.

Had the technician been thinking of the shipping clerk, he would have written something like this: "The door frames go by Seaboard Rail to Miami. The windows go by Ace Express to Anchorage and should be stacked on platform B for 6 A.M. pickup Tuesday."

The doors and windows were shipped to the wrong places because of two pronouns. One was **them,** which referred to the noun **windows.** The second was **others,** which referred to the noun **doors.** The technician had not made it clear what the antecedents were. (You will remember that an *antecedent* is the noun that the pronoun refers to.)

*Make sure every pronoun has a clear antecedent.* Do not use a pronoun if there is the slightest doubt about what it refers to. This practice does not always cause expensive errors, but it does confuse readers and make them stop and reread the sentence. This is reason enough to correct the sentence.

EXAMPLES

POOR: Mellon bumped his Olds against the wall of his carport **which** he hadn't yet paid for.

The reader stops. Does *which* refer to the Olds or to the carport?

BETTER: Mellon bumped his Olds, which he hadn't yet paid for, against the wall of his carport.

POOR: Norden picked up the wrench, removed the nut, and handed **it** to Robert.

What does **it** refer to? Again, the reader is obstructed in his or her reading. In this case, the word **wrench** must be repeated or **it** must be replaced by a synonym for **wrench**.

BETTER: Norden picked up the wrench, removed the nut, and handed **the tool** to Robert.

Never let a pronoun "float" in space, unconnected to some noun. Make sure it has a specific antecedent.

POOR: Complaining angrily, Rudolph wrote **it** up and sent **it** to the newspaper. (*What is* **it**?)

BETTER: Angrily, Rudolph wrote up his **complaint** and sent it to the newspaper.

CONFUSING: Not until Fred had heard his uncle talk about the pay scales in drafting did he want to become **one**.

CLEARER: Not until Fred had heard his uncle talk about the pay scales in drafting did he want to become a **draftsman**.

## ACTIVITY 11-A: Pronoun Reference

Rewrite these sentences to clarify the pronoun reference. Use your own paper.

1. I went with Brad to Phil's place because *he* wanted company.
2. Tack an overlay on the drawing board to keep *it* clean.
3. Peter spoke to the timekeeper, and *he* was very rude.
4. The division manager always favored Swanson. *This* angered the other employees.
5. John showed the news reporter how to take good pictures, and *his* pictures turned out beautifully.

6. After the lab technician had trained an assistant, *she* enjoyed *her* work more.

7. Gail hired the waitress, *which* was a wise move on her part.

8. Plant three-foot azaleas in front of the seven-foot rhododendrons to make *them* stand out.

9. To get the students' grades to them as soon as possible, we feed *them* into a computer.

10. The policeman stopped the man who was speeding down the highway, and *he* was really mad.

Check your responses in Feedback 11-A at the end of this module. If your responses were correct, proceed to the next section on other Indefinite References. If you missed any, do Activity 11-B.

---

**ACTIVITY 11-B: Pronoun Reference**

---

Rewrite these sentences to clarify the pronoun reference. Use your own paper.

1. My problems in math were serious. Although my progress in English and reading were good, *this* brought down my overall record.

2. John likes his supervisor and *he* is good to him.

3. As the ferry boat approaches the tugboat, *it* blows a warning.

4. After the electrician installed new switches in the motors, *some of them* did not work.

5. The car ran off the highway when the tire blew; *this* was a mess.

6. The beets were pickled which made them last longer.

7. John is not only a very good lecturer but a very good economist as well. I have always wanted to be *one*.

8. When the legislature convened, two members favored and three members opposed the bill; I agreed with *them*.

9. I almost signed a contract to buy a Mack, my favorite truck; then GM made me an attractive offer. *This* made me think a while longer.

10. An alcoholic should work very closely with his counselor; then *he* would take an interest in *his* welfare.

Check your responses in Feedback 11-B at the end of this module. If your responses were correct, proceed to the section on Indefinite References. If you missed any, check with your instructor before proceeding.

**Other Indefinite References**

Try to avoid the use of the indefinite **it** and **they.**

EXAMPLES

POOR:     In the college handbook, **it** lists the holidays we get in the winter quarter.

BETTER:   The college handbook lists the holidays we get in the winter quarter.

POOR:     At DuPont, **they** provide very reasonable health insurance.

BETTER:   DuPont provides very reasonable health insurance.

Also avoid explaining a term with ". . . is when" and ". . . is where."

EXAMPLES

POOR:     A bear market **is when** stock prices fall.

BETTER:   Stock prices fall in a bear market.

POOR:     Early spring **is when** most new construction projects begin.

BETTER:   Most new construction projects begin in early spring.

POOR:     The fire station **is where** we vote for candidates for local offices.

BETTER:   We vote for candidates for local offices at the fire station.

---

### ACTIVITY 11-C: Indefinite References

---

Eliminate the vague **it, they, is when,** and **is where** in the following sentences.

1. At Aero International, **they** have an excellent in-service training program.
2. In the editorial in today's paper, **it** discusses the controversial busing problem.
3. In Oregon, **they** have passed a law which encourages the recycling of waste materials.
4. In the instruction manual, **it** explains how to operate an oscilloscope.
5. Inflation **is when** the dollar is worth less than previously.
6. Toxemia **is when** fluid builds up in the body.
7. At the Farmers' Auction Block **is where they** have many buyers of truck crops.
8. In the specifications, **it** clearly states the type of muffler to use on my car.
9. Talking on a telephone **is when** a secretary demonstrates finesse.
10. At the hardware center, **they** have all kinds of electrical equipment available.

Check your responses in Feedback 11-C at the end of this module. If your responses are correct, proceed to Part II. If you missed any, review the Indefinite References and then do Activity 11-D.

**ACTIVITY 11-D: Indefinite References**

Eliminate the vague **it, they, is when,** and **is where** in the following sentences.

1. On the drawing board **is where** this whole idea was conceived.
2. On Wall Street in New York **they** have many brokerage companies.
3. In our Nursing Department's weight control booklet, **it** catalogs the approximate number of calories in all foods.
4. Surveying a plot of ground **is when** the boundaries are legally established.
5. For safety on all these switch boxes, **they** have a master lever.
6. In a computer, **it** stores information that may be used later.
7. The sign of a good switchboard operator **is when** he can make himself easily understood.
8. When tuning an engine, **it** requires time and patience.
9. Driving onto the freeway **is where** we must be alert.
10. On the editorial page in the evening paper, **they** printed many letters to the editor suggesting ways to resolve our tax problems.

Check your responses in Feedback 11-D at the end of this module. If your responses were correct, proceed to Part II. If you missed any, check with your instructor before proceeding.

## PART II: MISPLACED AND UNCLEAR MODIFIERS

A modifier is a word, phrase, or clause used to describe or enhance the meaning of another word in the sentence. It should be placed *next to* the word it modifies. A modifier in the wrong place can cause confusion. Note the misplaced modifiers in the examples below and the various ways to unscramble the confusion and make the meaning clear.

EXAMPLES

MISPLACED
CLAUSE: Marjory waited to put her ring on in the bus *which I had just bought her. (Bought the bus?)*

CLARIFIED: Marjory waited until we got on the bus to put on the ring which I had just bought her.

MISPLACED
PHRASE: *Earning time-and-a-half,* Joe was certain his secretary would remain on the job. (*Who was earning time-and-a-half? The secretary? Joe?*)

CLARIFIED: Joe was certain that his secretary, earning time-and-a-half, would remain on the job.
or

Earning time-and-a-half, the secretary assured Joe that she would remain on the job.

MISPLACED
PHRASE: *To fly in to the airstrip,* the mountains must be crossed. (*Mountains flying?*)

CLARIFIED: To fly in to the airstrip, the pilot must cross the mountains.

*Note:* Misplaced modifiers often occur with the passive voice, as in the sentence above.

To avoid confusion, place the modifying clause or phrase immediately next to the word it modifies. If you begin a sentence with a verbal phrase, make sure the phrase modifies the subject of the sentence. A verbal phrase, you will remember from Module 3, is a verbal (gerund, infinitive, or participle) with its object and/or modifiers.

Some nouns exist only in the careless writer's imagination. They are not actually expressed in the sentence. These nouns must be added to the sentence to keep the reader from stumbling.

EXAMPLES

POOR: *Excused at 3:30,* the office Christmas party began. (*Was the party excused?*)

The reader finally supplies the answer, but not without feeling a twinge of irritation.

BETTER: Excused at 3:30, the staff attended the office Christmas party.

Do not leave the reader guessing what you are trying to say. Make sure each pronoun has a clear antecedent—what the pronoun refers to.

POOR: *Despite typing all day,* no letters were finished. (Did the letters type?)

BETTER: Despite typing all day, the secretary did not finish any letters.

---

**ACTIVITY 11-E: Misplaced Modifiers**

---

Eliminate confusion by repositioning misplaced phrases or clauses next to the words they modify. Some rewording may also be necessary.

1.  At the age of five, my father decided I would be an engineer.
2.  Concerned about the grain market, a call was made to the broker.
3.  While low on ink, James continued to operate the printer.
4.  Worn thin from use, Bill replaced the shims on the wheels.
5.  Although writing for several years, no articles have been published.

6. A photocopier was advertised in *The Reporter* which was expensive.

7. Emily is writing a report on filmmaking in the college library.

8. The shoplifter admitted that she had stolen the dress while talking to the security officer.

9. Arriving at the police station, my license was returned.

10. I received instructions for operating the ten-ton crane by mail.

Check your responses in Feedback 11-E at the end of this module. If your responses were correct, proceed. If you missed any, review and do Activity 11-F.

---

### ACTIVITY 11-F: Misplaced Modifiers

---

Eliminate confusion by repositioning misplaced phrases or clauses next to the words they modify. Some rewording may also be necessary.

1. Mrs. Allen complained about the lengthy report she had typed while riding home in her car pool.

2. To reserve a room, the motel was called.

3. He repaired the typewriter for the boss's secretary, a run-down old model that needed replacing.

4. Feeling very sick at work, the company dispensary was where Jim saw the doctor.

5. Puzzled about the fall-off in the current, the transformer was checked.

6. Smiling courteously, her offer was accepted.

7. Coming in on the bus, the factory is seen off to the left.

8. Not enough attention is devoted to quality-control instruction, giving seminars only once every three months.

9. He ordered a special lubricant for the two-ton turbine air-freighted from New York.

10. The driver said he would never carry a firearm in a truck that was loaded.

Check your responses in Feedback 11-F at the end of this module. If your responses were correct, proceed to Part III, Word Usage. If you missed any, check with your instructor before proceeding.

---

## PART III: WORD USAGE

---

Be careful about the words you use. Be sure that the word you choose means exactly what you think it means. Below is a list of pairs of words that are often confused. Study the definitions and examples carefully.

1. **Good** is usually an *adjective.*
   EXAMPLE: He is a **good** basketball player.
   **Well** is normally an *adverb.*
   EXAMPLE: He did **well** in chemistry.
   **Well** is an adjective only when it pertains to health.
   EXAMPLE: He doesn't feel **well.**

2. **Respectively**, an *adverb*, means *in the order given.*
   EXAMPLE: The board of directors appointed Harrison, Bonner, and Cook, **respectively**, as manager, comptroller, and secretary of the firm.
   **Respectfully**, an adverb, means *showing respect.*
   EXAMPLE: The salesman nodded **respectfully** to the manager and left the office.

3. **Precede**, a *verb*, means to *go before.*
   EXAMPLE: The secretary **preceded** the supervisor out the door.
   **Proceed**, a *verb*, means to *advance* or *move forward.*
   *EXAMPLE: They* **proceeded** through the front door of the courthouse.

4. **Altogether** is most commonly used as an *adverb*, meaning *wholly, thoroughly.*
   EXAMPLE: He was **altogether** too high-strung a person for that job.
   **All together** usually means *in a group, collectively.*
   EXAMPLE: They went **all together** to the graduation.

5. **Accept**, a *verb*, means to *take or receive* something.
   EXAMPLE: I will **accept** your job offer.
   **Except**, used most frequently as a *preposition*, means *with the exception of.*
   EXAMPLE: Everybody quit at five o'clock **except** me.

6. **Amount**, as a *noun* meaning *quantity*, is used with reference to things that *cannot be counted.*
   EXAMPLE: We have a tremendous **amount** of work to do.
   **Number**, as a *noun*, refers to items that *can be counted.*
   EXAMPLE: A large **number** of motorists were held up by the parade.

7. **About**, usually an *adverb*, means *approximately.*
   EXAMPLE: I made **about** forty dollars on the trade.
   **Around**, an *adverb* or a *preposition*, means *circling.*
   EXAMPLE: He went **around** the plant collecting union dues.

8. **Persecute**, a *verb*, means to *afflict* or *harass.*
   EXAMPLE: The Nazis **persecuted** the Jews in Germany.
   **Prosecute**, a *verb*, means to *seek to accomplish by legal process.*
   EXAMPLE: The district attorney will **prosecute** the defendant on a charge of fraud.

9. **Illegible**, an *adjective*, means *unreadable.*
   EXAMPLE: Elaine's handwriting is **illegible.**
   **Ineligible**, an *adjective*, means *not qualified.*
   EXAMPLE: He was **ineligible** for a license because he had just moved to the state.

10. **Affect**, a *verb*, means to *influence.*
    EXAMPLE: His action won't **affect** my decision.
    **Effect**, most commonly used as a *noun*, means *result.*
    EXAMPLE: The report had a bad **effect** on the morale of the office.

11. **Between**, a *preposition*, refers to the space or relationship between *two* persons or things.

> EXAMPLE: The new accountant caused friction **between** the pay clerk and the timekeeper.

**Among**, also a *preposition*, refers to *three or more* persons or things.

> EXAMPLE: The investigator caused trouble **among** all members of the staff.

12. **Uninterested**, an *adjective*, means *without interest* or *indifferent*.

> EXAMPLE: He was **uninterested** in merchandising as a career.

**Disinterested**, also an *adjective*, means *having no desire for personal gain, impartial*.

> EXAMPLE: The judge was wholly **disinterested** and evicted the dishonest attorney from the courtroom.

13. **Imply**, a *verb*, means to *suggest or hint to someone*. (The person speaking *implies*.)

> EXAMPLE: Braden **implied** to me that he wanted a ride home.

**Infer** is just the opposite, a *verb* meaning to *perceive what is being suggested by someone else*. (The person listening *infers*.)

> EXAMPLE: I **inferred** from what Braden said that he wanted a ride home.

**Imply** is an expression of *projecting;* **infer** is an expression of *receiving*.

14. **Complement**, a *noun* or *verb*, means *to fill up* or *complete*.

> EXAMPLE: Mrs. Smith, a polite woman, provided a perfect **complement** to her successful but ill-mannered husband.

**Compliment**, a *noun* or *verb*, means *praise*.

> EXAMPLE: He showered **compliments** on her for her typing speed.

15. **Fewer**, an *adjective*, used with plural nouns, refers to the *number* of items or things (can be counted).

> EXAMPLE: The plant produced **fewer** cars in August than in July.

**Less**, an *adjective*, refers to the *amount* (cannot be counted).

> EXAMPLE: There was **less** concrete in the mixer than he had estimated.

16. **Farther**, an adverb, usually *refers to physical distance*.

> EXAMPLE: He drove **farther** down the road.

**Further**, an adverb, means *more distant in degree, time, or space*. It also means *to a greater extent or in addition*.

> EXAMPLE: The chairman will pursue the salary question **further.**

17. **To**, a preposition, means *in the direction of*.

> EXAMPLE: The electronics expert walked **to** the computer lab.

**Too**, an adverb, means *also* or *extremely.*

> EXAMPLE: The new laser printer is **too** expensive.

18. **Its** is a possessive pronoun.

> EXAMPLE: The computer had **its** cover off.

**It's** is a contraction for *it is*.

> EXAMPLE: **It's** a well-written report.

19. **Advice**, a noun, means *counsel* or *information*.

> EXAMPLE: The employment counselor gave the graduate some good **advice.**

**Advise**, a verb, means *to counsel*.

> EXAMPLE: The employment counselor will **advise** the new graduate.

20. **Got**, a verb, is past tense of **get** and means *obtained* or *acquired*.
      EXAMPLE: The technician **got** a raise.
    **Have**, a verb, means *to possess*.
      EXAMPLE: The technician will **have** a raise by next week.

*Note:* It is incorrect to use **got** as *became*. (**He got arrested** is wrong.) It is also incorrect to use **have got** in place of *must*. (**I have got** to go now is wrong.)

## ACTIVITY 11-G: Word Usage

Underline the correct word in the parentheses.

1. The first shift will (precede/proceed) the second shift at the pay window.
2. Jack, Joe, and Henry, (respectfully/respectively), covered the sales territories of Wilmington, Newark, and Philadelphia.
3. The TV advertisement brought (fewer/less) responses than expected.
4. Hearing the labor boss, members of the union (implied/inferred) that there will be a meeting tomorrow.
5. Left out in the rain, the pages of her report were almost (ineligible/illegible).
6. He performed very (good/well) as a master of ceremonies.
7. The treasurer distributed the money (among/between) the head of the board of directors and the representative of all stockholders.
8. The price rise had a bad (affect/effect) on sales.
9. Please (except/accept) my apologies for disturbing you.
10. The company will pursue the matter (further/farther).
11. The bankruptcy referee was (disinterested/uninterested) and made no effort to show favoritism to the creditors.
12. (It's/Its) (to/too/two) soon to make a decision.
13. The professional counselor's (advise/advice) was good.
14. The state will (persecute/prosecute) him in the superior court.

Check your responses in Feedback 11-G at the end of this module. If your responses were correct, proceed to Part IV. If you missed any, review the words in the Glossary and then do Activity 11-H.

## ACTIVITY 11-H: Word Usage

Underline the correct word in the parentheses.

1. His letter of recommendation was very (complimentary/complementary).
2. The members of the jury could not agree (between/among) themselves.
3. The (further/farther) he drove, the worse the storm became.
4. Inflation increased the cost of steel (around/about) 10 percent.

5. The police officers will (precede/proceed) to their squad cars.

6. The students were (disinterested/uninterested) in seeking a B.A. degree.

7. (Less/Fewer) motorists are putting up with freeway traffic than before.

8. She did very (good/well) in writing the memo.

9. The president (has/has got) to make a decision.

10. The table had (it's/its) leg broken.

11. The used Chevrolet is priced (all together/altogether) too high.

12. The nonunion members of the company were (prosecuted/persecuted) by the union leaders.

13. He ordered all the options (accept/except) electric windows.

14. The senior employees can (advise/advice) you.

15. Without an associate degree, he was considered (ineligible/illegible) for the position.

Check your responses in Feedback 11-H at the end of this module. If your responses were correct, proceed to Part IV. If you missed any, check with your instructor before proceeding.

## PART IV: PARALLEL CONSTRUCTION

A good sentence functions like a well-lubricated car, carrying the reader from one thought to the next without any squeaks or rattles. A sentence that draws attention to its wording—no matter how beautifully written—is a BAD SENTENCE. The reader should be wholly unaware of the passage of words. Sometimes the jolts in a sentence that interrupt the reader's flow of thought are errors in spelling or grammar. Often, however, they are structural blunders, such as violations of parallel construction. These occur most often in sentences using words joined by **and** or **or.** We will look at three types.

1. *Parallel construction with the word* **and**. *Words or word groups preceding and following the word* **and** *should be similar in form.* They should both be gerunds, for example, or infinitives or clauses or the same part of speech.

    EXAMPLES

    POOR:    I like **engineering** and **to fish.** (*Here a gerund,* **engineering,** *is mistakenly paired with an infinitive phrase,* **to fish.**)

    BETTER:  I like **engineering** and **fishing.** (*Two gerunds*)

    POOR:    The workers began to feel **as if they had confidence** and **happy.** (*A clause,* **as if they had confidence,** *is mistakenly paired with an adjective,* **happy.**)

BETTER: The workers began to feel **confident** and **happy.** (*Two adjectives*)

POOR: Jefferson plans **to study engineering** and then **going to work** at NCR. (*Here an infinitive,* **to study,** *is paired with the verbal* **going.**)

BETTER: Jefferson plans **to study engineering** and then **to go to work** at NCR. (*Two infinitive phrases*)

2. *Parallel construction in lists.* Technical people often have to draw up lists. The items on a list should be parallel. Notice the two items in the following list which do not match the others:

| POOR | BETTER |
|---|---|
| check oil filter | |
| change points | |
| spark plugs ⟶ | change spark plugs |
| add oil | |
| fill gas tank | |
| windshield wiper fluid ⟶ | check windshield wiper fluid |

3. *Parallel construction in a series.* A series of words or word groups in a sentence should maintain the same form.

EXAMPLES

PARALLELISM BY NOUN

POOR: Desmond had ability, knowledge, honesty, and **was courageous**. (*Here an adjective,* **courageous,** *has been mixed in with a series of nouns. As a result, the sentence has a bad "rattle."*)

BETTER: Desmond had **ability, knowledge, honesty**, and **courage**. (*All nouns*)

PARALLELISM BY ADJECTIVE

POOR: Desmond was **intelligent, able, honest**, and **had courage**. (*Here a verb phrase,* **had courage,** *has been mixed in with a series of adjectives.*)

BETTER: Desmond was **intelligent, able, honest**, and **courageous**. (*All adjectives*)

PARALLELISM BY PHRASE

POOR: Desmond spoke **on the same subject, to the same people, when the time was identical**. (*Here a clause,* **when the time was identical,** *has been mixed in with phrases.*)

BETTER: Desmond spoke **on the same subject, to the same people**, and **at the same time**. (*All prepositional phrases*)

## PARALLELISM BY CLAUSE

POOR: Desmond, **who was intelligent** and **had honesty,** was hired for the position.

BETTER: Desmond, **who was intelligent and who was also honest,** was hired for the position. (*Similar clause structure*)

## PARALLELISM BY SENTENCE

POOR: To operate the slide projector, first **plug the cord** into the electrical outlet. Then the **slide tray should be positioned** on zero. Next, **you turn** the fan on. After that the **lamp should be** switched on. Finally, **advance** to the first slide. (*Note the mixture of second person, second person commands, and passive voice.*)

BETTER: To operate the slide projector, first **plug the cord** into the electrical outlet. Then **position the slide tray** on zero. Next, **turn the fan on**. After that, **switch on the lamp**. Finally, **advance** to the first slide. (*All second person commands in the active voice*)

---

## ACTIVITY 11-I: Parallel Construction

---

Draw a line through the words or word groups that are not parallel. Write the correct form above the line.

1. He has been taking instruction in drafting, surveying, and how to operate a die-casting machine.

2. The transportation chief supervises the service crew, and he is giving directions to the drivers.

3. The counselor advises the students on preparing schedules, getting financial aid, and to carry reasonable course loads.

4. We saw that Borden's Porsche is beautiful, that it is a lot of excitement to drive, and brand new.

5. In on-the-job training in journalism, we learned how to lay out ads, to cover local stories, and proofreading.

6. To become a successful business administrator, a person must have ability, patience, and be enthusiastic.

7. Our classes were held on Wednesday afternoon, Thursday evening, and we also attended every other Friday morning.

8. On weekends the employees usually tend to their gardens, fix up their houses, go shopping, exchanging visits with their relatives.

9. The students' grades were run through the computer, recorded on print-outs, and the students received them in the mail.

10. In the emergency room at the hospital, a nurse looked at my eyes, checked my throat, a thermometer was put in my mouth, and she took my blood pressure.

Check your responses in Feedback 11-I at the end of this module. If your responses were correct, proceed to the section on Correlatives. If you missed any, review Parallel Construction and then do Activity 11-J.

---

**ACTIVITY 11-J: Parallel Construction**

---

Draw a line through the words or word groups that are not parallel. Write the correct form above the line.

1. Answering the phone, taking shorthand, dictation that must be typed, and filing documents are only parts of my secretary's job.
2. We learned how to gauge points, how to adjust a carburetor, checking the spark plugs, and how to grease a car.
3. To make a good impression during an interview, act like a lady or a gentleman, speak as well as you can, and dressing is very important.
4. We saw the bulldozer when it pushed down the trees, when it cleared the lot, and it leveled a ridge toward the center.
5. An advertisement should be written to be easily understood, to attract attention, a little color would help, and to be sensational.
6. Helen particularly enjoys sterilizing equipment, preparing mediums, growing cultures, and the analysis of results.
7. When we arrived at the Student Center, we were cordially welcomed, questioned, and someone gave us counsel.
8. To listen, to think, and speaking clearly are the three primary responsibilities of a good speaker.
9. During a political campaign everyone should think about political views, talk to the candidates, and then he votes for his choice.
10. Regardless of your technology, you will constantly be involved with communications—reading, writing, an occasional speech.

Check your responses in Feedback 11-J at the end of this module. If your responses were correct, proceed to the section on Parallel Construction in Outlines. If you missed any, check with your instructor before proceeding.

**Parallel Construction in Outlines**

One area where parallel construction is of great importance is in your outline. When you make an outline, check to see that the items are equal in grammatical structure; that is, all nouns or noun phrases, all verbs or verb phrases, etc.

---

**ACTIVITY 11-K: Parallel Construction in Outlining**

---

In the following outline, draw a line through the items that are not parallel (those that are not verb phrases, in this case). Write the correct form above the line.

Proper Telephone Techniques for Businesses

1. Answer on first or second ring
2. Identify company
3. Be sure to identify yourself
4. Politeness and friendliness
5. Respond helpfully
6. Product and service information given
7. Close call courteously

Check your responses in Feedback 11-K. If your responses were correct, proceed to the section on Parallel Construction in Correlatives. If you missed any, do Activity 11-L.

## ACTIVITY 11-L: Parallel Construction in Outlining

In the following outline, draw a line through the items that are not parallel. Write the correct form above the line. *Hint:* Use all verbal phrases

Proper Telephone Techniques in Business

1. Answering on first or second ring
2. Identify company
3. Identifying yourself
4. Being polite and friendly
5. Helpfulness
6. Giving product and service information
7. Close call courteously

Check your responses in Feedback 11-L. If your responses were correct, proceed to the section on Parallel Construction in Correlatives. If you missed any, check with your instructor before proceeding.

**Parallel Construction in Correlatives**

Correlatives are conjunctions that are usually used in pairs. Here are the most common ones:

CORRELATIVES

not only . . . but also
either . . . or
neither . . . nor
both . . . and
whether . . . or

Parallel structure is also important when correlatives are used. The wording that follows the first correlative must be in the same form as that which follows the second correlative.

EXAMPLES

NOT PARALLEL:    He was **not only** courteous to supervisors **but also** he went out of his way to be pleasant to fellow employees.

Since an adjective (*courteous*) follows **not only**, an adjective must therefore also follow **but also**.

PARALLEL:    He was **not only** courteous to supervisors **but also** pleasant to fellow employees.

NOT PARALLEL:    Eddie was **either** dodging the sheriff **or** he would buy everybody in town a drink.

PARALLEL:    Eddie was **either** dodging the sheriff **or** buying everybody in town a drink.

NOT PARALLEL:    He was **neither** somebody who was getting ahead **nor** putting anything by.

PARALLEL:    He was **neither** getting ahead **nor** putting anything by.

NOT PARALLEL:    She **either** was angry **or** upset.

PARALLEL:    She was **either** angry **or** upset.

## ACTIVITY 11-M: Correlatives

Correct the sentence by using parallel word groups with the correlatives.

1. She was both worried at the employee's absence and became furious at John.
2. Whether I go to the business conference or if you should be going makes no difference to me.
3. She was not only efficient but also had a great deal of attractiveness.
4. I am neither interested in the job nor is Baltimore a town I would be eager to live in.
5. We have good luck growing not only Fordhook lima beans but also Burpee limas produce a good crop.
6. She was concerned whether to accept the offer at the hospital or it may be better to continue in school toward a degree.
7. Before the contractor lays the foundation, we will either increase the size of the two bedrooms or another plan will be chosen.
8. The mechanic checked both the oil dipstick and gave special attention to the right front tire.
9. After the jury foreman pronounced the verdict, the judge was neither lenient about the defendant's sentence nor did he become severe.
10. A swimming pool at a motel functions as either supplying some desired recreation or its value in advertising and promotion.

Check your responses in Feedback 11-M at the end of this module. If your responses were correct, proceed to Activity 11-O. If you missed any, review Correlatives and then do Activity 11-N.

## ACTIVITY 11-N: Correlatives

Correct the sentences by using parallel word groups.

1. The excavated area not only filled in nearly full from the heavy rains, but a lot from the sidewalls trickled in.
2. Figuring income taxes has become so complicated that the average wage earner will either hire a specialist or he can let the IRS do it.
3. This applicant is very good at both typing and her shorthand is very good too.
4. The decrease in electrical power lies neither in the fuse box nor does there seem to be anything wrong with the wires.
5. We are concerned whether to employ a nurse to live at home or my grandfather may do better in a nursing home.
6. These men can either operate the precision machines or they are good at assembling the equipment.
7. On most farms, a soil sample not only gives the farmer an idea about the condition of his field but also he can plan his crop rotation better.
8. A police officer is both a regulator of law and order and he performs many other services for people.
9. A computer cannot produce an accurate result if either the facts are entered inaccurately or if the figures are entered incorrectly too.
10. The engineers debated whether the old aqueduct would be strong enough for an increase in service or should it be rebuilt.

Check your responses in Feedback 11-N at the end of this module. If your responses were correct, proceed to Activity 11-O. If you missed any, check them with your instructor before proceeding.

## ACTIVITY 11-O: Writing Sentences for Review

Follow the directions in the items below. Use your own paper to write the sentences.

1. Write sentences using the following words:
   a. number
   b. except
   c. effect
   d. less
   e. proceed
   f. imply
   g. between

2. Write a sentence with nouns in parallel construction.

3. Write a sentence with phrases in parallel construction.

4. Write a sentence using the pair **not only . . . but also.**

5. Write a sentence using the pair **either . . . or.**

6. Write a compound sentence with a singular noun in the first part and a singular pronoun referring to that noun in the second part.

    EXAMPLE: The technicians repaired the **computer**, but **it** never worked satisfactorily.

7. Write a compound sentence with a plural noun in the first part and a plural pronoun referring to that noun in the second part.

    EXAMPLE: The nurse attended all safety **meetings**, and **they** proved most helpful in improving discipline.

Check your responses with your instructor; then ask for Test A.

---

### FEEDBACK FOR MODULE 11

**Feedback 11-A**

There may be more than one correct answer. If your responses differ, check with your instructor.

1. Because Brad wanted company, I went with him to Phil's place.
2. To keep the drawing board clean, tack an overlay on the board.
3. Peter spoke very rudely to the timekeeper.
4. Because the division manager always favored Swanson, the other employees were angry. (or) The division . . . Swanson. This action angered . . .
5. . . . the reporter's pictures turned out beautifully.
6. . . . the assistant enjoyed her work more. (or) . . . the technician enjoyed her work more.
7. Gail's hiring of the waitress was a wise move on her part. (or) Gail hired the waitress. This move was wise on her part.
8. . . . to make the rhododendrons (or the azaleas) stand out.
9. . . . we feed the grades into a computer.
10. . . . the policeman (or the man) was really mad.

**Feedback 11-B**

There may be more than one correct answer. If your responses differ, check with your instructor.

1. My problems in math were serious. Although my progress in English and reading were good, my math performance brought down my overall record.
2. John likes his supervisor, who is good to him.
3. The ferry boat blows a warning as it approaches the tugboat.
4. . . . some of the switches did not work.
5. . . . the tire was a mess.

6. Pickling the beets caused them to last longer. (or) The beets lasted longer because they were pickled.
7. . . . I have always wanted to be an economist (or a lecturer).
8. . . . I agreed with those who favored (or those who opposed).
9. . . . This offer made me think a while longer.
10. . . . the counselor would take an interest in the alcoholic's welfare.

## Feedback 11-C

There may be more than one correct answer. If your responses differ, check with your instructor.

1. Aero International has an excellent in-service training program.
2. The editorial in today's paper discusses the controversial busing problem.
3. Oregon has passed a law which encourages the recycling of waste materials.
4. The instruction manual explains how to operate an oscilloscope.
5. Inflation occurs when the dollar is worth less than previously.
6. Toxemia occurs when fluid builds up in the body.
7. Many buyers of truck crops are at the Farmers' Auction Block.
8. The specifications clearly state the type of muffler to use on my car.
9. A secretary demonstrates finesse when talking on the telephone.
10. The hardware center has all kinds of electrical equipment available. (or) All kinds of electrical equipment are available at the hardware center.

## Feedback 11-D

There may be more than one correct answer. If your responses differ, check with your instructor.

1. This whole idea was conceived on the drawing board.
2. Wall Street in New York has many brokerage companies.
3. Our Nursing Department's weight control booklet catalogs the approximate number of calories in all foods.
4. The boundaries of a plot of ground are legally established by surveying.
5. All of these switch boxes have a master lever for safety.
6. A computer stores information that may be used later.
7. A good switchboard operator can make himself easily understood. (or) The sign of a . . . is that he can . . .
8. Tuning an engine requires time and patience.
9. We must be alert when driving onto the freeway.
10. The editorial page in the evening paper printed many letters to the editor suggesting ways to resolve our tax problems.

## Feedback 11-E

There are other possible answers. If yours differ, check with your instructor.

1. *When I was five,* my father decided I would be an engineer.
2. Concerned about the grain market, *the investor* called his broker.
3. James continued to operate the printer while *it was low* on ink.
4. Bill replaced the wheel shims, *which were worn thin from use.*

5. Although writing for several years, *she* has never published any articles.
6. A photocopier, *which was expensive,* was advertised in *The Reporter.* Or *an expensive photocopier.*
7. Emily is *in the library* writing a report on filmmaking.
8. *While talking to the security officer,* the shoplifter admitted that she had stolen the dress.
9. Arriving at the police station, *I* had my license returned.
10. I received by mail instructions for operating the ten-ton crane.

## Feedback 11-F

There may be more than one correct answer. If your responses differ, check with your instructor.

1. *While riding home in her car pool,* Mrs. Allen complained about the lengthy report she had typed.
2. To reserve a room, *we* called the motel.
3. He repaired the typewriter, *a run-down old model that needed replacing,* which belonged to the boss's secretary.
4. *Feeling very sick at work,* Jim saw the doctor at the company dispensary.
5. *Puzzled about the fall-off in current,* the operator checked the transformer.
6. *Smiling courteously,* Mary accepted her offer.
7. *Coming in on the bus,* tourists can see the factory off to the left.
8. Not enough attention is devoted to quality-control instruction since *the company holds seminars* only once every three months.
9. He ordered a special lubricant *air-freighted from New York* for the two-ton turbine.
10. The driver said he would never carry in a truck *a firearm that was loaded.*

## Feedback 11-G

| | | |
|---|---|---|
| 1. precede | 6. well | 11. disinterested |
| 2. respectively | 7. between | 12. It's, too |
| 3. fewer | 8. effect | 13. advice |
| 4. inferred | 9. accept | 14. prosecute |
| 5. illegible | 10. further | |

## Feedback 11-H

| | | |
|---|---|---|
| 1. complimentary | 6. uninterested | 11. altogether |
| 2. among | 7. Fewer | 12. persecuted |
| 3. farther | 8. well | 13. except |
| 4. about | 9. has | 14. advise |
| 5. proceed | 10. its | 15. ineligible |

## Feedback 11-I

1. . . . drafting, surveying, and *operating* a die-casting machine.
2. . . . supervises the service crew and *gives* directions. . . .
3. . . . preparing schedules, getting financial aid, and *carrying* reasonable course loads.

4. . . . that Borden's Porsche is beautiful, that it is exciting to drive, and *that it is brand new.*
5. . . . how to lay out ads, to cover local stories, and *to proofread.*
6. . . . must have ability, patience, and *enthusiasm.*
7. . . . held on Wednesday afternoon, Thursday evening, and every other *Friday morning.*
8. . . . tend to their gardens, fix up their houses, go shopping, and *visit* with their relatives.
9. . . . run through the computer, recorded on printouts, and *mailed to the students.*
10. . . . looked at my eyes, checked my throat, *put* a thermometer in my mouth, and *took* my blood pressure.

**Feedback 11-J**

1. Answering the phone, taking shorthand, *typing dictation,* and filing documents are only . . .
2. . . . how to gauge points, how to adjust a carburetor, *how to check the spark plugs,* and how to grease a car. (or) . . . how to gauge points, adjust a carburetor, check the spark plugs, and grease a car.
3. . . . act like a lady or a gentleman, speak as well as you can, and *dress well.*
4. . . . when it pushed down the trees, when it cleared the lot, and *when it leveled a ridge toward the center.*
5. . . . to be easily understood, to attract attention, *to be colorful,* and to be sensational.
6. . . . sterilizing equipment, preparing mediums, growing cultures, and *analyzing results.*
7. . . . we were cordially welcomed, questioned, and *counseled.*
8. To listen, to think, and *to speak* clearly are . . .
9. . . . think about political views, talk to the candidates, and then *vote for his choice.*
10. . . . reading, writing, and occasionally *speaking.*

**Feedback 11-K**

1. Answer on first or second ring
2. Identify company
3. *Identify yourself*
4. *Be polite and friendly*
5. Respond helpfully
6. *Give product and service information*
7. Close call courteously

**Feedback 11-L**

1. Answering on first or second ring
2. *Identifying company*
3. Identifying yourself
4. Being polite and friendly
5. *Responding helpfully*

6. Giving product and service information
7. *Closing call courteously*

## Feedback 11-M

There may be more than one correct answer. If your responses differ, check with your instructor.

1. She was **both** *worried* at the employee's absence **and** *furious* at John.
2. **Whether** *I go* to the business conference **or** *you go* makes no difference to me.
3. She was **not only** *efficient* **but also** *attractive*.
4. I am **neither** *interested* in the job **nor** *eager* to live in Baltimore.
5. We have good luck growing **not only** *Fordhook lima beans* **but also** *Burpee limas*.
6. She was concerned **whether** *to accept* the offer at the hospital **or** *to continue* in school toward a degree.
7. Before the contractor lays the foundation, we will **either** *increase* the size of two bedrooms **or** *choose* another plan.
8. The mechanic checked **both** *the oil dipstick* **and** *the right front tire*.
9. After the jury foreman pronounced the verdict, the judge was **neither** *lenient* **nor** *severe* about the defendant's sentence.
10. A swimming pool at a motel functions as supplying **either** *some desired recreation* **or** *advertising and promotion*.

## Feedback 11-N

There may be more than one correct answer. If your responses differ, check with your instructor.

1. The excavated area filled in **not only** *from the heavy rains* **but also** *from the trickle in the sidewalls*.
2. Figuring income taxes has become so complicated that the average wage earner will **either** *hire* a specialist **or** *let* the IRS do it.
3. This applicant is very good at **both** *typing* **and** *shorthand*.
4. The decrease in electrical power lies **neither** *in the fuse box* **nor** *in the wires*.
5. We are concerned **whether** *to employ* a nurse to live at home **or** *to put* my grandfather in a nursing home.
6. These men can **either** *operate* the precision machines **or** *assemble* the equipment.
7. On most farms, a soil sample gives the farmer an idea about **not only** *the condition* of his field **but also** *crop rotation*. (or) **not only** *gives* . . . **but also** *allows him to plan* . . .
8. A police officer is **both** *a regulator of law and order* **and** *a performer of many other services for people*.
9. A computer cannot produce an accurate result if **either** *the facts are entered inaccurately* **or** *the figures are entered incorrectly*.
10. The engineers debated **whether** *the old aqueduct would be strong enough for an increase in service* **or whether** *it should be rebuilt*.

# Accelerating Techniques

OBJECTIVE: This module will help you make your writing more concise.

Upon completion of this module, you will be able:

To eliminate unnecessary words in a sentence.

To eliminate clichés and slang in writing samples.

To combine like subjects and verbs for the purpose of brevity.

To subordinate ideas.

To reduce dependent clauses to single words.

There is an old saying in industry: *The professional writer writes in plastic; the amateur writer writes in concrete.* This means that the professional works his sentences over and over, knowing that the first version is seldom the best. You must train yourself to take a second look at your own writing so that you can catch and correct any errors.

One of the most common errors is using unnecessary words. This practice draws attention to itself and slows down the reader. You should cut out any dead wood that is making your sentences too long. Notice how unnecessary words are eliminated in the following examples.

LENGTHY:   Each and every employee will report in writing and complete and turn in form number 402 by August 31 and not later.

BETTER:   Each employee will complete and turn in form 402 by August 31. *(10 words saved.)*

LENGTHY:   The employers cooperated together and endorsed a confirmation of the important essentials of the concurring agreement.

BETTER:   The employers cooperated and endorsed the essentials of the agreement. *(6 words saved.)*

Redundant expressions are those which say the same thing more than once. They cause extra wordage in your writing and should be eliminated. Look at the redundant phrases below and their correct versions. Learn to avoid redundancy in your own sentences.

---

obviously apparent (apparently)

consensus of opinion (consensus)

mix together (mix)

combine together (combine)

connect together (connect)

for the purpose of (for *or* to)

a speech about the subject of (a speech on)

noticeable to the eye (noticeable)

visible to the eye (visible)

audible to the ear (audible)

alone all by himself (alone)

during the winter months (during winter)

a minor who has not yet reached the age of 18 (a minor)

endorse the check on the back (endorse the check)

---

in the month of May (in May)

in the city of Detroit (in Detroit)

as to whether (whether)

past experience (experience)

past history (history)

in the final analysis (finally)

honest truth (truth)

final conclusion (conclusion)

bought and paid for (bought)

around in circles (around)

half in two (in half)

whole entire (entire)

winning another victory (another victory)

center around (center on)

might possibly (might)

here in this place (here)

different variations (variations)

square corner (corner)

two twins (twins)

resulting consequences (consequences)

fluid liquid (liquid)

written literature (literature)

in this day and age (today)

blue in color (blue)

round in shape (round)

at 8:30 A.M. this morning (at 8:30 A.M.)

retrieve back (retrieve)

small in size (small)

bitter in taste (bitter)

due to the fact that (due to)

has proved itself to be (is)

prior to the time that (before)

during the years between (between)

foreseeable future (future)

## ACTIVITY 12-A: Unnecessary Words

Without changing the meaning, reduce the italicized expressions to one or two words.

1. The clerk reviewed the statement *for the purpose of checking* for errors.
2. We visited Assateague Island *on a single occasion.*
3. He works in Ocean City *during the summer months.*
4. He works in the research lab *all alone by himself.*
5. All the students must know the *absolutely basic fundamentals* of grammar.
6. The politician tried *to make his influence felt among* the citizens.
7. *Mix together* all the dry ingredients before adding the eggs.
8. The bank teller asked the customer to *endorse the check on the back.*
9. The governor's assistant gave *a speech on the subject of* the resources of Texas.
10. The patient was to take his medicine *at regular intervals of time.*

Check your responses in Feedback 12-A at the end of this module. If your responses were correct, proceed to Part II. If you missed any, review Part I and then do Activity 12-B.

## ACTIVITY 12-B: Unnecessary Words

Without changing the meaning, reduce the italicized expressions to one or two words.

1. The military family often *changed living quarters.*
2. *A minor who has not yet reached the age of eighteen* is not permitted to vote.
3. He has *a great amount of* time to prepare for his trip.
4. Greg was standing on the corner *at the time that* the accident occurred.
5. *He is of the opinion* that women make good lawyers.
6. On Friday we should know *as to whether* she passed the oral exams.
7. The room was constructed to accommodate *a large number of* people.
8. He is to *make a recommendation* that the employee receive a raise.
9. The war was *finally brought to an end.*
10. There was a *consensus of opinion* that the class be cancelled.

Check your responses in Feedback 12-B at the end of this module. If your responses were correct, proceed to Part II. If you missed any, check with your instructor before proceeding.

A cliché is an overused, worn-out expression, such as **sticks out like a sore thumb.** Slang is the unconventional use of a word not intended by its dictionary meaning, such as **buzz off.** Both types of expressions indicate that the writer is too lazy to find an appropriate, clear, and fresh way to convey the meaning. They also tend to bog the reader down, causing him or her to be distracted from the writer's message. In order to speed up your own writing, learn to recognize and avoid clichés and slang.

### Clichés

Excessive use of certain phrases has caused them to lose their impact. They no longer are effective or striking. Particularly in technical writing, you cannot afford to be trite and wordy. Study the representative list below and learn to rephrase such expressions to make your own writing more effective.

---

racks one's brain (concentrates)

laid to rest (buried)

as plain as day (very clear)

green with envy (envious)

on the right track (correct)

to the bitter end (to the conclusion)

whole nine yards (all of . . .)

be into (involved with)

chip off the old block (like his father)

after all is said and done (in the end)

as cold as ice (cold, frigid)

as happy as a lark (ecstatic)

at the crack of dawn (early)

bored to tears (bored)

selling like hotcakes (popular item)

slept like a log (slept soundly)

stick to your guns (stand firm)

in the minds and hearts of (predominant idea)

the powers that be (the authorities)

the picture of health (healthy)

from the bottom of my heart (sincerely)

like a needle in a haystack (hard to find)

bring home the bacon (support the family)

eat his cake and have it too (have it all)

vicious circle (no end)

open and shut case (no controversy)

up against the wall (in trouble)

tapped out (exhausted)

short and sweet (concise)

icing on the cake (extra)

tunnel vision (short-sighted)

around the Horn (long way)

nothing to sneeze at (significant)

old as the hills (ancient)

worried to death (concerned)

do or die situation (crucial moment)

in the nick of time (in time)

ins and outs (workings)

---

### Slang

Slang words are phrases or expressions that are informal, nonstandard, and inexact. The use of slang in technical writing is as out of place as the use of clichés. Furthermore, slang is quickly outdated. Learn to accelerate your writing by staying away from such words and phrases as those below.

---

lousy (bad, ill, etc.)

okay (all right)

for the birds (undesirable)

cool (appealing, etc.)

turned on (excited)

where I am at (where I am)

broke (lacking funds)

handle (name)

nuts (insane)

racket (line of work)

far out (outrageous)

blew me away (astonished me)

uptight (tense)

party pooper (negative person)

gross (disgusting)

goofed off (shirked responsibility)

dynamite (excellent)

happening spot (place of action)

ticked her off (made her angry)

totally awesome (dreadful or wonderful)

super (excellent)

---

### ACTIVITY 12-C: Clichés and Slang

List at least five clichés or slang expressions that you hear frequently.

1. _____

2. _____

3. _____

4. _____

5. _____

Check with your instructor before proceeding.

## ACTIVITY 12-D: Clichés and Slang

Select a more appropriate way of wording the italicized clichés and slang expressions.

1. Jill has a *never say die* attitude about life.
2. Our problems are growing *by leaps and bounds*.
3. That was a *crummy* thing to say!
4. I hope the retailers will not automatically *jack up the price*.
5. If you are going to learn to ski, good equipment is *a must*.
6. The politics in the city government was *rotten to the core*.
7. *In this world today,* there are no easy solutions to our problems.
8. *At this point in time,* we do not anticipate any cuts in the budget.
9. Dressed in the latest fashions, she seemed always to be *the center of attraction*.
10. Finding a good solution is usually *easier said than done*.

Check your responses in Feedback 12-D at the end of this module. If your responses were correct, proceed to Activity 12-E. If you missed any, check with your instructor before proceeding.

## ACTIVITY 12-E: Clichés and Slang

Select a more appropriate way of wording the italicized clichés and slang expressions.

1. There was *method in his madness*.
2. Good jobs are *few and far between*.
3. *In this day and time,* one has to watch one's budget carefully.
4. The choices were *six of one, half a dozen of another*.
5. She is *as pretty as a picture*.
6. *Last but not least,* the company will publish its annual report in June.
7. His new car is really *tough*.
8. The hotel accommodations were *fit for a king*.
9. *Little by little,* we learned the facts of the case.
10. *Each and every* employee must be on time.

Check your responses in Feedback 12-E at the end of this module. If your responses were correct, proceed to Part III. If you missed any, check with your instructor before proceeding.

A sentence is sometimes slowed down by a needless interruption of thought. Compare the following sentences.

EXAMPLES

She lives in a new development. Usually, she has no trouble getting a bus.
She lives in a new development and usually has no trouble getting a bus.

Both examples are grammatically correct. However, the second sentence, in which the two subjects are combined, is much smoother. Look in your own writing for instances where sentences that have the same subject can be combined and the verb made compound.

EXAMPLES

SLOW:    Color television took time catching on, but soon color TV had swept the country.

SMOOTHER:    Color television took time catching on but soon swept the country.

SLOW:    Mr. Redford has a leadership quality, and he uses it at the office.

SMOOTHER:    Mr. Redford has a leadership quality and uses it at the office.

Similarly, when you have two sentences (or two parts of a compound sentence) with the same verb, you can combine the verbs and make the subject compound.

EXAMPLES

SLOW:    Bob drove to Chicago, and Allison also took her car.

SMOOTHER:    Bob and Allison both drove to Chicago.

SLOW:    The union voted for Smith, and the administration did the same thing.

SMOOTHER:    Both the union and the administration voted for Smith.

### ACTIVITY 12-F: Combining Subjects or Verbs

Speed up these sentences by combining like subjects or like verbs.

1. Douglas got a job in Design at Universal Drafting, and Harry was also hired in the very same department.

2. William preregistered, and thus he avoided the long lines on registration day.

3. ABC Company offers free health insurance and a pension plan, and the same is true at Acme Bolt, Inc.

4. She operates the sorting machine, and she operates the Xerox copier.

5. Morrison established a very good sales record. Then he went right to the top with the company.

Check your responses in Feedback 12-F at the end of this module. If your responses were correct, proceed to Part IV. If you missed any, review Part III and do Activity 12-G.

## ACTIVITY 12-G: Combining Subjects or Verbs

Speed up these sentences by combining like subjects or like verbs.

1. The supervisor for Shift A makes out the assignment schedule every morning, and so does the supervisor for Shift B.

2. The nurse took the patient's temperature today, and the doctor took it, too.

3. The secretary types letters for her boss, and she also keeps the office books.

4. The school board approved of the new policy, and the administrative staff also favored it.

5. The doctor performed duties in the emergency room, and she also worked with patients in the ward.

Check your responses in Feedback 12-G at the end of this module. If your responses were correct, proceed to Part IV. If you missed any, check with your instructor before proceeding.

## PART IV: SUBORDINATING IDEAS

Short, choppy sentences are easy to read when they are interspersed at reasonably long intervals; however, when they are used frequently, they give an unpleasant, "bumpy" impression. You can usually smooth bumpy sentences by using clause signals and subordinating secondary thoughts into dependent clauses. This process can be accomplished in three steps. Let's consider the following three choppy sentences.

EXAMPLES

(1) It stopped raining.
(2) We drove into New York in Fred's car.
(3) It had just been washed.

*First Step:* Which is the dominant thought? Obviously, number 2. Therefore we will make this the main (independent) clause and try to subordinate numbers 1 and 3.

*Second Step:* What kind of clause signals should be used? Number 1 tells *when* we went to New York; therefore, we should try an *adverb* clause signal. Number 3 *describes* Fred's car; therefore, we should look among the *adjective* signals.

Here are some of the clause signals divided into two types: those that introduce clauses that function as adverbs within a sentence, and those that introduce adjective clauses. (A more complete list of clause signals appears on pp. 80–81.)

| ADVERB CLAUSE SIGNALS | | ADJECTIVE CLAUSE SIGNALS | |
|---|---|---|---|
| (To be used when the clause does the job of an adverb) | | (To be used when the clause does the job of an adjective) | |
| after | since | MOST COMMON: | that |
| although | unless | | which |
| as | until | | who |
| because | when | OTHERS: | what |
| before | where | | whatever |
| if | while | | whom |
| | | | whomever |

*Third Step:* We select the signal **when** from among the adverbs to subordinate the adverb clause and **which** from among the adjectives to subordinate the adjective clause. This gives us the following smooth sentence.

> **When** it stopped raining, we drove into New York in Fred's car, **which** had just been washed.

Here are more examples of choppy sentences linked to make the writing flow more speedily.

EXAMPLES

(1) First the basement is excavated.
(2) The foundation is dug by using a backhoe.
(3) This is operated by one man.

Which is the most important thought? Number 2. Again number 1 serves as an adverb, telling *when* the action occurs. Number 3 again acts as an adjective, describing the noun **backhoe.** Here is the smooth, combined sentence.

> **After** the basement is excavated, the foundation is dug by a backhoe, **which** is operated by one man.

**237**

Again, here are three choppy sentences:

(1) The new employee relieved George.
(2) The new man had been hired for quality-control work.
(3) Then the regular operator returned to work and took over.

Which is the dominant thought? In this case, number 1. Number 2 tells something about the new man and therefore acts as an *adjective.* So we select an adjective clause signal. Number 3 tells how long the new man relieved George and therefore acts as an *adverb;* thus, we select an adverb clause signal.

The new employee, **who** had been hired for quality-control work, relieved George **until** he returned and took over.

If a series of choppy sentences contains two thoughts of equal importance, do not subordinate one to the other; combine them with a coordinating conjunction. Here are the choppy sentences:

(1) John went to work for the First National Bank.
(2) He graduated from Western Community College in 1988.
(3) Warner went on to San Francisco University.

Numbers 1 and 3 are of equal importance and can be combined with the conjunction **and**. Number 2 describes John and therefore should be subordinated as an adjective clause.

John, **who** graduated from Western Community College in 1988, went to work for the First National Bank, **and** Warner went on to San Francisco University.

Remember that when coordinated clauses have a similar subject or verb, these can be combined (see Part III of this module).

(1) The Mackenzies bought the old Rob house.
(2) It was located in a wooded area.
(3) They restored it in 1983.

Numbers 1 and 3 are of equal importance, can be joined by **and**, and have a similar subject. Number 2 should be subordinated.

The Mackenzies bought the old Rob house, **which** was located in a wooded area, **and** restored it in 1983.

It is important to determine correctly when coordination is called for and when one clause should be subordinated to another. Look at the following sentence.

Mary was telephoning me, and lightning struck the courthouse steeple.

Grammatically, this sentence is correct. It has two independent clauses joined by the conjunction **and**, properly preceded by a comma. However, it is obvious that something is wrong. The writer has placed a second-class thought in a first-class position, jerking the sentence out of balance. The information about Mary merely sets the stage for the lightning account and should be subordinated. This is easily done by adding the clause signal **while** and putting Mary in an adverb dependent clause:

> **While** Mary was telephoning me, lightning struck the courthouse steeple.

Here are two examples in which the clause signal **who** was inserted as a relative pronoun, subordinating one of the thoughts to a dependent *adjective* clause.

EXAMPLES

UNBALANCED: The workers liked to deal with their supervisor, and he spoke their own language.

BALANCED: The workers liked to deal with their supervisor, **who** spoke their own language.

UNBALANCED: Ms. Birch spoke fluent Spanish, and the President summoned her.

BALANCED: The President summoned Ms. Birch, **who** spoke fluent Spanish.

**Punctuation Note**

Note the commas inserted into the two previous sentences. These will be explained shortly, in the section on essential clauses. In the following sentences, a comma is always needed when the dependent adverb clause precedes the independent clause (DC, IC). No comma is needed when the independent clause comes before the dependent adverb clause (IC DC).

A sentence with an adverb clause usually acquires a little more punch and acceleration if the dependent clause precedes the independent. Note how anticlimactic the first sentence below sounds.

EXAMPLES

The floor collapsed while Nancy and Gus and everybody else in the class were scrambling about searching for Jim. (IC DC)

While Nancy and Gus and everybody else in the class were scrambling about searching for Jim, the floor collapsed. (DC, IC)

---

**ACTIVITY 12-H: Subordinating Ideas**

---

Eliminate choppiness by subordinating secondary thoughts into adverb or adjective dependent clauses, following the three steps described in the text.

If two thoughts are of equal importance, join them with a coordinating conjunction. If necessary, rewrite the entire sentence. Use separate paper.

1. I was typing. Mr. Wellington talked to a woman. She had known him in real estate.

2. Mark off the center of the room. The room is about 15 feet long. Do this when the paint dries.

3. A heavy wrench is harder to handle. It completes the job in less time, however. It cuts labor costs.

4. The proposition sounded attractive to me. It appealed to my partner. We turned it down.

5. The union organizers approached the company executive yesterday. I spoke to the workers before that. The workers agreed to listen.

6. George didn't follow up on his application at JBK Co., and then he received a notice to report.

7. The personnel manager had a splendid speaking voice, and he represented the company on TV.

8. We paid Frank our dues; prior to that we had elected him treasurer.

9. I complained to the timekeeper, and then he found out he had misplaced my card.

10. Joanna had worked for Everett Norton, but she claimed she had never been employed.

Check your responses in Feedback 12-H at the end of this module. If your responses were correct, proceed to Part V. If you missed any, do Activity 12-I.

## ACTIVITY 12-I: Subordinating Ideas

Combine these sentences into one sentence as in Activity 12-H.

1. The old die-cutting machine was in continuous use. It was operated by McNiel. Then the replacement unit arrived.

2. The employees formally demanded a wage hike. The management agreed to negotiate. The Board of Directors was violently opposed to a wage increase.

3. The plant closed. However, before that Jack drove into town with the president. He was due to speak at five.

4. Inflation could be corrected. It robs all of us. Oh, that the government would act intelligently and promptly!

5. The nurse was checking the patient's chart. The doctor was talking to another patient. He had gone to college with her.

6. The sales manager turned down the appointment, and so the position went to Jones.

7. Alicia had no privacy in the main office, and so she moved into a cubicle of her own.
8. Newlson was a good welder, but on the other hand he was very slow.
9. Jack lived just down the block, and so he joined our car pool.
10. Dobbles was fired, following which action the company hired Barnard.

Check your responses in Feedback 12-I at the end of this module. If your responses were correct, proceed to Essential and Nonessential Adjective Clauses. If you missed any, check with your instructor before proceeding.

### Essential and Nonessential Adjective Clauses

There are two types of adjective clauses: essential and nonessential. A *nonessential* clause is not necessary to the sentence and can be left out without destroying the meaning of the sentence. These clauses are set off from the rest of the sentence by commas. In other words, if the subject is well identified without the clause, use commas to set off the clause. (Added information; add commas.)

EXAMPLES (NONESSENTIAL)

The driver of the second car, **who was also from Baltimore,** presented his license.
The President summoned Ms. Birch, **who spoke fluent Spanish.**

In the sentences above the boldface adjective clause can be deleted without changing the meaning of the sentence; hence, *commas are needed.*

An essential clause is one that is important to the *meaning* of the sentence. The clause is essential if it is necessary to identify the particular noun it modifies. Essential clauses are *not* set off by commas.

EXAMPLES (ESSENTIAL)

He is the man **who was elected to City Council**.
The computer **that Henry was using** is broken.

The boldface clauses are essential to identify which man and which computer; therefore, they are not separated from the rest of the sentence.

Notice how the commas, in setting off the nonessential clauses, can change the meaning of a sentence.

EXAMPLES

The order forms, which are green, are kept on the top shelf. (*All order forms are green, and they are all kept on the top shelf.*)
The order forms which are green are kept on the top shelf. (*Only the green order forms are kept on the top shelf. Other order forms may be kept elsewhere.*)

I spoke to the receptionist who is wearing a blue dress. (*Not to the one who is wearing a yellow dress.*)

I spoke to the receptionist, who is wearing a blue dress. (*There is only one receptionist and she is wearing blue.*)

In Part I of Module 6 you were introduced to five of the six sentence patterns, and you learned how they were punctuated. You can now see that the punctuation in Pattern 6 depends on whether a dependent adjective clause is essential (EDC) or nonessential (NDC).

**Punctuation Pattern 6**

> Part of IC  EDC  rest of IC.

> Part of IC, NDC, rest of IC.

You can also now reconsider Pattern 5, IC DC. If the DC happens to be a nonessential adjective clause, then that clause must be separated from the dependent clause by a comma.

> IC, NDC.

EXAMPLE

The president summoned Ms. Birch, who spoke fluent Spanish.

In other words, a nonessential adjective dependent clause is set off by commas whether it comes at the beginning (DC, IC.), the middle (part of IC, NDC, rest of IC.), or the end (IC, NDC.) of the sentence.

---

**ACTIVITY 12-J: Punctuating Essential and Nonessential Clauses**

Punctuate the following sentences where necessary. Remember, if you can omit the clause and not change the meaning of the sentence, it is nonessential and should be set off by commas.

1. The Mayor who happened to favor the new shopping mall met in closed session with the City Council.

2. The person whose knowledge of the market is up-to-date is most likely to make the sale.

3. Anything which can be done to save energy should be suggested.

4. Fred Henry whose technical expertise was well known in the company was assigned the task of drafting the report.

5. The pharmaceutical company's representative who was familiar to each of the doctors in the clinic rarely had to wait ten minutes to get an appointment.

6. The person who invented photocopiers changed office routines dramatically.

7. Dr. Angela Sims who organized the reconstruction of the Indian village used many volunteers at the site.

8. Your supervisor whose experience should have qualified her for the task decided you would be better at working with new trainees.

9. The employer who sets high standards gets better performance on the job.

10. Mrs. Roberts who spoke at the secretaries' conference gave the audience some excellent guidelines on office procedures.

Check your responses in Feedback 12-J at the end of this module. If your responses were correct, proceed to Part V. If you missed any, review and do Activity 12-K.

## ACTIVITY 12-K: Punctuating Essential and Nonessential Clauses

Punctuate the following sentences where necessary.

1. The Space Shuttle astronauts who were recognized by only a few workers toured the plant yesterday.

2. Safety programs which were started in the past year are superior to previous programs.

3. The trainer bandaged the horse's injured leg which still showed some swelling.

4. Groundbreaking for the newest nylon factory which will be located on the north side of town is scheduled for Thursday at 10:00 A.M.

5. The Three Mile Island reactors which caused a national panic have been thoroughly checked by the engineers.

6. On Wednesday which is usually his day off Chuck works on his antique cars.

7. Long distance charges that are over three minutes are closely monitored in the front office.

8. The person who worked on the newest soybean hybrids spoke to the horticulture class yesterday.

9. The chief technician who drove his new car today was in a very good mood.

10. The secretary who answers the phone well is extremely valuable to a boss.

Check your responses in Feedback 12-K at the end of this module. If your responses were correct, proceed to Part V. If you missed any, check with your instructor.

Just as you can often make a sentence flow better by reducing an independent clause to a dependent clause, you can save words by reducing a dependent clause to a phrase or a word.

1. *Reducing Dependent Clauses to Prepositional Phrases.* Be on the lookout for clauses that can be turned into prepositional phrases.

EXAMPLES

CLAUSE: **When you come to the loading platform,** sound your horn.

PHRASE: **At the loading platform,** sound your horn. (*3 words saved*)

The man **who is wearing the white coat** is the lab chief.
The man **in the white coat** is the lab chief. (*2 words saved*)

**While we were going through Los Angeles,** we saw the GM executive.
**In Los Angeles** we saw the GM executive. (*4 words saved*)

**When the executives had finished the meeting,** they went in to dinner.
**After the meeting,** the executives went in to dinner. (*4 words saved*)

2. *Reducing Clauses to Infinitive Phrases.* An infinitive phrase is composed of the word **to** with the present tense of a verb: **to write, to know, to drive.** Infinitive phrases are particularly useful in eliminating an awkward dependent clause beginning with **so that.**

EXAMPLES:

I skipped lunch **so that I could cut** down on my weight.
I skipped lunch **to cut** down on my weight. (*2 words saved*)
He took Technical Writing **so that he would be prepared** for future work assignments.
He took Technical Writing **to prepare** for future work assignments. (*4 words saved*)

3. *Reducing Clauses to Participles or Participial Phrases.* The present participle is the **-ing** form of the verb. The past participle of a regular verb is formed by adding **-ed** to the verb (first deleting any final **e**). The most common irregular past participles are listed on page 10. Participles can be very useful in reducing dependent clauses.

EXAMPLES

**While he read all of the morning mail,** he planned the next meeting.
**Reading the mail,** he planned the next meeting. (*5 words saved*)

**Although George was hired on Wednesday,** he did not report until Friday.
**Hired on Wednesday,** George did not report until Friday. (*3 words saved*)

**Because Mary had worked as a programmer,** she advanced rapidly at B & D.
**Having worked as a programmer,** Mary advanced rapidly at B & D. (*2 words saved*)

4. *Reducing Clauses to Adverbs.* Sometimes an adverbial clause can be reduced to one word that does the same job in the sentence.

   EXAMPLES

   The boss argued **in a manner that was very angry** with the workers.
   The boss argued **angrily** with the workers. (*6 words saved*)

   All morning she awaited his return at the airport, **in the course of which she became nervous.**
   All morning she **nervously** awaited his return at the airport. (*7 words saved*)

5. *Reducing Clauses to Adjectives.* An adjective dependent clause often can be reduced to a single adjective.

   EXAMPLES

   He wore a tie **that had a lot of stripes on it.**
   He wore a **striped tie.** (*7 words saved*)

   In Miami he picked up a Chevy **that somebody had either turned in or sold outright to a dealer.**
   In Miami he picked up a **used** Chevy. (*11 words saved*)

   Candace, **who worked at a full-time job at Hercules,** did typing for the Welfare Society.
   Candace, **a full-time Hercules worker,** did typing for the Welfare Society. (*4 words saved*)

6. *Reducing Clauses to Nouns.* Often you can reduce adjective clauses by simply eliminating the clause signal (*who* or *which*) and the verb. In the sentences below, the adjective clauses (underlined) become appositives renaming the subjects and coming immediately after the words they describe.

   EXAMPLES

   Our instructor, (**who was**) <u>an intelligent person</u>, disagreed with the newspaper editorial. (*2 words saved*)

   The soy bean crop, (**which is**) <u>an important factor in our local economy</u>, is late this year. (*2 words saved*)

Our car payments, (**which impose**) <u>a real burden on the budget</u>, will continue for two years. (*2 words saved*)

7.  *The Four-Step Reduction Technique.* If you have trouble reducing clauses to single words, try this simple technique. A clause modifying a noun or pronoun can be converted into an adjective by the following procedure:

EXAMPLE

He designed a house that a family could live in.

*Step 1.*   Find the dependent adjective clause. ("that a family could live in")
*Step 2:*   Which is the most important word in this clause? (**live**)
*Step 3:*   Convert the key word **live** into an *adjective,* using one of the following adjective endings:
　　　　　**-ful**　　**-d** or **-ed**
　　　　　**-less**　　**-y**
　　　　　**-able**　　**-ing**
*Step 4:*   Shortened sentence:
　　　　　*He designed a* **livable** *house.* (*5 words saved*)

EXAMPLE

Until the general election, he was the candidate who led all of the rest of the people running.

1.  Dependent clause? ("who led all the rest of the people running")
2.  Key word? (**led**)
3.  Which adjectival ending is applicable? (**-ing**)
4.  Shortened sentence:
    Until the general election, he was the **leading** candidate. (*8 words saved*)

Sometimes a rambling dependent clause can be reduced to an *adverb.* Follow the same general procedure as with adjectives.

EXAMPLE

He addressed the workers as a dictator would address his troops.

1.  Dependent clause? ("as a dictator would address his troops")
2.  Key word? (**dictator**)
3.  Turn this into an adverb? (**dictatorially** [**-ly** is the most common adverb ending])
4.  Shortened sentence:
    He addressed the workers **dictatorially.** (*6 words saved*)

If a sprawling dependent clause cannot be reduced to an adjective or adverb, try converting the key word into a *noun.* You can probably use one of the following noun endings.

**-ness**
**-tion, -sion**
**-ence, -ance**
**-ment**
**-ing**

A clause that functions as a noun can often be reduced to a single noun.

EXAMPLE

One of the basic rules of the laboratory is that employees must keep things very clean.

1. Dependent clause? ("that employees must keep things very clean")
2. Key word? (**clean**)
3. Turn into a noun? (**cleanliness**)
4. Shortened sentence:
   One of the basic rules of the laboratory is **cleanliness.** (*6 words saved*)

In reducing dependent clauses to prepositional phrases, identify the key word, change it into a noun if it is not in that form already, place a preposition before the noun, and position the phrase appropriately. Add minor words as needed.

EXAMPLE

He was a very pleasant man who maintained an appearance of being gruff and rude.

1. Dependent clause? ("who maintained an appearance of being gruff and rude")
2. Key word? (**appearance**)
3. Add preposition **behind** and add **his**.
4. Shortened sentence:
   **Behind his gruff and rude appearance,** he was a very pleasant man. (*3 words saved*)

EXAMPLE

Because he was very angry, he shouted at the secretary.

1. Dependent clause: ("Because he was very angry")
2. Key word? (**angry**)
3. Add preposition **in.**
4. Shortened sentence:
   **In anger,** he shouted at the secretary. (*3 words saved*)

**247**

## ACTIVITY 12-L: Reducing Clauses

Employing the four-step reduction technique, reduce the dependent clauses in the following sentences to a *single word*. Strike out the clause, and insert the word in the appropriate place.

1. They began excavating on a day that the sun was shining.
2. You are fortunate in having an employee who is obviously a person that you can depend upon.
3. One of the reasons for our poor profits this year is that inflationary influences are operating against us.
4. He was a worker who did outstanding work on his job.
5. She spoke to him in a manner that revealed her impatience.

Check your responses in Feedback 12-L at the end of this module. If your responses were correct, proceed to Activity 12-N. If you missed any, review Part V and then do Activity 12-M.

## ACTIVITY 12-M: Reducing Clauses

Reduce the dependent clause to a single word. Strike out the clause, and insert the word in the appropriate place.

1. A decision that operates impartially for all is sometimes difficult to make.
2. Anne Johnson, who earned her degree in biology, visits here every summer.
3. The farmer, who became very furious in the course of the incident, ordered the hunters off his property.
4. He bought an Olds with air-conditioning that had been installed at the factory.
5. A worker who comes part-time every day was injured in the assembly department.

Check your responses in Feedback 12-M at the end of this module. If your responses were correct, proceed to Activity 12-N. If you missed any, check with your instructor before proceeding.

## ACTIVITY 12-N: Reducing Clauses

Without changing the meaning, convert the dependent clauses into prepositional phrases. Cross out the clause, and insert the phrase where appropriate.

1. When the noon hour finally arrived, he would retreat and read.
2. While summer warmed the land, the surveyors set the boundaries of our property.

3. As soon as everybody quit work, he would start moonlighting in his cab.

4. When the hunting season came around once more, he sold licenses.

5. When you come to the corner of Third Street and Folsome Avenue, turn right.

Check your answers in Feedback 12-N at the end of this module. If your responses were correct, proceed to Activity 12-P. If you missed any, do Activity 12-O.

## ACTIVITY 12-O: Reducing Clauses

Without changing the meaning, convert the dependent clauses into prepositional phrases. Cross out the clause, and insert the phrase where appropriate.

1. The woman who is now wearing the white suit works at General Foods.

2. While we were going down Michigan Avenue, we saw the builders repairing the hotel.

3. When the convention guests had finally finished the last of their dinner, they went into the conference room.

4. Our supervisor, who is an extremely diplomatic person in working with people, handles all of the personnel problems that arise.

5. The request which asked for an interview came in Friday's mail.

Check your responses in Feedback 12-O at the end of this module. If your responses were correct, proceed to Activity 12-P. If you missed any, check with your instructor before proceeding.

## ACTIVITY 12-P: Reducing Clauses

On your own paper rewrite the following sentences, using any of the word-reducing methods in this module.

1. Ellen took the Pontiac so that she could go to work.

2. After he called Mr. Newton, he dictated the memo.

3. Although Horace was fired on Monday, he did not leave his job until Wednesday.

4. After Mrs. Bremmer had completed her in-service training, she reported to the makeup section.

5. The supervisor gave orders to the crew, and he did this in an angry way.

6. She walked alone down the dark corridor, in the course of which she became very nervous.

7. The salesman arrived in Samoa during the season when it rains much of the time.

8. My partner sent me a pipe that had been carefully carved by hand.

9. Helguard is a draftsman who is very talented.

10. He turned in a production record that was a surprise to everybody.

11. Just as dawn was breaking in the east, we entered the factory, which was old.

12. He lowered his eyelid in a wink that was meant to warn us about the high-pressure salesman.

13. The job that Henrietta did on the reports simply impressed everybody.

14. The orders from the boss, which amazed all of us, upset the program in a way that was complete to say the least.

15. The boss seemed to delight in making us feel confused.

16. Some office worker without the slightest sense of responsibility left the safe unlocked.

17. They had set up temporary headquarters in the section of the warehouse in which various materials of different kinds were no longer stored.

18. The supervisor showered upon us compliments that were wholly unexpected on our part.

19. For his business trip he picked up a Buick that had been bought new the year before and recently traded in.

20. Mr. Stern, the man who is my employer at the office, reports to work at eight o'clock.

Check your responses in Feedback 12-P at the end of this module. If your responses were correct, proceed to Activity 12-Q. If you missed any, check with your instructor before proceeding.

## ACTIVITY 12-Q: Writing Sentences for Review

Follow the directions for each item. Use separate paper.

1. Write a sentence using two independent clauses joined by a coordinate conjunction.

2. Subordinate one of the independent clauses in the following sentence, using an adverb clause signal: *The nurse checked the patient's chart, and the aide took his temperature.*

3. Subordinate one of the independent clauses in the following sentence, using an adjective clause signal: *Mr. Newton was hired by the data processing department, and he is one of the best computer programmers in the area.*

4. The following sentence contains an independent clause, an adverb clause, and an adjective clause. Use it as a model to write a sentence of your own. *Before the repairman fixed the television set, he tested the new antenna which had been struck by lightning.*

5. Write three choppy sentences; then combine them to form one smooth sentence.

6. Rewrite the sentences below, reducing the italicized adjective clause to a single word:

a. The architect drew a house plan *which was very expensive.*
b. The foreman, *who was so old he should have retired years ago,* was still on the job.
c. The salesman *who was totally inexperienced* lost the company's biggest account.

Check your sentences with your instructor; then ask for Test A.

---

**Feedback 12-A**

The italicized phrases may be reduced to the following:

1. checking
2. once
3. during summer
4. by himself
5. fundamentals
6. influence
7. Mix
8. endorse the check
9. a speech on
10. regularly

**Feedback 12-B**

The italicized phrases may be reduced to the following:

1. moved
2. a minor
3. much
4. when
5. He thinks
6. whether
7. many
8. recommend
9. finally ended
10. consensus

**Feedback 12-D**

These are suggested answers. Yours may differ and still be acceptable. Check with your instructor.

1. positive
2. rapidly
3. awful, bad, nasty, spiteful
4. raise the price
5. very important, crucial, essential
6. corrupt
7. Today
8. Today, Nowadays
9. popular
10. difficult

**Feedback 12-E**

These are suggested answers. Yours may differ and still be acceptable. Check with your instructor.

1. purpose to his actions

2. hard to find, rare
3. Today, Nowadays
4. equal
5. pretty, lovely, beautiful
6. Finally
7. fast, attractive, appealing
8. superior, excellent, luxurious
9. Gradually
10. Each, Every

## Feedback 12-F

1. Douglas and Harry got jobs in Design at Universal Drafting.
2. William preregistered and thus avoided the long lines on registration day.
3. Both ABC Company and Acme Bolt, Inc., offer free health insurance and pension plans.
4. She operates the sorting machine and the Xerox copier.
5. Morrison established a very good sales record and went right to the top with the company.

## Feedback 12-G

1. The supervisors for Shifts A and B make out the assignment schedule every morning.
2. Both the nurse and the doctor took the patient's temperature today.
3. The secretary types the letters for her boss and also keeps the office books.
4. The school board and administrative staff approved of the new policy.
5. The doctor performed duties in the emergency room and worked with patients in the ward.

## Feedback 12-H

These are suggested answers. Your answers may differ and still be acceptable. Check with your instructor.

1. While I was typing, Mr. Wellington talked to a woman who had known him in real estate.
2. After the paint dries, mark off the center of the room, which is about 15 feet long.
3. Although a heavy wrench is harder to handle, it completes the job in less time and cuts labor costs.
4. Although the proposition sounded attractive to me and my partner, we turned it down.
5. Before the union organizers approached the company executives yesterday, I spoke to the workers, who agreed to listen.
6. Although George didn't follow up on his application at JBK Co., he received a notice to report.
7. The personnel manager, who had a splendid speaking voice, represented the company on TV.
8. After we had elected Frank treasurer, we paid him our dues.

9. After I complained to the timekeeper, he found out he had misplaced my card.

10. Although Joanna had worked for Everett Norton, she claimed she had never been employed. (or) Joanna, who had worked for Everett Norton, claimed she had never worked.

## Feedback 12-I

These are suggested answers. Your answers may differ and still be acceptable. Check with your instructor.

1. The old die-cutting machine, which was operated by McNiel, was in continuous use until the replacement arrived.
2. Although the Board of Directors was violently opposed to a wage increase, the management agreed to negotiate when the employees formally demanded a wage hike.
3. Before the plant closed, Jack drove into town with the president, who was due to speak at five.
4. Inflation, which robs all of us, could be corrected if the government would act intelligently and promptly.
5. While the nurse was checking the patient's chart, the doctor talked to another patient with whom he had gone to college.
6. Because the sales manager turned down the appointment, the position went to Jones.
7. Since Alicia had no privacy in the main office, she moved into a cubicle of her own.
8. Although Newlson was a good welder, he was very slow.
9. Jack, who lived just down the block, joined our car pool.
10. After Dobbles was fired, the company hired Barnard.

## Feedback 12-J

1. The Mayor, who happened to favor the new shopping mall, met in closed session with the City Council.
2. The person whose knowledge of the market is up-to-date is most likely to make the sale.
3. Anything which can be done to save energy should be suggested.
4. Fred Henry, whose technical expertise was well known in the company, was assigned the task of drafting the report.
5. The pharmaceutical company's representative, who was familiar to each of the doctors in the clinic, rarely had to wait ten minutes to get an appointment.
6. The person who invented photocopiers changed office routines dramatically.
7. Dr. Angela Sims, who organized the reconstruction of the Indian village, used many volunteers at the site.
8. Your supervisor, whose experience should have qualified her for the task, decided you would be better at working with new trainees.
9. The employer who sets high standards gets better performance on the job.
10. Mrs. Roberts, who spoke at the secretaries' conference, gave the audience some excellent guidelines on office procedures.

**Feedback 12-K**

1. The Space Shuttle astronauts, who were recognized by only a few workers, toured the plant yesterday.
2. Safety programs which were started in the past year are superior to previous programs.
3. The trainer bandaged the horse's injured leg, which still showed some swelling.
4. Groundbreaking for the newest nylon factory, which will be located on the north side of town, is scheduled for Thursday at 10:00 A.M.
5. The Three Mile Island reactors, which caused a national panic, have been thoroughly checked by the engineers.
6. On Wednesday, which is usually his day off, Chuck works on his antique cars.
7. Long distance charges that are over three minutes are closely monitored in the front office.
8. The person who worked on the newest soybean hybrids spoke to the horticulture class yesterday.
9. The chief technician, who drove his new car today, was in a very good mood.
10. The secretary who answers the phone well is extremely valuable to a boss.

**Feedback 12-L**

These are suggested answers. Your answers may differ and still be acceptable. Check with your instructor.

1. They began excavating on a *sunny* day.
2. You are fortunate in having a *dependable* employee.
3. One of the reasons for our poor profits this year is *inflation*.
4. He was an *outstanding* worker.
5. She spoke to him *impatiently*.

**Feedback 12-M**

These are suggested answers. Your answers may differ and still be acceptable. Check with your instructor.

1. An *impartial* decision is sometimes difficult to take.
2. Anne Johnson, *a biologist,* visits here every summer.
3. The farmer *furiously* ordered the hunters off his property.
4. He bought an Olds with *factory* air-conditioning.
5. *A part-time worker* was injured in the assembly department.

**Feedback 12-N**

Your answers may differ. Check with your instructor.

1. *At noon,* he would retreat and read.
2. *In summer,* the surveyors set the boundaries of our property.
3. *After work,* he would start moonlighting in his cab.

4. *During hunting season,* he sold licenses.
5. *At the corner of Third and Folsome,* turn right.

## Feedback 12-O

**Your answers may differ. Check with your instructor.**

1. The woman *in the white suit* works at General Foods.
2. *On Michigan Avenue,* we saw the builders repairing the hotel.
3. *After dinner,* the convention guests went into the conference room.
4. Our supervisor handles all the personnel problems *with diplomacy.*
5. The request *for an interview* came in Friday's mail.

## Feedback 12-P

**If your responses differ, check them with your instructor. There are many possible correct answers.**

1. Ellen took the Pontiac *to work.*
2. *After calling Mr. Newton,* he dictated the memo.
3. *Fired on Monday,* Horace did not leave his job until Wednesday.
4. *Her in-service training completed,* Mrs. Bremmer reported to the makeup section. (or) *After in-service training,* Mrs. Bremmer . . .
5. *Angrily,* the supervisor gave orders to the crew.
6. *Nervously,* she walked alone down the dark corridor.
7. The salesman arrived in Samoa *during the rainy season.*
8. My partner sent me a *hand-carved* pipe.
9. Helguard is a very *talented* draftsman.
10. He turned in a *surprising* production record.
11. *At dawn* we entered the *old* factory.
12. *He warned us with a wink* about the high-pressure salesman. (or) He winked to warn us . . .
13. Henrietta did an *impressive* job on the reports.
14. The *amazing* orders from the boss *completely* upset the program.
15. The boss seemed to delight in *confusing us.*
16. Some *irresponsible* office worker left the safe unlocked.
17. They set up temporary headquarters in an *unused* section of the warehouse.
18. The supervisor showered *unexpected* compliments upon us.
19. For his business trip he picked up a *year-old* Buick.
20. Mr. Stern, *my employer,* reports to work at eight o'clock.

# Report Writing

OBJECTIVE: Structurally, the report is an expanded version of the paragraph. This module takes you into report writing and lets you work with five common types of reports.

Upon completion of this module, you will be able:

To define the function of an outline in multiparagraph writing.

To prepare a multiparagraph report outline given three principles of organization.

To identify and to use appropriately two report formats.

To write five reports using appropriate report format for each.

Before we see how a report is constructed, we will review the essential points of constructing a unified paragraph. First, the *topic sentence* must have a *subject* (what you are talking about) and a *controlling idea* (what you are saying about the subject).

SAMPLE PARAGRAPH

| | | |
|---|---|---|
| Topic Sentence | S<br>Opening a fast food franchise involves | CI<br>several steps. |

Next, there should be several *supporting sentences* that help to prove the controlling idea.

| | |
|---|---|
| Supporting Sentences | First, arrange to finance the operation. Then find a suitable building site. Next, recruit and hire personnel, and finally, advertise to promote the merchandise. |

Last of all, there should be a *concluding sentence* that summarizes the main point of the paragraph.

| | |
|---|---|
| Concluding Sentence | If you follow these steps, you will soon have a successful restaurant. |

If you have mastered the parts of the unified paragraph, you possess the basic tools for report writing. This is so because each sentence of the paragraph can be enlarged into a paragraph itself. Here is how you do it:

| | | |
|---|---|---|
| Topic Sentence | becomes → | Introductory Paragraph |
| Supporting Sentences | become → | Supporting Paragraphs |
| Concluding Sentence | becomes → | Concluding Paragraph |
| Paragraph | becomes → | Report |

Let's now apply this process to the sample paragraph above and turn it into a report.

**SAMPLE REPORT**

| | |
|---|---|
| Introductory Paragraph | If you have investigated many careers and have decided you would like to be your own boss, then perhaps you would like to open your own business. <u>Although opening a fast food franchise</u> (S) can be difficult for some, if approached in a business-like way and broken down into <u>several steps</u> (CI), it could prove to be a highly profitable commercial undertaking. |

Compare this introductory paragraph with the topic sentence in the sample paragraph.

| | |
|---|---|
| Supporting Paragraphs 1 | First, you must arrange to finance the business. Discuss the possibility of a loan with bankers and other business people, making an itemized list of capital needs. Plan to borrow money from a bank or find financial backers to go into business with you. |
| 2 | Then find a suitable building lot in an appropriate spot in a retail area after comparing several different locations. Keep in mind, in selecting a site, such features as accessibility from major arteries, customer parking, drive-in window, and an area of stable population. |
| | Next, after making a list of qualifications for all employees, recruit and hire personnel. You will need a manager with experience and good references. Also you will need to hire short-order cooks and counter help, plus students as part-time employees. |
| | Finally, advertise to promote the franchise. Consider billboards along main highways and discount coupons in local newspapers. Radio and television are excellent media to appeal to hungry patrons. Another good advertising device is a catchy slogan or jingle. |

Compare these four supporting paragraphs with the supporting sentences.

Notice that these supporting paragraphs do not have concluding sentences. *A paragraph does not need a concluding sentence if it leads into the next paragraph. Only paragraphs that stand alone must have a concluding sentence.*

| | |
|---|---|
| Concluding Paragraph | If you will follow these steps, you could soon be the owner of a thriving fast food franchise. As you master all of the techniques involved in your business ventures, you will make a place for yourself in a world that offers a variety of opportunities. |

Compare the concluding paragraph with the concluding sentence in the sample paragraph.

The formats for the paragraph and for the report are almost identical. The most important principle is that of logical organization, and you can be assured of having logical organization if you lay out the framework or skeleton before writing the report. How do you develop the framework. By outlining, of course. An outline is merely a way to categorize neatly all the various points to be included in the report, to get all your ideas down in the proper order. In Module 9 you learned to jot your ideas down in grocery-list fashion. In order to write a report, you will need a more detailed outline.

## PART II: OUTLINING

When you set out to write a report, your task will go smoothly if you approach it in a systematic manner. *A disorganized, inefficient student might simply sit down with a pencil and paper or with a word processor and hope the jumble of thoughts will jump from his or her mind to the paper.* As you learn to be an organized writer, you will begin the task more logically.

First, you must select a broad topic; then you narrow it to a specific topic geared to an appropriate length for your report. As an example, you might consider a report on the general topic of careers and narrow it to the specific topic of "Starting a Business." The next step is to formulate a topic sentence which states what focus you will develop regarding your specific topic. In this example, a possible topic sentence would be *Starting a business is relatively easy if you follow a definite plan.*

Once these three steps (selecting a broad topic, narrowing it to a specific topic, and constructing a topic sentence) are complete, you are ready to proceed with the outline for the report.

Outlining is not as difficult as many writers think it is. First, you must understand the real function of an outline. The outline, when done with care, will help you present the purpose of your report and set fourth your procedure for developing your ideas. It can also be an effective way of testing your idea for a paper because it will let you know *before* you write whether you have enough information and detail to develop your ideas. Continuing with the topic "Starting a Business," let us see how an outline can be developed.

The outline should present the subject of your report and a procedure for discussing the subject. Your *topic* is what you are talking about and what you have to say about it. The *procedure,* on the other hand, is the actual organization of details. This organization of details is important, for you must choose details that will support your main topic, and you must present them in the most effective order to gain support.

If given the topic "Starting a Business" for a report, you must first determine what to say about it and how to say it best. The easiest way to do this is to make a *scratch outline.* A scratch outline is merely a list of ideas that come to mind when you think of your topic. Brief phrases are better than complete sentences. Do not be concerned at this point with organization or spelling or appropriateness. Concentrate on getting down as many solid ideas as possible. A scratch outline for "Starting a Business" might look like this:

### SCRATCH OUTLINE

| | |
|---|---|
| Recruiting and hiring personnel | Customer parking |
| Billboards along main highways | Locating site in retail area |
| Leisure time on weekends | Area of stable population |
| Advertising merchandise | Students as part-time employees |
| Find financial backers | Borrow from bank |
| Drive-in window | Cooks and counter help |
| Family problems at home | List of capital needs |
| Catchy slogan or jingle | Discussion of possibility of loan with bankers and business people |
| Financing the business | |
| Experienced manager | Compare several locations |
| Radio and TV | Accessibility from major arteries |
| Political survey | Discount coupons in local newspaper |

Now you should study your list carefully and start grouping ideas together. Look for general ideas first rather than details. These broad ideas will later be the main topics in the body of your paper. In the scratch outline (p. 260), for example, the first item, "Recruiting and hiring personnel," is a general idea that will be one of the major topics of your paper. The second item, "Billboards along main highways," is not general and can serve only to support one of the broad major topics. After studying this particular list, you should see four major ideas that would be helpful in "Starting a Business." Pull these out of the list as your main divisions; don't worry yet about details to develop them. Put them in the proper order, in this case the order you would follow if you were a businessperson. Sometimes the order you choose will be decided by chronology, as in this case of what must be done first, then next, and so on. In other cases, you may organize the main points in order of importance, usually from greatest to least. Your outline at this time would look like this:

SKELETON OUTLINE

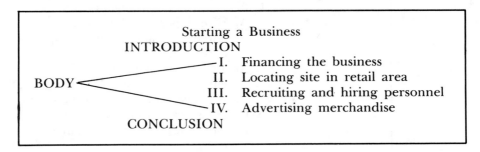

Once you have your major topics for the body of your paper, you should go back to your list to look for details that will develop these ideas. Group all related ideas together under one general heading. If your scratch outline does not have any details for a certain topic, add some at this time from your own experience and knowledge or from research in books or magazine articles. If you cannot come up with any details to develop a topic, you will know that your main divisions should be changed to topics that will lend themselves to development. At this point, you should also eliminate items in your list that have nothing to do with the general topics. In our example, the following items are irrelevant: leisure time on weekends, family problems at home, political survey. Cross them out. Remember that a scratch outline is rough, and you do not have to use every item you put down. The detailed outline resulting from the sample scratch outline might look as follows.

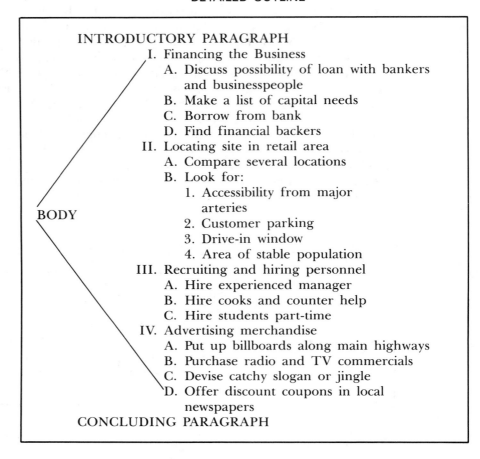

INTRODUCTORY PARAGRAPH
I. Financing the Business
   A. Discuss possibility of loan with bankers and businesspeople
   B. Make a list of capital needs
   C. Borrow from bank
   D. Find financial backers
II. Locating site in retail area
   A. Compare several locations
   B. Look for:
      1. Accessibility from major arteries
      2. Customer parking
      3. Drive-in window
      4. Area of stable population

BODY

III. Recruiting and hiring personnel
   A. Hire experienced manager
   B. Hire cooks and counter help
   C. Hire students part-time
IV. Advertising merchandise
   A. Put up billboards along main highways
   B. Purchase radio and TV commercials
   C. Devise catchy slogan or jingle
   D. Offer discount coupons in local newspapers
CONCLUDING PARAGRAPH

Note these important factors in translating a scratch outline into a completed topic outline:

1. You do not need to use every item on the scratch outline.

2. The introduction and conclusion are not found on a scratch outline.

3. Choose a minimum number of main divisions and try to develop these well on the completed topic outline.

4. The final topic outline is written in *parallel form* for clearness. All headings should be parallel (that is, all noun phrases, all verbs, all clauses, etc.) and all items under each heading should be parallel. (Refer to Module 11, Part IV, for more on parallel construction.)

5. The purpose of outlining is to divide ideas into parts, so there is no need to break an idea down if it has only one part. In other words, if you have a I, you must have a II. If you have an A, you must have a B.

Change the scratch outline below into a working topic outline. Use these principles of organization to prepare to write your own reports: (1) Eliminate the unrelated items. (2) Arrange the remaining items into an outline with five major ideas or divisions and two or more subdivisions supporting each major part. (3) Write "Introduction" and "Conclusion" in the proper place on the outline.

---

Topic: Coping Skills for Stress Management

No caffeine

Appearance

No sugar

Perfectionism

Have a contingency plan

Delegation of authority

Use deep breathing exercises for relaxation

Accumulate several chores to do at once

Smile

Ulcers

Have children do certain household chores

Organization

Make a daily plan

No drugs

Eliminate duties that frustrate you

Overcommitment

Exercise

Share jobs with others at work

Include fun things in your schedule

Hire someone to do certain jobs

Lack of honesty

No alcohol

Nutrition

Wear clothes you feel good in

Run, walk, bicycle, swim, or play tennis or racketball regularly

Pay attention to neatness and cleanliness

Work out aerobically at least three 20-minute sessions per week

---

After completing the scratch outline assignment, check your outline in Feedback 13-A at the end of this module.

## PART III: TWO REPORT FORMATS

Once you understand the principles of the logical outline, you are ready to set up the introductory, supporting, and concluding paragraphs. There are two ways the paragraphs of your report can be set up, the two basic formats illustrated below demonstrate methods that will give you a concrete framework for future reports. Having a choice of formats will give you more flexibility in writing. You can choose the one that best suits your purpose.

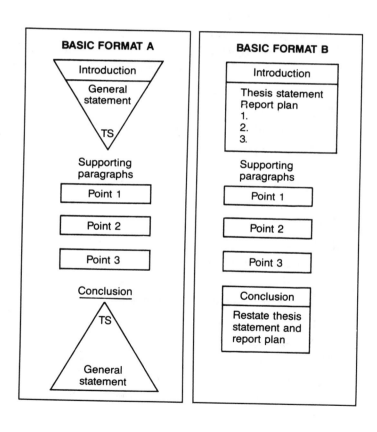

| Inverted Triangle Format | Report Plan Format |
|---|---|
| INTRODUCTION: Open with a general statement to set the context for the subject area then gradually narrow to the main point—usually called the thesis statement or topic sentence—preferably in the last sentence of the opening paragraph. | INTRODUCTION: Open with the thesis statement or topic sentence (the subject and controlling idea of the report). Following that, state the report plan which lists the main points to be presented in the order in which they will occur. |
| SUPPORTING PARAGRAPHS: Each supporting paragraph should have its own topic sentence. The second paragraph begins supporting (proving or developing) the thesis statement. Use a separate paragraph for each major point. Use transitional expressions to link paragraphs smoothly. Statements within the paragraph can consist of reasons, examples, details, statistics, comparison and contrast, negation, classification, definition, cause, and process. | SUPPORTING PARAGRAPHS: At least one paragraph should be used to support each main point mentioned in the report plan of the introduction. The points should be discussed in the same order in which they were presented in the report plan so as not to confuse the reader. Each discussion paragraph should have its own topic sentence telling briefly what the paragraph is about. Transitions are necessary to lead the reader smoothly from one main idea to the next. |
| CONCLUSION: Start with a restatement of the thesis statement (topic sentence) in different words. Broaden gradually to the final general statement. In effect, you have completed the circle you began in the introduction. | CONCLUSION: Sum up the main points you wish to emphasize by restating in different words the thesis statement (topic sentence) and then the report plan in the same order. By doing this, you let the reader know that you have completed the discussion. |

The following reports will illustrate the two basic formats. Notice that the supporting paragraphs remain the same in both formats, while the introductions and conclusions are different. The same report has been used to illustrate both formats so that you can see how both would work well. The outlines follow the Planning Forms, which appear at the end of the module. They will help you outline each report.

*Background Information*

**Subject:** pregnant women who smoke

**Controlling Idea (thesis):** Should quit smoking

**Format:** Inverted Triangle

**Point of view:** Third person (pregnant women)

*Content*

**Introduction**

**Opening General Statement:** The Surgeon-General's report on the hazards of smoking has made people more aware of the dangers of smoking.

**Topic Sentence:** It is vital for any pregnant woman to quit smoking.

I. **Major argument 1:** Decrease in birth weight

    A. **Supporting evidence 1:** Correlation between smoking and infants weighing less than 7 pounds

    B. **Supporting evidence 2:** Greater weight gain of nonsmoking mothers and their infants

    C. **Supporting evidence 3:** Intermediate weight gain of light smokers and their mothers

II. **Major argument 2:** Neonatal respiratory distress

    A. **Supporting evidence 1:** Carbon monoxide from placenta to fetus

    B. **Supporting evidence 2:** High carbon monoxide levels in blood of smoking mothers

    C. **Supporting evidence 3:** Nicotine's effect on fetus (vasoconstriction)

III. **Major argument 3:** Stillbirth

    A. **Supporting evidence 1:** Less oxygen to fetus in uterus

    B. **Supporting evidence 2:** Less oxygen to fetus during birth

    C. **Supporting evidence 3:** Rigors of labor on fetus

    D. **Supporting evidence 4:** Hypoxic (lacking oxygen) infant at time of birth

**Conclusion**

**Topic Sentence Restatement:** It is hoped that any pregnant woman who knows the effects of smoking on her unborn baby will be motivated to stop smoking completely.

**Closing General Statement:** Smoking is bad for everyone but especially for those who are pregnant and could be affecting innocent life.

## SAMPLE OUTLINE: INVERTED TRIANGLE FORMAT

| | |
|---|---|
| **Introduction** | General statement on the hazards of smoking. |
| **Opening General Statement** | The Surgeon-General's report on the hazards of smoking has made people more aware of the dangers of cigarettes. |
| **Topic Sentence:** | It is vital for any pregnant woman to quit smoking. |

**Supporting Paragraph 1**

    I. Decrease in birth weight
       A. Correlation between smoking and infants weighing less than 7 pounds
       B. Greater weight gain of nonsmoking mothers and their infants
       C. Intermediate weight gain of light smokers and their infants

**Supporting Paragraph 2**

    II. Neonatal respiratory distress
       A. Carbon monoxide from placenta to fetus
       B. High carbon monoxide levels in blood of smoking mothers
       C. Nicotine's effect on fetus (vasoconstriction)

**Supporting Paragraph 3**

    III. Stillbirth
       A. Less oxygen to fetus in uterus
       B. Less oxygen to fetus during birth
       C. Rigors of labor on fetus
       D. Hypoxic (lacking oxygen) infant at time of birth

| | |
|---|---|
| **Conclusion** | |
| **Topic Sentence Restatement** | It is hoped that any pregnant woman who knows the effects of smoking on her unborn baby will be motivated to stop smoking completely. |
| **Closing General Statement** | Smoking is bad for everyone but especially for those who are pregnant and could be affecting an innocent life. |

**Introduction**
**General Statement**

The Surgeon-General's report on the hazards of smoking has made people more aware of the dangers of smoking. In particular, many studies in the last several years have linked smoking cigarettes to problem pregnancies. The risks of smoking during pregnancy have been clearly demonstrated. Because of the extensive evidence of the harmful effects on the newborn, it is vital for any pregnant woman to quit smoking.

**Thesis Statement**
**(Topic Sentence)**

**Supporting**
**Paragraph 1**

First of all, there is a definite correlation between smoking during pregnancy and infants weighing less than 7 pounds at birth. In a study of 1159 infant-mother pairs, it was found that pregnant women who did not smoke gained significantly more weight than mothers who were heavy smokers, with an intermediate weight gain in mothers who were light smokers. The size of the infants at birth varied similarly. Infants born to women who did not smoke at all were larger than infants born to mothers who were even light smokers.

**Supporting**
**Paragraph 2**

After low birth weight, the next most common complication of infants whose mothers smoked during pregnancy is neonatal respiratory distress. Every time a mother smokes a cigarette, carbon monoxide passes through the placenta to the fetus, producing intrauterine hypoxia (lack of oxygen). The carbon monoxide, which attaches to the hemoglobin before oxygen does, is increased in smoking mothers. Also, nicotine in tobacco has a direct effect on the fetus through its vasoconstriction (contraction of the blood vessels). These effects may last several hours.

**Supporting**
**Paragraph 3**

The last effect smoking has on the infant is stillbirth, which is caused in much the same way fetal hypoxemia is. The mother smokes a cigarette, causing carbon monoxide to attach to hemoglobin instead of oxygen, thus causing the fetus to receive less oxygen

|  | for several hours later. During labor, the fetus receives less oxygen because of the contracting uterus. In a mother who does not smoke, there is no real problem, and the fetus recovers quickly. In a smoking mother, however, the fetus is already depressed, and the rigors of labor may prove too much. The result is the delivery of a severely hypoxic infant needing aggressive measures such as intubation. |
|---|---|
| **Topic Sentence Restatement** | It is hoped that any pregnant woman who knows the effects of smoking on her unborn baby will be motivated to stop smoking completely. The adverse effects on the fetus could be devastating. Smoking is bad for everyone, but especially for those who are pregnant and could be affecting an innocent life. |
| **Closing General Statement** | |

## SAMPLE PLANNING FORM: REPORT PLAN FORMAT

*Background Information*

**Subject:** Pregnant women who smoke

**Controlling idea (thesis):** Should quit smoking

**Format:** Report plan

**Point of view:** Third person (pregnant women)

*Content*

**Introduction**

**Thesis Statement (Topic Sentence):** It is vital for any pregnant woman to quit smoking.

**Report Plan:**  1. Decrease in birth weight
2. Neonatal respiratory distress
3. Stillbirth

I.  **Major argument 1:** Decrease in birth weight

    A.  **Supporting evidence 1:** Correlation between smoking and infants weighing less than 7 pounds

    B.  **Supporting evidence 2:** Greater weight gain of nonsmoking mothers and their infants

    C.  **Supporting evidence 3:** Intermediate weight gain of light smokers and their infants

II.  **Major argument 2:** Neonatal respiratory distress

    A.  **Supporting evidence 1:** Carbon monoxide from placenta to fetus

B. **Supporting evidence 2:** High carbon monoxide levels in blood of smoking mothers

C. **Supporting evidence 3:** Nicotine's effect on fetus (vasoconstriction)

III. **Major argument 3:** Stillbirth

    A. **Supporting evidence 1:** Less oxygen to fetus in uterus

    B. **Supporting evidence 2:** Less oxygen to fetus at birth

    C. **Supporting evidence 3:** Rigors of labor on fetus

    D. **Supporting evidence 4:** Hypoxic (lacking oxygen) infant at time of birth

**Conclusion**

**Topic Sentence Restatement:** It is hoped that any pregnant woman who knows the effects of smoking on her unborn baby will be motivated to stop smoking completely.

**Report plan:** When a pregnant woman smokes, she increases the risks of a decrease in the birth weight of her infant, of the possibility of neonatal respiratory distress, and even of stillbirth.

SAMPLE OUTLINE: REPORT PLAN FORMAT

**Introduction**

**Thesis Statement: (Topic Sentence) Report Plan:** It is vital for any pregnant woman to quit smoking.
    I. Decrease in birth weight
    II. Neonatal respiratory distress
    III. Stillbirth

**Supporting Paragraph 1**
    I. Decrease in birth weight
        A. Correlation between smoking and infants weighing less than 7 pounds
        B. Greater weight gain of nonsmoking mothers and their infants
        C. Intermediate weight gain of light smokers and their infants

**Supporting Paragraph 2**
    II. Neonatal respiratory distress
        A. Carbon monoxide from placenta to fetus

<table>
<tr><td></td><td>B. High carbon monoxide levels in blood of smoking mothers<br>C. Nicotine's effect on fetus (vasoconstriction)</td></tr>
<tr><td>**Supporting Paragraph 3**</td><td>III. Stillbirth<br>   A. Less oxygen to fetus in uterus B. Less oxygen to fetus during birth<br>   C. Rigors of labor on fetus<br>   D. Hypoxic (lacking oxygen) infant at time of birth</td></tr>
<tr><td>**Conclusion**</td><td></td></tr>
<tr><td>**Topic Sentence Restatement**</td><td>It is hoped that any pregnant woman who knows the effects of smoking on her unborn baby will be motivated to stop smoking completely.</td></tr>
<tr><td>**Report Plan**</td><td>When a pregnant woman smokes, she increases the risks of a decrease in the birth weight of her infant, of the possibility of neonatal respiratory distress, and even of stillbirth.</td></tr>
</table>

## SAMPLE REPORT PLAN REPORT

| | |
|---|---|
| **Introduction** | It is vital for any pregnant woman to quit smoking. The hazards to the unborn child, including decrease in birth weight, neonatal respiratory distress, and stillbirth, are too great to take the chance. |
| **Supporting Paragraph 1** | First of all, there is a definite correlation between smoking during pregnancy and infants weighing less than 7 pounds at birth. In a study of 1159 infant-mother pairs, it was found that pregnant women who did not smoke gained significantly more weight than mothers who were heavy smokers, with an intermediate weight gain in mothers who were light smokers. The size of the infants at birth varied similarly. Infants born to women who did not smoke at all were |

larger than infants born to mothers who were even light smokers.

**Supporting Paragraph 2**

After low birth weight, the next most common complication of infants whose mothers smoked during pregnancy is neonatal respiratory distress. Every time a mother smokes a cigarette, carbon monoxide passes through the placenta to the fetus producing intrauterine hypoxia (lack of oxygen). The carbon monoxide, which attaches to the hemoglobin before oxygen does, is increased in smoking mothers. Also, nicotine in tobacco has a direct effect on the fetus through its vasoconstriction (contraction of the blood vessels). These effects may last several hours.

**Supporting Paragraph 3**

The last effect smoking has on the infant is stillbirth, which is caused in much the same way fetal hypoxemia is. The mother smokes a cigarette, causing carbon monoxide to attach to hemoglobin instead of oxygen, thus causing the fetus to receive less oxygen for several hours later. During labor, the fetus receives less oxygen because of the contracting uterus. In a mother who does not smoke, there is no real problem, and the fetus recovers quickly. In a smoking mother, however, the fetus is already depressed, and the rigors of labor may prove too much. The result is the delivery of a severely hypoxic infant needing aggressive measures such as intubation.

**Conclusion**

**Topic Sentence Restatement**

It is hoped that any pregnant woman who knows the effects of smoking on her unborn baby will be motivated to stop smoking completely.

**Report Plan**

When a pregnant woman smokes, she heightens the risks of a decrease in the birth weight of her infant, of the possibility of neonatal respiratory distress, and even of stillbirth.

Note that the report did not begin with "In this report I am going to tell you how to. . . ." Do not call the reader's attention to the fact that you are writing a report.

It is best to avoid the first person (*I* or *we*) unless it is absolutely essential. The same goes for second person (*you*). Generally, it is best to stick to third person (*he, she, it, one,* or *they*) unless it is necessary to talk directly to the reader. Be sure to remain consistent in person. If you begin with second person, do not switch to third person.

## PART IV: TECHNICAL PROCEDURE REPORT

A technical procedure report explains how to do something. Although it is similar to the process paragraph that you wrote in Module 9, it is usually more detailed. The process paragraph deals with a rather simple process that can be related in a few fairly short steps. The technical procedure report is lengthier because it describes a more complex process, and it contains more details. Here is a sample for you to look at before you write your own.

SAMPLE PLANNING FORM: TECHNICAL PROCEDURE REPORT

*Background Information*

**Procedure:** Developing a computer program in Basic language

**Audience:** Person who has not done procedure before

**Purpose:** To explain how to actually do the procedure

**Format:** Report Plan

*Content*

**Necessary materials:** Personal computer, monitor, printer, floppy disk

**Definition of special terms:** Assume reader knows Basic terminology

**Topic Sentence:** There is a logical procedure to follow in order to develop a computer program in Basic programming language.

**Report Plan:** The following information will help you prepare, enter, and print your program.

I.  **Preparation:**    A.   Preparing computer
                          1.   Obtaining and inserting floppy disk
                          2.   Turning on computer switch
                     B.   Setting up computer
                          1.   Setting caps lock set key down
                               2. typing in B, PR#3

II. **Procedure:**      A.   Entering the program
                          1.   Typing statement number and statement
                          2.   Entering remaining statements

3. Proofreading and correcting
errors

4. Entering statements

5. Reentering incorrect statements

B. Printing the program

1. Checking printer

2. Turning on surge master and
line printer

3. Inserting disk

4. Turning on computer and
monitor

5. Loading

6. Entering PR#3, PR#1, List,
and PR#0

7. Printing information

8. Form feeding

9. Tearing off printout

10. Removing disk

11. Turning off computer,
monitor, and printer

III. **Precautions:** Correcting errors, checking printer for
paper

**Conclusion:** As you will see, these steps will let you
control the computer instead of the
computer controlling you. Try this
procedure to prepare, enter, and print
a Basic program successfully.

SAMPLE OUTLINE FOR TECHNICAL PROCEDURE: REPORT PLAN FORMAT

**Introduction**
**Topic Sentence**       There is a logical procedure to follow
in order to develop a computer
program in Basic programming
language.

**Report Plan**          The following information will help you
prepare, enter, and print your program.

I. **Supporting**
   **Paragraph 1**
   **(Preparation)**     A. Preparing computer

1. Obtaining and inserting floppy disk
2. Turning on computer switch

B. Setting up computer
   1. Setting caps lock set key down
   2. Typing in B, PR#3

**II. Procedure**
**Supporting**
**Paragraph 2**

A. Entering the program
   1. Typing statement number and statement
   2. Entering remaining statements
   3. Proofreading and correcting errors
   4. Entering statements
   5. Reentering incorrect statements

**Supporting**
**Paragraph 3**
**(Procedure cont.)**

B. Printing the program
   1. Checking printer
   2. Turning on surge master and line printer
   3. Inserting disk
   4. Turning on computer and monitor
   5. Loading
   6. Entering PR#3, PR#1, List, and PR#0
   7. Printing information
   8. Form feeding
   9. Tearing off printout
   10. Removing disk
   11. Turning off computer, monitor, and printer

**Conclusion**

As you will see, these steps will let you control the computer instead of the computer controlling you. Try this procedure to prepare, enter, and print a Basic program successfully.

275

**Introduction**

There is a logical procedure to follow in order to develop a computer program in Basic programming language. The following information will help you prepare, enter, and print a Basic computer program.

**Preparation**

The first step is preparing and setting up the computer for your program. First, you will need to obtain and insert a floppy disk. Then, you need to turn the computer on. Next, press the caps lock set key down. Finally, type in B, PR#3. After all these tasks are completed, continue to the next step.

**Procedure**

Now enter your program into the computer. First, you will need to type the statement number and statement. Continue in the same manner throughout the rest of your statements. If you make an error before pressing Return, you can correct it by using the left and right arrows to backspace or move forward. If you detect the error after you have pressed the Return key, just reenter the statement number and statement. The computer will automatically retain the last statement.

After entering your program correctly into the computer, you are ready to print your program. First, make sure there is enough paper in the line printer. Second, turn on the surge master and line printer. Next, insert the disk in the disk drive, and turn on the computer and monitor. Then type B, Load, program name; press Return. Finally, you need to press Return after each of the following: PR#3, PR#1, List, and PR#O. Then you are ready to obtain a printout by pushing the button next to Select. When the green light goes off, press Form Feed. Next, press the button next to Select and the green light will come back on. Tear off your program. Finally, remove the disk, and turn off the computer, monitor, and printer.

**Conclusion**

These steps will let you control the computer instead of its controlling you. Try this procedure to prepare, enter, and print a Basic computer program successfully.

Do not forget to use transitional expressions. Below is a list for particular use in a process report. A more complete list can be found on page 78.

```
┌─────────────────────────────────────────────────────┐
│        SUGGESTED TRANSITIONAL EXPRESSIONS FOR          │
│                  PROCEDURE REPORT                       │
│                                                         │
│        first, second (etc.)        to                   │
│        next                        also                 │
│        then                        in addition          │
│        afterwards                  furthermore          │
│        finally                     moreover             │
│        lastly                      besides              │
│                                                         │
└─────────────────────────────────────────────────────┘
```

### ACTIVITY 13-B: Technical Procedure Report

Write a technical procedure report, following the procedures below. Write the report in class so that your instructor will be available to help you as you proceed.

1. Choose a procedure to explain for the report.
2. Write a thesis statement.
3. Outline the report, including Preparation and Procedures if appropriate. Use the Planning Form on page 269.
4. Write the final draft from the outline.
5. Proofread carefully, using the following checklist.

_____Spelling

_____Verb forms and endings

_____Punctuation

_____Pronoun agreement

_____Subject–verb agreement

_____Fragments

_____Shifts

    _____Voice (consistency with active or passive)

    _____Tense (consistency with past, present, future)

    _____Person (consistency with 1st, 2nd, 3rd)

    _____Number (consistency with singular or plural)

_____Parallel structure

_____Possessives (correct use of apostrophe, no contractions)

_____Misplaced modifiers

_____Correct word usage

_____Wordiness

_____Clichés

_____Slang

6. Type or write the revised draft in ink on 8½" × 11" unlined paper. Use only one side of the paper. Do not tear paper from a spiral ring.

7. Hand in to your instructor your Planning form, outline, rough draft, and revised draft.

If your report is not acceptable, your instructor will indicate what areas need work. From that information you will write a second revised draft. If this copy is not acceptable, you will choose a different topic.

After achieving a passing grade on the Technical Procedure Report, you should make an appointment to interview someone working in your technology (not an instructor or a member of your family). In a later section you will be writing an interview report. For efficiency, set up the appointment *now* so that when you are ready to conduct the interview and write the report, there will not be a delay and you can proceed steadily through the module. See the first two sections of Part VI for directions on how to select an interviewee and how to set up an interview. Proceed to Part V.

## PART V: THE PERSUASIVE REPORT

The persuasive report presents an argument to readers and then asks them to act. It presents only one side of the picture and tries to persuade readers that the point of view given is the logical one. Keep in mind that this report is designed to convince readers of your point of view and to get them to take some action. The topic should be a controversial idea or at least a subject that has more than one side to it.

The use of the second person (you) is much more appropriate in a persuasive report than in other reports since you are addressing the reader directly and urging him or her to take action. In other types of reports, it is preferable to use the third person (**the reader, he, she, one, etc.**).

Occasionally in a persuasive report you may want to mention some of the common arguments contrary to your thesis statement so that you can refute or dispel them. If you wish to include a concession to the opposition, it should appear in the paragraph immediately after the introduction. Then the remainder of the report supports the thesis statement.

Note that the sample outlines and report used to illustrate the two basic formats on pages 264–65 are persuasive reports.

## ACTIVITY 13-C: Persuasive Report

Write a persuasive report, following the procedures below. Write the report in class so that your instructor will be available to help you as you proceed.

1. Choose a general topic for the report.
2. Narrow it to a specific topic.
3. Write a thesis statement.
4. Outline the report using the Planning Form on page 298.
5. Proofread carefully, using the following checklist.

_____Spelling

_____Verb forms and endings

_____Punctuation

_____Pronoun agreement

_____Subject–verb agreement

_____Fragments

_____Shifts

     _____Voice (consistency with active or passive)

     _____Tense (consistency with past, present, future)

     _____Person (consistency with 1st, 2nd, 3rd)

     _____Number (consistency with singular or plural)

_____Parallel structure

_____Possessives (correct use of apostrophe, no contractions)

_____Misplaced modifiers

_____Correct word usage

_____Wordiness

_____Clichés

_____Slang

6. Type or write the revised draft in ink on 8½″ × 11″ unlined paper. Use only one side of the paper. Do not tear paper from a spiral ring.
7. Hand in to your instructor your Planning Form, outline, rough draft, and revised draft.

The techniques of interviewing should be very valuable to you on the job in order to collect the information you need on a particular subject. To conduct an interview, you will need to rely upon several skills you have already learned.

At the end of Part IV of this module, you were asked to interview someone currently employed in your technology to prepare for writing an interview report. Since the interview is intended to give you another point of view from someone actually working in your field, *do not interview one of your technology instructors or a member of your family.* Furthermore, this assignment is designed to give you practice both in interviewing and in writing, helpful tools to use on the job. By utilizing the skills of planning ahead and organizing facts, as indicated below, you will improve your ability to communicate.

### Selecting the Interviewee

Your technology may be a very broad area, giving you many choices of people to interview. If you are enrolled in business administration, for instance, you will have to narrow the field to a specific area, such as accounting, sales, or management. Thus, the first thing for you to decide is the particular facet of your technology you wish to make your career. (If you are not certain, choose your favorite among the possibilities.) Then find a person employed in this area. For a list of people, consult your technology instructors, the telephone directory, or a local firm.

### Preparing for the Interview

When you have selected the individual you want to interview, telephone or write to ask for an appointment convenient to both of you. Be sure to tell the interviewee who you are, why you would like the interview, what the specific subject of the interview is, and the amount of time you would like. Discuss a time limit for the interview, so you will both know what to plan for. It would be courteous also to tell the interviewee that you will send a copy of the report to read before it goes to your instructor. Find out as much as possible about the interviewee beforehand.

The second part of the preparation before the actual interview is drawing up a list of questions. Make these as specific as possible so that you can control the direction of the interview. Ask about things you personally want to know about. Since this interviewee is working in your chosen career, this person can give you many ideas as to what to expect on the job. Here are some specific areas you may have questions about:

Type of person required for job

Educational requirements for job

Internship

Opportunities for graduates in field

Possibilities for advancement

Salary

Benefits

Duties

Advantages and disadvantages

Recommendations to persons entering field

New developments and proposed changes in field

Writing requirements for job

As soon as you have compiled a list of questions which you would like to ask in the interview, review them with your instructor (see Activity 13-D). Include the name and address of the person you are interviewing so that the English Department can send a letter of appreciation for this person's time and interest. In this letter, the interviewee will be asked to fill out a form evaluating the interview. You should also send the person a thank you letter (see the Social Business Letter in Module 14).

### ACTIVITY 13-D: Interview Questions

After securing an appointment for an interview, review the following information with your instructor.

1. Name of person to be interviewed
2. Position held
3. Place of employment
4. Address
5. Date and time set for interview
6. Questions you intend to ask

Proceed to the section on Conducting the Interview.

#### Conducting the Interview

Arrive early for the interview. Be sure that you are neatly and appropriately dressed. As soon as the interview begins, be prepared to direct the discussion. Your purpose is to collect information about the job, so do not be timid in asking questions. It is preferable to begin with such subjects as job opportunities and responsibilities. Save the topic of money for last. Be pleasant and courteous, yet assert yourself. Indicate your interest by remaining alert, sitting up straight, and looking the interviewee in the eye.

Let your interviewee do most of the talking, but do not allow the person to wander off on a tangent and discuss irrelevant subjects. Remain objective; keep your convictions to yourself. Don't take sides. Ask questions in the order in which they come up in the discussion; new questions are certain to arise that you did not include on your original list. Concentrate on the person's remarks. Take notes only briefly so as not to disturb the interviewee's train of thought. Do not use a large notebook, but have a small note pad and pencil available. It is best not to use a tape recorder because it is likely to make the interviewee nervous and self-conscious.

Remember to thank the interviewee for the time and information as you leave. Do not drag the interview out any longer than it takes you to ask your questions. The interviewee is a busy person and will appreciate your being as brief as possible.

### SAMPLE PLANNING FORM: INTERVIEW REPORT

*Person Interviewed*

**Name:**  Harry Wilson

**Address:**  Biller Associates
301 Harley Avenue
West, TX 77601

**Position:**  Draftsman designer

**Date of interview:**  May 1, 1991

*Content*

**Questions:**

Education and personal requirements

Engineering jobs available

Possibilities for advancement

Duties

Recommendations

Likes and dislikes

**Major impression from interview:**  Positive feeling about job

**Major headings of report:**

Background information on interviewee

Positions available

Duties

Recommendations

**Concluding remarks:**  Interesting job, satisfying work, opportunities for advancement

**INTRODUCTION**

Person interviewed:   Harry Wilson

Position:   Draftsman Designer

Company:   Miller Associates

Education:   A.A.S. from DTCC

   I.  Positions available

      A.  Surveyors

      B.  Draftsmen Designers

      C.  Rodmen

  II.  Duties.

      A.  Job specifications

      B.  Designing

      C.  Supervising

III.  Recommendations

      A.  Familiarity with computers

      B.  Notetaking ability

**CONCLUSION**

Interesting job

Satisfying work

Opportunities for advancement

### Writing the Report

As soon after the interview as possible, while your impressions are still fresh, sit down and make detailed notes. If you wait too long, you may forget some of the important points.

Once your note-taking is completed, you are ready to organize all the facts by constructing an outline. You have already gained some skill in this procedure.

First, pick out the headings. Then, organize them in a logical sequence. Finally, group all of the facts obtained in the interview under appropriate headings. With this outline completed, you have done the hardest part of the task. The actual writing of the report is easy once you have organized the material.

You may choose to write your interview report in either of two formats: the question and answer format or the standard report format.

The *Question and Answer Format* is used frequently in magazine interviews. If you choose to write your report in this manner, be sure your outline. The report will be very hard to follow if you jump around from subject to subject without any plan. Also, this format requires a careful summing up of the main points at the end. In addition, you should reveal your own conclusions and impressions of the information gathered in the interview.

The *Standard Report Format* is similar to the one you learned for the process report and the persuasive report. It is made up of three sections:

1. INTRODUCTION: This should contain pertinent background information about the person interviewed, as well as the date, time, and place of the interview.

2. SUPPORTING PARAGRAPHS: These should discuss the main headings in the outline. You will probably want to devote a paragraph to each heading. Remember to tie the paragraphs together with transitional expressions.

3. CONCLUSION: Here you should restate the essential facts learned in the interview. You may also include any conclusions you have drawn as a result of the interview; you can express your own opinion here.

Here is a sample interview report. Note the use of headings to make it easier for the reader to follow. First person pronouns are acceptable in the introduction and conclusion of the interview report.

## SAMPLE INTERVIEW REPORT

On May 1, 1991, I interviewed Mr. Harry Wilson, a draftsman designer at Biller Associates. He has an Associate of Applied Science Degree in Architectural Engineering from Delaware Technical and Community College. During the interview, he told me about his past and present duties. At the end of our conversation, he made some recommendations for prospective civil engineers.

### POSITIONS AVAILABLE

There are several positions available in the field of civil engineering. At Biller Associates, these positions are separated into two categories. One category is made up of surveyors, and the other is composed of draftsmen designers. Mr. Wilson started as a draftsman under constant supervision and worked his way up to the position of a draftsman designer. He stated that the beginning position of surveyor is that of a rodman. The rodman can then work his way up to the position of party chief.

## DUTIES

According to Mr. Wilson, there are several duties he has to perform as a draftsman designer. Among these, he must have the ability to take the specifications for a particular job and turn them into a working design. These include such things as designing a proper drainage ditch, rock embedments, storm drainage systems, and bulkheads for waterfront property. In addition to designing, he is also given the responsibility of supervising other draftsmen working under him.

## RECOMMENDATIONS

Mr. Wilson outlined several recommendations for prospective civil engineers. Since he started working for Biller Associates, Mr. Wilson has noticed a large move toward the use of computers. With this in mind, he made the recommendation that prospective civil engineering students take as many computer courses as possible. He also suggested that they learn how to take good notes and that they keep them for future reference in courses such as Statics, Fluid Mechanics, Wastewater and Sewage Systems, and Soil Mechanics.

## CONCLUSION

Mr. Wilson made his job as draftsman designer sound very interesting. It was evident that he is very happy with his work. He stressed the different options and the opportunities to advance in each. After conducting this interview, I feel that the time that I have spent working on an associate degree in Civil Engineering has been worthwhile.

---

**ACTIVITY 13-E: Interview Report**

Conduct your interview, outlining notes immediately afterward. Use the Planning Form on page 299. Then write the report following the procedures on pages 283–85. If your report is acceptable, proceed to Part VII. If your report is not acceptable, correct the errors indicated by your instructor and do an alternate report if necessary. After achieving a passing grade on your interview report, proceed to Part VII.

---

## PART VII: RECOMMENDATION REPORT

When you are on the job, it is likely that you will be asked to make a decision or recommendation on whether to purchase a particular piece of equipment or to adopt a particular program. You would have to examine several alternatives, compare the results, and recommend one for adoption, presenting the results of your comparative study in the form of a *Recommendation Report*.

### Memorandum Format

The best approach to a recommendation report is a memorandum accompanied by tabulated data. The advantage of the tabulated form is that the reader can see everything at a glance and need not wade through a sea of words. This format is preferable when the report contains a great deal of hard data.

In a recommendation report, the *introduction* should set the purpose of the report, mentioning the items under consideration and also stating your choice at the outset. It should also indicate why you are making the recommendation. The *supporting paragraphs* should analyze the main features of the best choices available for consideration. The *conclusion* should recommend which item to adopt and tell *why*. Be sure that you compare at least two items which have several features to be evaluated or at least four items if there are only a few features to contrast.

Note that the first paragraph of the memorandum contains the background information that would be in the introduction of a standard recommendation report. The conclusion states the recommendation and summarizes the data that support that decision. In all recommendation reports, be sure to compare a sufficient number of alternatives—at least two items if there are many features to compare or at least four less complicated items. Be sure to draw conclusions in a final paragraph stating *why* you made the choice that you did. It is helpful if you not only give reasons for your choice, but also give reasons for rejecting the other items.

### SAMPLE PLANNING FORM: RECOMMENDATION REPORT

*Background Information*

**Items to be analyzed:** Taxan 630. Amdek 600, and Sony color video monitors

**Audience:** Chairman of committee to purchase color monitor

**Format:** Memo or paragraph

*Content*

**Introduction:**

Situation requiring recommendation: Committee request

Specifications considered: Size, resolution, dot/pitch, screen, price, warranty

**Major points of comparison:** Size, resolution, dot/pitch, screen, price, warranty

**Data on each item:**

Taxan 630: 13-inch screen, 640 horizontal by 400 vertical, .37 mm dot/pitch, nonglare screen, $675, one-year warranty

Amdek 600: 13-inch screen, 640 horizontal by 200 vertical, .25 mm dot/pitch, glare screen, $665, two-year warranty

Sony: 13-inch screen, 640 horizontal by 200 vertical, .43 mm dot/pitch, nonglare screen, $670, 90-day warranty

**Conclusion:**

Item recommended: Taxan 630

Reasons for choice: performance, better vertical resolution, clearer text/screen image

Reasons for rejecting other items: Amdek screen glare, Sony short warranty period

---

### SAMPLE OUTLINE: RECOMMENDATION REPORT

Recommendation for a Color Monitor

**INTRODUCTION**

Features considered
   Size
   Resolution
   Dot/Pitch
   Screen
   Price
Models
   Taxan 630
   Amdek 600
   Sony

   I. Size
      A. Taxan 630—13 inch
      B. Amdek 600—13 inch
      C. Sony—13 inch

  II. Resolution
      A. Taxan 630—640h × 400v
      B. Amdek 600—640h × 200v
      C. Sony—640h × 200v

 III. Dot/Pitch
      A. Taxan 630—.37

        B.  Amdek 600—.43
        C.  Sony—.25
    IV.  Screen
        A.  Taxan 630—nonglare
        B.  Amdek 600—glare
        C.  Sony—nonglare
    V.  Price
        A.  Taxan 630—$675
        B.  Amdek 600—$665
        C.  Sony—$670
    VI.  Warranty
        A.  Taxan—1 year
        B.  Amdek—2 years
        C.  Sony—90 days

## CONCLUSION

    Choice:  Taxan 630
    Reasons:  Amdek glare, taxan clearer image

### SAMPLE RECOMMENDATION REPORT: MEMO FORMAT

**TO:**       Mr. Fred Morris, Chairman
**FROM:**     Roy Collins
**SUBJECT:**  Video Monitors
**DATE:**     November 11, 1990

At the conclusion of our meeting on November 3, the committee requested I research the market and make a recommendation for color monitors to be used with the new IBM PC computers. Following an extensive preliminary study, I have listed those which best meet our specifications of size, resolution, pitch, screen, price, and warranty. Three units—the Taxan 630, the Amdek 600, and the Sony—are the models to be considered.

| Model | Taxan 630 | Amdek 600 | Sony |
|---|---|---|---|
| **Size** | 13 in | 13 in | 13 in |
| **Resolution** | 640h × 400v | 640h × 200v | 640h × 200v |
| **Dot/Pitch** | .37 mm | .25 mm | .43 mm |
| **Screen** | nonglare | glare | nonglare |
| **Price** | $675 | $665 | $670 |
| **Warranty** | 1 yr | 2 yrs | 90 days |

After studying the data and visually evaluating each monitor, 1 have decided, on a cost vs. performance basis, that the Taxan 630 is the best buy. The Amdek 600 costs less and has a longer warranty period, but the screen glare makes it unacceptable. The Sony's short warranty period is a disadvantage. Although the Taxan 630 and the Sony are similar in price, the 400 vertical resolution of the Taxan presents a much clearer text/screen image. Considering these facts, I recommend that the committee accept the Taxan 630 for purchase.

Here is the same recommendation report set up in the conventional paragraph format.

## SAMPLE RECOMMENDATION REPORT: PARAGRAPH FORMAT

One of the most useful machines a person in business or industry has at his disposal is the personal computer. Anyone spending time working at a computer screen will certainly realize the importance of choosing the right monitor to use. Such things as size, resolution, dot/pitch, screen, and price are important considerations in selecting a monitor. Three units—the Taxan 630, the Amdek 600, and the Sony—are monitors worthy of consideration. Of these, the Taxan seems to be the best choice.

One point to look at is size. The Taxan 630, the Amdek 600, and the Sony all have a 13-inch screen.

Another factor is resolution. The Taxan maintains 640 horizontal lines by 400 vertical, while both the Amdek and the Sony have only 200 vertical lines, making them less well defined.

In addition, Dot/Pitch must be taken into account. The Taxan 630 has a Dot/Pitch of .37 millimeters; the Amdek, .43; and the Sony, .25.

The type of screen can be important to someone who spends much time at a computer. Both the Taxan 630 and the Sony have non-glare screens while the Amdek does not.

Of course, the cost may be the most significant factor. In ascending order, the list prices for the units follow: $665 for the Amdek, $670 for the Sony, and $675 for the Taxan.

After the data is examined and the monitors are visually evaluated, it appears that the Taxan 630 is the best buy on a cost vs. performance basis. Although the Amdek 600 costs less and has a longer warranty, the screen glare makes it unacceptable. The Taxan and the Sony are close in price, but the 400 vertical resolution of the Taxan presents a much clearer text/screen image. It is definitely worth the $5 extra.

Given these considerations, the Taxan 630 is the logical choice.

### ACTIVITY 13-F: Recommendation Report

Obtain facts on equipment you wish to evaluate. For information, consult your technology instructor, technical magazines, company literature, an equipment manual, *Consumer Reports,* or catalogs. If your technology does not deal with equipment, you may evaluate programs, ideas, or policies. Prepare your outline and then write a recommendation report, using either the paragraph or the memorandum format. Follow the general procedures given on pages 285–89. If your report is acceptable, proceed to Part VIII. If your report is not acceptable, correct the errors indicated. Your instructor will decide whether you have achieved a passing grade or should write a second recommendation report on a new topic. After achieving a passing grade, proceed to Part VIII.

## PART VIII: SUMMARY REPORT

Another type of writing you may be asked to do on the job is to summarize a magazine article, progress on a project, or research on a subject. You will do this in a *summary report.* This type of report should be as brief as you can make it, yet as clear and complete as possible. You have to condense the essential points and eliminate all of the extra material.

Let's suppose you have been asked to summarize a magazine article. First, read the article thoroughly so that you understand it completely. You may even want to reread parts and highlight major ideas to make sure you do not miss any important points.

Your summary report should include an *introduction* which states the name of the magazine, underlined; the date of the magazine; the name of the article, in quotes; and its general subject; *supporting paragraphs,* which describe the main points of the article; and a *conclusion,* which emphasizes the heart of the article. Do not inject your own opinion even if you disagree since your purpose is merely to summarize.

The summary should be 5 to 10 percent of the length of the original article. Condensing material to the essentials will give you practice in distinguishing between primary facts and minute details.

Be very careful to avoid plagiarism. If you use the author's exact words anywhere in your report, be sure to give the author credit by enclosing those words in quotation marks and inserting a footnote about the source. If you express the author's thoughts in your own words, no quotation marks are needed.

Read the following magazine article; then study the sample planning form, outline, and summary of the article. The article is approximately 2400 words, and the summary is 236 words, about 10 percent of the original length.

# Speaking of Writing—Interviews with People on the Job

Madeline Hamermesh
*Normandale Community College*

With considerable frequency, articles appear in *The Wall Street Journal* and other business-related periodicals lamenting the state of written communication in business. The authors of these articles point out the avoidable costs in employee time, poor product quality, and customer dissatisfaction that are entirely due to miscommunication of the written word. Examples range from nonuse or misuse of commas, wrong word choices, cloudy syntax, and jumbled organization to factual errors and misinformation.

For years I have been collecting such articles in order to motivate students in the business writing course I teach. I don't know just how seriously the students take these articles. (After all, I have my priorities and they have theirs.) But I can say that the articles give me much to think about. And my thoughts are these: How can I teach so as to send these young people out to their first jobs able to compose, at least, a clear two-sentence or one-paragraph memo, and, if I'm lucky, a soothing letter to an irate customer? Is drill in the mechanics the answer? Just how much time should be spent on the basic principles of written communication and how much on specific types of letters, memos, reports? Should I follow the textbook faithfully? And do I really know what these students will need in order to write effectively on their future jobs?

Like most academics, my experience in the real world of business is limited to being a consumer rather than a producer or a service person. Thus I tend to follow the precepts and patterns of business communication textbooks as guides. They advocate the several C's (conciseness, clarity, completeness, courtesy, correctness, coherence, etc.); the triangle of sender-message-receiver; the psychological patterns of good news, bad news, and persuasion; empathy and the "you"-attitude (or the "you-view," as I term it); good diction and tone; and avoidance of jargon and redundancy. But my doubts about the content of my course in business writing have grown each time I read an article decrying the lack of writing skills young people bring to their jobs. A sabbatical year has given me the chance to test what the textbooks say.

Through contacts with friends, colleagues, and students, I compiled a list of several dozen people in business whom I might be able to interview. The names given to me ranged from vice-presidents of international corporations through middle managers (usually in human resource training) to individual small entrepreneurs. I wrote to these people asking if they would be willing to talk with me for an hour or so in order to answer this question: What should I teach my business writing students in order to prepare them as well as possible for the writing they will do on the job? As you might expect, more responses came from those near the top of the corporate structure than from those nearer the bottom.

Over four months, January to April, 1985, I interviewed a dozen people in business. I must keep them anonymous since I do not have their permission to specify them by name or company. They include a vice-president of a multinational high-tech corporation; a communications manager for the same corporation who is a former college English instructor; the vice-president of a large manufacturing firm; the training manager of a firm that makes products for factories and defense contractors; the manager for public affairs communications for a food processing conglomerate; a specialist underwriter and a personnel director of an insurance broker serving businesses and industries; a "director of corporate materials" for a manufacturer of insulated shipping containers: a vice-president for communications for a financial services corporation; an account executive, one of ten serving this area for a national training and development corporation; a "personnel and training coordinator" for a small company that serves all the stores in the state of a national fast food chain; the manager of education in the human resources department of another multinational high-tech manufacturer; and a program manager of supervisory development in the corporate headquarters of the same company. I believe I was fortunate in talking with people who are especially aware of problems in communication: those in training and development and those directly involved in communication themselves.

The interviews lasted about one hour each and were conducted informally. I took notes. but the conversations were not structured. I *did* go with some basic questions:

What do you see as the qualities of good writing?

Do you feel that miscommunication due to poor writing is a problem in your company?

What are your personal writing practices?

What are your expectations in the writing skills of entry-level employees?

What are your suggestions about how such people should be prepared in a business writing course?

Overall, their answers more than support the precepts to be found in typical business communication textbooks. Although they lack the terminology with which to name these qualities, they were unanimous in citing conciseness, even brevity, as a top priority in business writing. Apparently, the lack of time and the effort needed to plough through excess verbiage and irrelevant material is the reason they said things like, "Get to the point" and—"Put it on one page, or don't bother writing me." While not all cited conciseness as a number one quality of effective writing, everyone mentioned it.

Similarly, there was consensus in valuing correctness in the mechanics. One person said, "There's no such thing as a typo," and another proofreads outgoing memos and letters several times, even asking a third person to check for errors. The financial services company vice-president for communication pointed out the obvious result of faulty mechanics: the waste of time and money when work has to be redone several times. And another specified "poor grammar, misspellings, and homonym confusion" on her list of writing sins. For some, mechanical correctness is not a problem. Typically, they stated, "That's the secretary's responsibility," and, in one company, a special perk is a secretary who can compose an effective, error-free letter."

A quality often mentioned by the textbooks is conversational tone, naturalness, avoidance of "corpspeak." Whatever it is called, it was named by each person I talked with as a desirable quality. Some call it sincerity; others, less concise, said that a letter should sound as if "we were talking face to face." One said he does not like "lofty, third-person stodginess," and his own letter reflected this attitude. Another, with some academic experience, did mention a "friendly, conversational tone." And one said he likes an "upbeat, affirmative tone." Only one failed to note the quality of ease and friendliness as desirable in writing, perhaps because he himself was stiff and unforthcoming in the interview.

Surprisingly, almost all noted the awareness of audience as a necessary prerequisite to effective written communication. One, who was a former college English instructor, hence sophisticated in his terminology, mentioned the necessity of "writer's sensitivity to the audience, which implies not only avoiding jargon, but also using tact, indirection, and subtlety." Another saw the problem of lack of audience awareness when writers use "unnecessarily complicated constructions, buzz words, pomposity." Some spoke of considering the probable attitude of the reader and of the amount of time, precious to the reader, needed to cover a long document. Another mentioned the need for the writer's empathy that takes into account the readers needs, whether she or he has the background for understanding the communication and its purpose, as well as the purpose attitude and receptivity of the reader. And all but one mentioned this sensitivity to the audience—in short, what we teach as the "you-view." This would subsume several related ideas: conciseness, conversational tone because the reader will be put off by pretentious diction and complicated syntax; avoidance of jargon because the reader might not understand, particularly if it is used in order to impress. One executive was quite vehement in his dislike of long letters and memos and said that he throws away, unread, anything over one page!

Surprising, too, was the mention of logical organization. Almost everyone noted the need for a structure within a piece of writing. The former English teacher even expressed the need for writers to follow the classical rhetorical structures of arrangement, as, for example, according to importance of details or by comparison and contrast. Most were not as sophisticated in naming the devices of organization, but all were aware of its importance. A person who prepares training manuals mentioned her use of numbered paragraphs and underlining for emphasis as tools to help readers.

Finally, the vice-president in charge of communication for the investment services company mentioned, quite understandably, the need for writers not only to be aware of the corporate culture, but also to express that culture, whenever communication occurs, both within and outside of the company.

When those interviewed were asked about their personal writing practices, they sounded like classic textbooks. It was clear that all took their written expression quite seriously, especially at the higher levels of corporate structure. One vice-president uses handwritten, short notes to colleagues and dictates longer-messages. He works hard at sounding conversational, he said, but what he dictates is always improved on the typed drafts. Interestingly, when he is faced with a ticklish writing situation, one that demands thought and care, he reverts to longhand. A training director follows the orthodox procedure of producing first a sentence outline, then a first draft in longhand, then a dictation or a re-write in longhand for the final typescript, and finally a careful proofreading.

Another person, a training and development supervisor, does all her own writing and proofs all outgoing correspondence from her department. The industrial insurance specialist must collect statistical data before submitting his proposals (which is what most of his writing consists of), but the writing follows a pattern that is circumscribed and "pre-formed" because of the legal implications of his work. Whatever the method, it was clear that my informants took effective written expression very seriously and took the time and effort necessary to achieve their best result.

Whether or not they were saying what they thought an English teacher might want to hear, they were unanimous in citing good writing skills as a prerequisite for advancement in the job. One executive quoted his chief engineer, who said that competent engineers could be hired by the dozen, but there's a shortage of those who can put their ideas on paper clearly. This executive feels that a career can be advanced significantly by good writing skills. One of the representatives of a small training and development business said that while he and his colleagues had few opportunities for writing, he often heard clients' complaints about the poor skills of entry-level employees and told an anecdote of a memo at a large, multi-national organization which was "read" and initialed through seven levels without anyone detecting a major error in it.

The training director of a manufacturing company said several times that poor writing detracts from the effectiveness of the message and gives a poor image of the company and the writer because both come across as ignorant. The training director of another company, in charge of the after-hours educational program for some 17,000 employees, said that the several writing-improvement courses offered each quarter are always filled to capacity, even though they carry no credit, and guarantee no job advancement or salary increase. What this does indicate, she said, is a desire to improve a very important job skill. A manufacturing company executive feels that not only recent graduates, but people generally are deficient in writing skills. All agreed with the major comment in articles critical of the current state of clear and effective writing: This is a skill crucial to achievement in the corporate world.

If no new or startling research findings are themselves significant results, then what business people told me is valid since it confirms the tenets of the textbooks and consequently the content of business writing courses. Bolstered by the comments of those I spoke with, I'll return to the classroom with more confidence in what I'm teaching. I'll also be able to speak of the importance of writing skills as perceived by people of substance in the business community. Some of them have volunteered to speak to my classes or to be interviewed on videotape. Maybe what they have to say will be more convincing than the articles about why the junior executive can't write.

---

## PLANNING FORM AND OUTLINE: SUMMARY REPORT

**Background Information** (to be included in Introduction)

Title of article: "Speaking of Writing—Interviews with People on the Job"

Author: Madeline Hamermesh, Normandale Community College

Publication: *The American Business Communication Association Bulletin*

Date: March 1986

General subject:
(Purpose of article)
What people in the business world say is important in written communication.

**Content**
(Under Roman numerals, list main points of article. Under capital

letters, briefly explain necessary supporting details. The number of main points and supporting details will vary according to the article.)

I. Conciseness a top priority
   A. Brevity
   B. No excess verbiage and irrelevant material

II. Correctness in mechanics
   A. No typos
   B. Proofreading
   C. Saving of time and money

III. Conversational tone
   A. Naturalness
   B. No "corpspeak"
   C. No stodginess
   D. Friendliness

IV. Awareness of audience
   A. Avoiding jargon
   B. Considering attitudes and receptivity of reader
   C. "You-view"

V. Logical organization
   A. Order of importance
   B. Comparison and contrast
   C. Numbered paragraphs
   D. Underlining for emphasis

VI. Awareness of corporate culture

VII. Interviewees' personal writing practices
   A. Importance of written expression
   B. Procedure of outline, rough draft, and final draft
   C. Taking time and effort for best results

**Conclusion**

Business people were "unanimous in citing good writing skills as a prerequisite for advancement in the job." Also, "Poor writing detracts from the effectiveness of the message and gives a poor image of the company and the writer. . . ." The author's research interviews confirmed that the content of business writing courses is relevant to the business world.

## SAMPLE SUMMARY REPORT

The March 1986 issue of *The American Business Communication Association Bulletin* published an article by Madeline Hamermesh entitled "Speaking of Writing—Interviews with People on the Job." The article reports on the results of interviews with business people concerning written business communication.

Foremost, conciseness and brevity were stressed because of no time for "excess verbiage and irrelevant material."

Another area of value was mechanical correctness. Typos were just not acceptable. Thus, proofreading, saving time and money, was a critical part of writing.

Each person also mentioned conversational tone, naturalness, and friendliness in the correspondence language, rather than "corp-speak" or stodginess.

Another prerequisite for effective written communication was audience awareness; that is, consideration of the reader's attitude and receptivity, lack of jargon, and the "you-view."

Logical organization was another important point. A planned approach, "according to importance of details or by comparison and contrast," along with enumerated paragraphs and underlining, was suggested.

A final feature mentioned was awareness of corporate culture.

The business people were quite serious about their personal written expression. They emphasized an outline, rough draft, and final draft, with careful proofreading. Taking the time and effort produced the best results.

In conclusion, interviewees unanimously cited "good writing skills as a prerequisite for advancement on the job." Ms. Hamermesh concluded, ". . . what business people told me is valid since it confirms the tenets of the textbooks and consequently the content of business writing courses."

## ACTIVITY 13-G: Summary Report

In the library find a magazine article or report that is related to your technology and is at least two pages long. Make a copy of the article to hand in with your report. Using the Planning Form, outline the article; then follow the procedures on pages 285–89 to write the summary report. If your report is acceptable, proceed to Activity 13-H. If your report is not acceptable, correct the errors indicated. Your instructor will decide whether you have achieved a passing grade or should write a second summary report on a new topic. After achieving a passing grade, proceed to Activity 13-H.

## ACTIVITY 13-H: Final In-Class Report

Your instructor will give you topics to choose from, in your technology, to write your final report in class. Using one of the topics given, write a persuasive report. You may use a dictionary, the modules, or any other resource you would like to use to write your paper. Hand in the Planning Form, rough draft, and revised draft. If your final report is not acceptable, you will be asked to write a second report on a new topic. When it is acceptable, you will have completed this module.

**Feedback 13-A**

Topic:   Coping Skills for Stress Management

   I.  Organization
      A.  Make a daily plan
      B.  Have a contingency plan
      C.  Accumulate several chores to do at once
      D.  Eliminate duties that frustrate you
      E.  Include fun things in your schedule

  II.  Delegation of authority
      A.  Have children do certain household chores
      B.  Share jobs with others at work
      C.  Hire someone to do certain jobs

 III.  Appearance
      A.  Smile
      B.  Wear clothes you feel good in
      C.  Pay attention to neatness and cleanliness

  IV.  Exercise
      A.  Use deep breathing techniques for relaxation
      B.  Work out aerobically at least three 20-minute sessions per week
      C.  Run, walk, bicycle, swim, or play tennis or racketball regularly

   V.  Nutrition
      A.  No caffeine
      B.  No sugar
      C.  No drugs
      D.  No alcohol

PLANNING FORM: TECHNICAL PROCEDURE REPORT

*Background Information*

**Procedure:**

**Audience:**

**Purpose:**

**Format:**

*Content*

**Necessary materials:**

**Definition of special terms:**

**Preparation:**

**Steps in procedure and identifying information:**
(Use command verbs)

**Precautions to emphasize:**
(Crucial steps, possible difficulties, or places where errors are likely to occur)

**Concluding remarks:**
(Importance of usefulness of the procedure)

*Background Information*

**Subject:**

**Controlling idea (thesis):**

**Format:**

**Point of view:**
(second person, you; third person, one, he, she, or they)


*Content*

**Introduction:**
(Thesis statement and report plan—summary of major arguments)


1.  **Major argument 1**

    A.  **Supporting evidence 1**

    B.  **Supporting evidence 2**

    C.  **Supporting evidence 3**


2.  **Major argument 2**

    A.  **Supporting evidence 1**

    B.  **Supporting evidence 2**

    C.  **Supporting evidence 3**


3.  **Major argument 3**

    A.  **Supporting evidence 1**

    B.  **Supporting evidence 2**

    C.  **Supporting evidence 3**


**Concluding remarks** (challenge to the reader):

*Person Interviewed*

**Name:**

**Address:**

**Position:**

**Date of interview:**

*Content*

**Questions:**

**Major impression from interview:**

**Major headings of report:**

**Concluding remarks:**
(Importance or usefulness of interview)

*Background Information*

**Items to be analyzed:**

**Audience:**

**Format:**

*Content*

**Introduction:**
(Situation requiring recommendation, specifications of desired item, items being analyzed and compared)

**Major points of comparison:**
(Headings)

**Data on each item:**

**Conclusion:**
(Item recommended, reasons for choice, reasons for rejecting other items)

*Background Information* (to be included in Introduction)

**Title of article:** (in quotes)

**Author:**

**Publication:** (underlined)

**Date:**

**General subject:**
(Purpose of article)

**Content**
(Under Roman numerals, list main points of article. Under capital letters briefly explain necessary supporting details. The number of main points and supporting details will vary according to the article.)

    **I.**

        **A.**

        **B.**

   **II.**

        **A.**

        **B.**

        **C.**

**III.**

        **A.**

        **B.**

*Conclusion* (restatement of main point of article)

**Precautions**

Do not add your opinion.

Make sure summary is only 5 to 10 percent of original article.

Avoid plagiarism. Use quotes around author's exact words.

# MODULE 14

# Business Letter Writing

OBJECTIVE: The letters and memos you write represent you personally just as your personal appearance does. This module will teach you how to write the main types of business letters and communications.

Upon completion of this module, you will be able:

To define the purpose and focus of business letter writing.

To write five types of business letters using appropriate form and focus.

To compare the business letter and the office memo.

To write two types of interoffice memos.

When you graduate and move into the job market, in order to get a good position, you will need to master two important areas of knowledge: (1) the technical skills necessary to perform your job well, and (2) the communication skills required to convey information effectively. While your technology courses are designed to give you proficiency in the technical aspects of your job, your English courses are set up to prepare you for the kinds of writing and speaking you will do as part of your duties. In particular, this course will enable you to communicate in writing with forceful letters that will not only enhance the company you work for, but give you personal credibility in your field. Letter-writing techniques should not be minimized; your letters may become important company records.

### Purpose

First, take a look at the *purpose* of business writing. When you write a letter, the critical thing is that the reader must understand the message. In addition, the letter should build and maintain the company's goodwill through an attitude of making and keeping friends. Ultimately, the letter should motivate readers to accomplish the writer's purpose.

### Focus

To fulfill this purpose, your letter should *focus on the reader*. Put yourself in the place of the reader; remember that he or she will be looking at the letter to determine how to benefit from it. Apply the principles of psychology about what motivates people: the need for financial gain, personal comfort, status, and physical well-being. Living in the computer age makes it even more important to give readers a sense of personal recognition. Use the person's name once in the body of the letter. Follow the "you approach" by avoiding too many **I**'s or **We**'s in the message. The use of these psychological principles will let the reader know that his or her interest is your concern.

### Wording

The *wording* of your business correspondence can help you achieve your purpose and focus on the reader. Using the following list of 15 C's will allow you to maintain the overall positive tone that you want to achieve:

courteous—pleasant, polite
cordial—friendly, congenial

clear—understandable

concise—brief

complete—comprehensive

coherent—unified, flowing

concrete—exact, specific

common—familiar, jargon-free

candid—forthright, open

concerned—interested, helpful

considerate—tactful

convincing—persuasive

credible—believable

conversational—not stiff and formal

correct—error-free

No matter what your message, whether positive or negative, use this checklist to avoid wording that is abrasive, stiff, unfriendly, or unclear. Use active rather than passive voice. A positive manner and conversational tone can help you influence the reader and accomplish your purpose.

## Tone

You cannot compose anything without being aware of *tone*. The tone of your correspondence will depend on the writer's position in relation to the person to whom it is addressed. When writing, you should try to strike a balance in the level of your language. You should avoid:

wordiness—*in this day and age, prior to the time that*

clichés—*selling like hotcakes, stick to your guns*

slang—*super, cool*

technical jargon—*prioritize, impacted*

outdated language—*as per our conversation, pursuant to*

contractions—*he's, it's*

Your letters should reflect the tone you use in conversation, rather than the formal business phrases traditionally associated with business letters and legal documents. Since correspondence is often retained as company records, keep your language objective and factual.

One good way to evaluate your tone is to read your letters as if you were receiving them. Would you respond favorably to their tone?

### Guidelines

To conclude the discussion on psychology of business writing, let us consider a few remaining general guidelines. As a superior writer, you must know your subject thoroughly. In addition, it is worthwhile to offer to be helpful to the reader whenever you can. Even if it is not required of you, you can volunteer useful information for the reader's benefit. You can facilitate action by making it easy for the reader to respond with a tearsheet, a self-addressed card, or even a phone number. Take care to be prompt in responding to business correspondence, and let the reader know you are dealing with the situation immediately. You can achieve success in your on-the-job writing by paying careful attention to (1) your purpose of clear communication, (2) your emphasis on the reader's self-interest, and (3) your positive wording.

## PART II: PLANNING

### Parts

A good business letter does not just happen; it comes from thoughtful preparation and planning. If you compare a letter to a conversation with a friend, you can break it into *three distinct parts:*

1. Greeting and purpose
2. Details
3. Goodbye

A typical social conversation on your part might go something like this:

Hello. How are you?
I would like you to go to the theater with me. (*Greeting and purpose*)
It will be on Saturday at the college auditorium starting at 2:00 P.M.
Tickets are $10 each. I will meet you in the lobby at 1:30. (*Details*)
I'll look forward to seeing you Saturday.
Bye. (*Goodbye*)

Breaking a task into its parts always makes it simpler to accomplish. If you are careful to include all three parts in your letters, you will have a well-balanced communication.

### Outline

Using the three parts of a letter as a skeleton, you can *outline* your message so that it communicates effectively.

First, decide on an appropriate opening sentence. Do not jump right in to the body of the letter; have at least one sentence that is introductory. For example, **Thank you for your (order, letter, reply,** etc.); or, **It is good to have you as a customer. . . .**

Next, determine the purpose of the letter. State it briefly in the paragraph following your introductory sentence. If you are responding to a letter, you should mention its subject. For instance, **I appreciate being asked to speak to your group. . . .**

Then gather all the information (*details*) you need to achieve your purpose. Ask yourself: who? what? when? where? why? how? as they apply to the situation. Then organize this information in an orderly flow in your next paragraph or paragraphs. If you have a great deal of information, you may want to use additional paragraphs.

To close, construct an appropriate paragraph of leave-taking, one that will ensure goodwill. For example, **We are happy to do business with you** or **We will look forward to hearing from you,** etc. If you desire certain action, you should suggest it before closing.

Following this plan will enable you to construct a proper business letter. Be sure to include all three sections.

### Emphasis

A significant consideration in the overall plan of your letter is *emphasis*. How do you give prominence to your most important ideas? You can do this by managing (1) space, (2) location, and (3) mechanics. The amount of space you devote to an idea indicates its importance. Obviously, the greater the development, the greater the emphasis. Also, emphasis can be achieved by location in a prominent position; for example, the beginning of ending statements. The use of mechanics is another way to highlight ideas. Such techniques as enumeration (lists), indentation, capitalization, underlining, and bold print can call the reader's attention to points of importance.

In summary, planning can be a productive effort when it (1) utilizes the three parts of a letter (*greeting and purpose, details,* and *farewell*), (2) establishes an outline using those parts, and (3) gives proper emphasis to the ideas of greatest importance.

To help with planning, refer to the Planning Forms for business correspondence at the end of this module. Complete the Planning Form to outline your information before writing a rough draft.

## PART III: FORMAT

### Letter Style

When writing a business letter, you have certain options in the area of style. Once you are on the job, you will discover what style your company prefers for its letters. It is wise to follow that preference. *Two basic styles* emerge as the common ones found in most businesses.

1. The block style
2. The modified block style

In the block letter, every line begins at the left margin—unless. of course, the printed letterhead is centered at the top of the page. See the following sample.

SAMPLE BLOCK FORMAT

**FAULK ENGINEERING**
**1011 SELSEY ROAD**
**CHICAGO, IL 60600**

2

April 15, 1988
   2–5
Mr. Robert Hooper
Shane Manufacturing
211 North Second Street
Toms River, NJ 08642

   2

Dear Mr. Hooper:

   2

The engineering firm of Naugle, Canterbury & Buhr, Inc., has been contracted to survey a building designed by the Seashore National Bank. The purpose of the survey is to recommend necessary changes in faulty, oversized, or inefficient equipment.

   2

In the survey, we discovered that a refrigeration unit has no nameplate. The only information we have is that it is manufactured by your company and its serial number is 8660-7891-512-3.

   2

To help us make the proper recommendations, would you please send us information on the refrigeration unit. Helpful data would include the power requirements, the full-load coefficient of performance, and the capacity.

   2

We would appreciate any information that you are able to supply as soon as possible.

*Right-margin labels:* Letterhead — Date — Inside Address — Salutation — Body

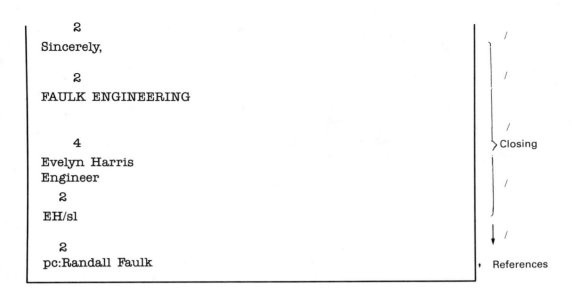

```
    2
Sincerely,

    2
FAULK ENGINEERING                                    ⎫
                                                     ⎬ Closing
    4
Evelyn Harris
Engineer
    2
EH/sl
                                                     ⎭
    2
pc:Randall Faulk                                     • References
```

In the modified block letter, the date and complimentary closing begin at the center point. Often it has indended paragraphs, as in the following sample. However, another acceptable version of the modified block letter does not have indented paragraphs.

SAMPLE MODIFIED BLOCK FORMAT (with indented paragraphs)

FAULK ENGINEERING
1011 SELSEY ROAD
CHICAGO, IL 60600

April 15, 1988

Mr. Robert Hooper
Shane Manufacturing
211 North Second Street
Toms River, NJ 08642

Dear Mr. Hooper:

The engineering firm of Naugle, Canterbury & Buhr, Inc., has been contracted to survey a building designed by the Seashore National Bank. The purpose of the survey is to recommend necessary changes in faulty, oversized, or inefficient equipment.

In the survey, we discovered that a refrigeration unit has no nameplate. The only information we have is that is manufactured by your company and its serial number is 8660-7891-512-3.

To help us make the proper recommendations, would you please send us information on the refrigeration unit. Helpful data would include the power requirements, the full-load coefficient of performance, and the capacity.

We would appreciate any information that you are able to supply as soon as possible.

Sincerely,

FAULK ENGINEERING

Evelyn Harris
Engineer

EH/sl

pc:Randall Faulk

## Sections of a Letter

As you can see from the sample block letter there are *seven sections* of a standard business letter:

1.  Letterhead (or return address)
2.  Date
3.  Inside address
4.  Salutation
5.  Body
6.  Closing
7.  Reference notations

The *letterhead* or **return address** gives the writer's complete address. Many businesses provide stationery with preprinted letterheads. Usually, if you use printed letterhead, the address is centered. Do not create letterheads for your assignments in this book. Use the return address format. Begin the return address at the left margin for a block style or at the midpoint of the page for a modified block style. Your name should not appear in the typewritten return address although it may be included in the printed letterhead. Use the two-letter, all capitals abbreviations for states (see list on page 345).

Place the **date** below the return address. Be sure to write out the month; do not abbreviate. Remember to place a comma between the day of the month and the year. The correct style is this: June 25, 1989.

The **inside address** is approximately five spaces below the date, depending on the length of the letter, and begins at the left margin. You should include the name and title of the person to whom you are writing, as well as the company name and address. Write out such words as *Street, Route, Road, Drive,* etc. Use the two-letter state abbreviations accepted by the United States Post Office.

The **salutation** begins two spaces below the inside address starting at the left margin. *Be sure to note that it is followed by a colon in a business letter.* (You can use a comma in a social business letter.) Use the person's name and title when you can. The salutation should agree with the first line of the inside address. If you do not know the person's name, call the receptionist of the company to find out before writing. *Ms.* is always correct for women unless you know that they would prefer to be referred to as *Miss* or *Mrs.*

```
Dear Professor Bartlett:

Dear Senator White:

Dear Ms. Abbott:

Dear Mrs. Canfield:
```

When you do not have a specific person to write to, it is customary to use some of the following salutations for a company:

```
Dear Sir:

Gentlemen:

Ladies and Gentlemen:

Dear Order Department Staff:
```

The **body** of the letter should follow your plan as you have outlined it. It should contain a minimum of three paragraphs, with a paragraph for the greeting and purpose, at least one paragraph for the details, and a paragraph for the farewell. These paragraphs are single spaced, with double spacing between each. In the block style, the paragraphs begin at the left margin. In the modified block style, you have the option of beginning them at the left margin or indenting them five spaces.

The **closing** consists of the complimentary close, such as *Sincerely* or *Cordially yours,* the company name (optional), the writer's signature, the typed name, and the person's job title. Note that the second word in a closing, such as *Cordially yours,* is not capitalized. In the block style the closing is found at the left margin. In the modified block style, it is directly under the return address at the midpoint of the page. The complimentary close is typed two spaces after the last paragraph. The company name is two spaces below the complimentary close. The typed name is four spaces below the company name, leaving room for the handwritten signature. If a job title is included, it follows immediately after the typed name.

The **reference notations** are typed two spaces below the closing at the left margin. They include such items as the initials of the writer and the typist, enclosures, attachments, personal copies, etc.

Examine the final copy of your letters to see that you have included all seven sections so that you can be sure of having a polished, professional letter which reflects the business image you wish to convey.

## Mechanics

If you pay careful attention to mechanical details, your business correspondence will project the image of a professional organization. The proper use of elements such as abbreviations, numbers, and capitalization is crucial in making your writing effective. Here are a few pointers concerning these mechanical elements as they occur in business letters. For a more detailed discussion, consult a handbook, grammar text, or dictionary.

**Abbreviations.** Use them sparingly in your business letters. First of all, in the return address and the inside address, use the two-letter, all capitals abbreviations for states given in the list on page 345. (In the body of the letter, spell out the state.)

EXAMPLES

DE for Delaware
CA for California
TX for Texas

When using the name of a state in the body of a letter (not in the form of an address), spell out the state name.

EXAMPLE

The new business is located in Flint, Michigan.

Write out words such as *Street, Route, Road, Lane*, etc., in an address. Also, write out *East, West, North,* and *South.*

EXAMPLES

Mr. William Freeman
Route 1, Box 218
Lewes. DE 19958

Ms. Carmen Ortega
301 East Peach Lane
Salisbury, MD 21801

Write out the months of the year in a date.

EXAMPLE

February 27, 1989

Write out titles following names.

EXAMPLE

Mr. Lamden Carey
Director of Personnel

Do not use contractions in business writing.

EXAMPLES

Use *it is* instead of *it's*.
Use *they are* instead of *they're*.
Use *do not* instead of *don't*.

You may abbreviate the name of an organization if you spell it out at the first use.

EXAMPLE

Registration for students at **Delaware Technical and Community College** will be on March 9, 1989. Students participating in **DTCC** orientation should report at 9:00 a.m.

**Numbers.** Check carefully to see if you should use words or figures. The basic rule is to use words for **one** through **ten** and figures for **11** and up.

In a date, do not use the ordinal ending (**th** or **nd**) unless it precedes the month.

EXAMPLE

**15th of February** (not **February 15th**)

Use the proper sequence of month, day, and year for dates.

EXAMPLE

**February 15, 1989** (not **15 February 1989**)

**Capitalization.** Capitalize all important words in a subject line or title. It is not necessary to capitalize the articles (**a, an, the**) or the prepositions under four letters (**of, in, to,** etc.).

Underline the titles of books and the names of newspapers and magazines. Enclose the titles of chapters, articles, short stories, and poems in quotation marks.

In your textbook *Writing Skills for Technical Students,* your assignment is to read Module 14. "Business Letter Writing."

Use lowercase abbreviations for **a.m.** and **p.m.**

EXAMPLES

9:00 p.m.
10:30a.m.

## Length

The question of *length of a letter* has no firm rules as far as number of sentences or number of paragraphs. You will have to pull some items from the list of C's to determine proper length. Ask yourself: "Is the letter clear, concise, and complete?" If you can say Yes to all three, your length is appropriate.

More definite guidelines can be given regarding *sentence and paragraph length. A* sentence should average 20 words; however, it is wise to keep in mind that variety in length makes for more pleasant reading. Basic paragraph length is about 100 words for the body (*details*) and 40 or 50 words each for the introduction (*greeting and purpose*) and conclusion (*goodbye.*). Generally speaking, a paragraph should be no longer than 8 typewritten lines.

## Appearance

The *appearance* of your letter is not to be overlooked because it reflects the kind of person you are and the type of company you represent. Neatness is a critical factor. If you are typing the letter, take care to avoid smudges and strikeovers. If you are using a word processor, try to use a letter-quality printer. The quality of paper is also a consideration. Professional-looking letterhead makes a good impression. Finally, the way the letter is balanced on the page can enhance the image. For example, if your letter is short (up to 125 words), you can use 2-inch margins and begin the date at line 19. For an average letter (up to 225 words), use 1½-inch margins and begin the date at line 16. A long letter (more than 225 words) should have 1-inch margins and the date at line 13. In other words, balance the white space on your sheet of paper.

## Summary

You will become increasingly proficient at developing the kind of business communications that enhance your company's public relations and build your own reputation as an employee of merit if you remember to do the following:

1. Apply the psychological principles of effective business writing.
2. Focus on the reader.
3. Use positive tone and proper wording.
4. Plan well by outlining the three parts of a letter while giving proper emphasis to your key points.
5. Follow the guidelines on style, format, and appearance.
6. Proofread carefully for correct mechanics.
7. When in doubt, consult a reference manual.

## PART IV: REQUEST LETTER

The most common type of letter that you will write is a letter of request. It is used to request information, services, or products. As the writer making the request, you must make it as easy as possible for the receiver to answer your request. This can be accomplished through proper planning and consideration for the reader.

To make it easier for the reader to comply, be sure to include the following specific information:

What is wanted
Who wants it
Why it is wanted
How it will be used
List of a few clear, direct questions (if appropriate)
Deadline for necessary action
Expression of appreciation

In the request letter, the *you approach* is very helpful because it allows you to indicate how the reader can benefit by sharing his or her knowledge and services. Whenever possible, show the reader the advantages of responding positively and promptly to your request.

Your choice of words will have a direct effect on the response you get. For example, if you are asking someone to be a guest speaker, **Would you consider addressing our group . . .** is preferred to **I would like you to speak. . . .** The second example is really not a request; it is a polite command. Likewise, **Would you send me information about . . .** is more appropriate than **I need information on. . . .**

The main parts of a request letter consist of an opening, a body, and a conclusion—at least three paragraphs. The purpose of the opening is to involve the reader by gaining his or her attention and to establish the purpose of the letter. The body contains all the necessary details the recipient will need to make a response. In your closing, be sure to ask for a due date or a specific time by which you need to have the response. Most of the time, the reader will respond to a reasonable request. Remember that the reader cannot know what you want if you do not give specific instructions.

For a sample of the content of a request letter, see the Sample Block Format on page 308. Then proceed to Activity 14-A.

## ACTIVITY 14-A: Writing a Request Letter

Using the Planning Form at the end of this module, write a request letter using one of the following situations. Supply the necessary details of who, what, when, where, and why to make the letter complete. Hand in your Planning Form, rough draft, and revised draft.

1. Write a letter asking a person to speak at a meeting of a professional organization of which you are a member.
2. Write a letter asking an expert in your field to judge a professional contest related to your technology.
3. Write a letter asking a person working in your technical field to grant you an interview for your class assignment in the Report Module on page 280–85.
4. You have been offered a job with a particular company. Write a letter asking a person working for that firm to give you some information about the company and the particular job you have been offered.

## PART V: LETTER THAT SAYS "NO"

A refusal letter is, of course, the opposite of a request letter. However, each is based on the same psychology: Both the writer and the receiver want something. The writer who views the request from both sides will write a better refusal letter—and keep the goodwill of the customer.

An objective of the "No" letter is to appeal to the requester's reason and, in so doing, avoid hurt feelings.

One of the most effective techniques for preparing the reader for a refusal is to begin with a brief statement agreeing with some aspect of the request—not the basic issue, but some attitude or feeling the reader has expressed. This action paves the way for you to present the reasons why the request cannot be met and then to refuse. You can end on a statement that keeps the door open for further business and keeps the customer's goodwill.

The best plan for a "No" letter is to use the **Stroke-Zing-Stroke** approach. In other words, you sandwich the bad news between good news.

Stroke 1. Begin in a positive way and also restate the original request. (*Opening paragraph*)

Zing 2.  State the reasons for your position: then refuse clearly. (*Second—and possibly third—paragraph*)

Stroke 3.  End with a positive statement. (*Final paragraph*)

To make this letter effective, you should not begin the opening paragraph or even the second paragraph with a negative statement. It is important to introduce the letter constructively and to present your reasons first so that the reader will remain objective.

In addition to the **Stroke-Zing-Stroke** plan of action, there are some things to avoid as you write your "No" letter:

1.  Do not ever heap blame on the reader.
2.  Do not shut the door of communication.
3.  Do not forget that you may someday be requesting a favor of the reader.
4.  Do not be indefinite, but give a clear-cut "No."

See the sample "No" Letter following.

SAMPLE "NO" LETTER

THE COLUMBUS VILLA
605 NORTH BOARDWALK
OCEAN CITY, MD. 21842

May 15, 1990

Mr. James L. Pike
President
Pike's Art Supplies
501 Main Street
Tamarac, New Jersey 20092

Dear Mr. Pike:

Preparations for the Mid Atlantic Craft Fair are well under way! How very thoughtful of you to remember us and to consider our lodging facilities for your company's representatives attending the fair.

Normally we would have no trouble accommodating your party of twenty people. However, due to the expansion of the show, we are

almost completely booked for the week in June that you have
requested. We regret that we are unable to offer you the
accommodations that you require.

If we can be of further service for future shows at Convention Hall,
please do not hesitate to contact us. How about a reservation now
for next year's Mid Atlantic Craft Fair?

Again, we certainly appreciate your continued patronage.

Sincerely yours,


Fred Baker

Manager

Following these guidelines carefully, you should be ready to
write a letter that says "No." Proceed to Activity 14-B.

## ACTIVITY 14-B: Writing a "No" Letter

Using one of the situations in Activity 14-A, write a letter of refusal to a
specific request. Use the Planning Form at the end of this module to outline
your ideas. Remember to restate the request and to use the **Stroke-Zing-
Stroke** approach. Hand in your Planning Form, rough draft, and revised
draft.

## PART VI: SOCIAL BUSINESS LETTER

Some of your most pleasant and worthwhile friendships may develop out of acquaintances made in the course of doing business. These
friendships can improve business relationships, enhance the standing of
your company in the community, and help you personally.

Several social occasions may require a written business response
on your part: congratulations, thank-yous, condolences, follow-ups for
job interviews. This type of letter, the social business letter, is different
from the standard business letter you have been studying. It deals

with a subject that is somewhat social in nature, yet it is written to someone with whom you have more of a business than a personal relationship.

The tone of the social business letter (also known as the *personal business letter*) should reflect as closely as possible the degree of familiarity that has developed between the correspondents, neither overdoing it on one hand nor understating it on the other. With this in mind, you can choose between two formats for social business letters: the *formal* and the *informal.*

**Formal**

The formal letter is sent to a person you know on a business level but not on a personal level. You would not be on a first-name basis with this person. There are several features of this style:

1. Often written on standard $8\frac{1}{2}'' \times 11''$ company letterhead or $7'' \times 9''$ monarch size stationery
2. Includes return address
3. Includes date
4. Usually typed
5. Uses colon after salutation
6. Places inside address five lines below writer's signature

**Informal**

The informal letter is sent to someone you know on a more personal basis. The features of this style are as follows:

1. Omits company return address or uses home address
2. Includes date
3. May be handwritten on plain stationery or $4'' \times 5''$ informal note paper
4. Uses first name for salutation
5. Uses comma after salutation
6. Omits inside address

**Content**

Once you decide whether to use the formal or the informal approach, start writing your social business letter. The tone should be in keeping with your personal relationship with the reader and the nature of the message. Guard against being overly familiar.

XYZ DISTRIBUTORS
1200 THIRD STREET
FLINT, MI 48502

April 15, 1986

Dear Mr. Hawaki:

As one of the suppliers of your newly opened Tahiti-Aki marina-hotel complex, we took space in the usual congratulatory advertisement in the newspapers.

I personally want to go further and tell you how much our staff enjoyed working with you on the challenging job of bringing Tahiti-Aki to completion. Doing business with you during construction—even when the rain undermined the driveway and the truckers struck—was a real pleasure.

Best wishes to you in your new operation.

Sincerely,

*Sally*

Sally Baker

Mr. B.A. Hawaki, President
Hawex Hotel Co.
59 Surfside Avenue
San Diego, CA 92100

As in other business letters, you should try to have three paragraphs: greeting and purpose, details, and closing. Obviously, this will not always work if the message is very short, but you should try to avoid a one-line or one-paragraph letter. Even though these letters are more difficult to compose, the reader will appreciate your efforts.

April 15, 1988

Dear Kelly,

I was very happy to learn at the regional dinner last night that the next company newsletter will contain an announcement of your stepping up to the supervisor's chair.

Congratulations! You have more than earned this. Keep up the fine performance.

I look forward to seeing you in early July.

Cordially,
Jennifer

### ACTIVITY 14-C: Writing a Social Business Letter

Using the Planning Form at the end of this module to outline your ideas, choose one of the following occasions to write a social business letter. Select the appropriate style—formal or informal—depending on your relationship with the person to whom you are writing and the nature of the letter. Supply the necessary details to make the letter complete. Hand in your Planning Form, rough draft, and revised draft.

1. Write a thank-you letter to follow up the interview you conducted in Module 13.
2. Write a letter of condolence.
3. Write a letter of congratulations.
4. Write a follow-up letter for a job interview.

After carefully proofreading the final draft, submit your letter to your instructor for evaluation.

## PART VII: RESUMÉ AND LETTER OF APPLICATION

### Resumé

A *resumé* (sometimes called a *personal data sheet*) and a letter of application work as a pair to help you get a job. To capitalize on this teamwork, use each for its specific purpose: (1) the resumé to show what you have accomplished and (2) the letter of application to show what you can do for the employer.

You should construct your resumé first so that the letter of application can highlight certain items on the resumé. Your first step is to take a personal inventory. What have you got to offer? Your education and training are important, of course. So is any work experience, whether full-time or part-time. Even if the experience is not directly related to the job you are seeking, these jobs indicate that you are willing to work. Also evaluate your personality; demonstrate your reliability, resourcefulness, energy and inventiveness.

The second step in job seeking is to find out which firms have openings for applicants with your qualifications. Among the people who study the needs of companies and could help you are your instructors and department chairpersons. Your college placement service may give you advice and lend you catalogs and other literature. Other productive sources include the college library, which houses the *Occupation Outlook Handbook,* plus newspaper want ads, the local Chamber of Commerce, and company employees. Get the names of the personnel directors of companies in which you are interested by telephoning the receptionists at their offices. If the plants or offices are within driving distance, take a look at them from the outside. Some may surprise you. Seeing the place to which you will address your letter sometimes helps you get the firm in focus and makes the writing a little easier. If you are answering a classified advertisement of a firm some distance away, check your sources for information, especially your college library.

Once you have decided which companies you would like to work for match your assets against the requirements of those companies. Determine what you have that the company needs.

Now you are ready to write the resumé. The resumé is a summary of your objectives, education, work experience, and accomplishments—all in one easily digested page. Because employers will use the resumé for quick reference, provide all information in the form of tabulated lists and clearly marked headings, not sentences and paragraphs. Study the following guidelines carefully.

GUIDELINES FOR A RESUMÉ

Essential items:
  name, address, phone number (*in prominent place*)
  job objective
  work experience (*reverse chronological order, including job titles*)
  professional memberships or licenses
  educational background (*including all degrees and dates received*)
  achievements (*honors, publications, awards*)
  military service

Optional items:
    description of jobs held
    readiness to move to another area
    statement of personal health
    skill areas
    foreign languages
    class standing (*if in top 25th percentile*)
    summer jobs (*if recent graduate or previous relevant jobs*)
    personal qualities, such as dependability, initiative, etc.
    special courses or major (*if lacking in work experience*)
    percentage of educational expenses earned working part
    time and attending school
    community activities

Unnecessary items:
    causes for terminating previous employment
    salary information
    photograph
    names of family members
    references
    high school information (*except honors*)
    personal data
    hobbies and interests

Appearance:
    neatness
    balance of white space—good margins
    good-quality 8½″ × 11″ paper (*tinted, if desired*)
    special effects (*selective use of caps, underlining, bold print,
    tabulation, asterisks*)
    letter-quality printing on word processor
    double-spacing between headings
    dates in prominent locations
    copies xeroxed or printed but not carbon

Other tips:
    Use reverse chronological order for education and work
    experience.
    Use active verbs, such as **audited, assisted, demonstrated,
    developed, facilitated, maintained, performed, reorganized,
    scheduled, supervised,** etc.
    Use phrases rather than sentences.
    Take care not to lie or be too modest.
    Proofread carefully for spelling and mechanics (*letter perfect*).
    Place most impressive, either experience or education, at top.
    Be consistent in wording (*verb phrases, noun phrases,* etc.) and
    in format (*indentations, use of periods, highlighting, underlining,
    etc.*).

**FELICITY A. SALVATORE**
**ROUTE 1, BOX 283-D**
**WEST, TX 76691**
**(817) 555-6384**

### PROFESSIONAL OBJECTIVE

Work in Systems Operations. Ultimate goal: Programmer

### EDUCATION

Delaware Technical and Community College, Southern Campus, Associate Applied Science Degree in Data Processing, June 1987

### SYSTEMS AND PROGRAMMING EXPERIENCE

— Systems project: Designed, coded, documented and implemented an inventory control and sales analysis application on an IBM XT personal computer for a retail establishment. This project utilized Ashton-Tate's Dbase III+ software.

— Created, processed, and updated both sequential and indexed sequential files in COBOL and RPG II on an IBM 4331 mainframe in an ICCF/POWER environment.

— Created and processed tables in COBOL, Assembler, and RPG II programming languages.

— Designed, coded, tested, and debugged programs in COBOL, RPG II, and Assembler Language to produce several levels of totals on business reports.

— All programming has been accomplished using standard industry program design technique with full documentation.

### WORK EXPERIENCE

| | |
|---|---|
| 1983—present | Cashier, Hardee's Seaford, DE |
| | Duties: Taking orders and serving the public. |
| 1983–1984 | Tutor, Delaware Technical and Community College, Writing Lab |
| | Duties: Answering telephone, delivering messages, grading papers, and running errands. |
| 1982 | Mailroom Aide, DuPont Co., Seaford, DE |
| | Duties: Sorting and stamping mail, checking purchase orders, working with UPS packages. |
| 1980–83 (summers) | Assembly Line Worker, Vlasic's, Millboro, DE |
| | Duties: Working on assembly line and hand packing. |

### PERSONAL QUALITIES

Dependability, punctuality, creativity, eagerness to learn, stamina, inquisitiveness.

**MITCHELL E. CARROLLTON**
**123 East Green Street**
**Dagsboro, DE 19939**
**(302) 539-5725**

**PROFESSIONAL OBJECTIVE:** Data Analyst

**EXPERIENCE**

9/79–6/86    Mid-Sussex Health Center, Millsboro, DE
Position: Administrative Assistant
Duties:    Handled all administrative and bookkeeping functions, supervised all office personnel, served as secretary to Management Committee which directed operations of Health Center.

8/76–12/83    Cohee & Co., Clarksville, DE
Position: Bookkeeper—Part-time
Duties:    Managed payroll and payroll taxes, reconciled bank statements, posted general ledger.

5/75–7/79    Pennisula Construction Company, Lewes, DE
Position: Office Manager
Duties:    Administered office; performed bookkeeping, secretarial, and receptionist functions.

5/72–1/75    J. Conn Scott Furniture, Selbyville, DE
Position: Bookkeeper
Duties:    Authorized payroll, maintained accounts receivable and payable, posted general ledger.

3/70–4/72    National Cash Register, Millsboro, DE
Position: Senior Accounting Clerk
Duties:    Handled payroll and payroll taxes, accounts payable and receivable, general ledger, and bank reconciliations.

**EDUCATION**    Delaware Technical and Community College, Georgetown, DE, Associate of Applied Science Degree in Data Processing. Cumulative GPA 4.0.
Applicable Courses: Structured ANSI COBOL, Assembler, RPG, FORTRAN, BASIC, DOS/VSE Job Control Languages; Systems Design, and Accounting.

## ACTIVITY 14-D: Writing a Resumé

Fill out the Planning Form for a Resumé at the end of this module. Use it as a guide to construct the professional resumé which will accompany your letter of application when you begin your job search. The resumé should be typed or printed with letter-quality printing on 8½" × 11" bond stationery. Hand in your Planning Form, rough draft, and revised draft.

### Letter of Application

As you begin your job search, your *letter of application* may be your first contact with the prospective company. For this reason, it is one of the most important pieces of correspondence you will write. Its purpose is to introduce yourself to the employer, to mention the position you are interested in, and to state your qualifications for the position. It should underscore your strong points and in so doing convince the employer that he or she will profit by granting you an interview.

The letter of application is designed to be accompanied by the resumé, which details your education and work experience. The letter complements the resumé in highlighting aspects of your background that would make the company want to hire you rather than someone else.

As in a standard business letter, the letter of application should maintain the "you approach" by letting the employer know how he or she can benefit by hiring you. Keep in mind that neatness and grammatical correctness are of prime consideration. A well-organized letter of application contains three sections.

The *introduction* should indicate the position you are applying for, if practical. You might also mention where you heard of the opening and arouse the reader's interest in you by mentioning some special qualification you have for the job.

The next section, the *body,* should emphasize the items on your resumé that you especially want to be noticed. Stress the strongest points of your education, your experience, and your abilities as each relates to the particular job you are applying for. Refer the reader to specific points on your resumé. Save any discussion of salary for the interview.

The main purpose of the *conclusion* is to secure the job interview. Before requesting a meeting, first summarize your qualifications for the job and comment on what you can do for the company. Then suggest setting up the interview. It is appropriate to give an idea of the times you are available, but be sure to be tactful and not demanding.

Do not use **I** as the first word in the letter.
Use name and title of company representative (*can be obtained by phoning receptionist*).
Mention specific job you are applying for.
Refer to special abilities or achievements.
Mention name of person who told you about job opening.
Include attention-getting statement in opening paragraph.
Place strongest points first, either education or experience.
Indicate your date of availability.
Match your training to employer's needs.
Refer to personal qualities, such as dependability, inventiveness, interest in working with people, etc.
Note outstanding academic record.
Comment on excellent health or lack of handicaps.
Refer to particular items on resumé.
Summarize qualifications for job.
Suggest direct action to secure interview.

Notice how these principles are applied in the following letter of application.

## SAMPLE LETTER OF APPLICATION

2371 Newlin Avenue
Milltown, DE 19944

May 5, 1988

Mr. George V. Ballantyne
Personnel Manager
114 Mellegood Street
Atlanta, GA 30342

Dear Mr. Ballantyne:

The position of draftsman-detailer in your industrial construction section is of interest to me. Word about the opening came through Mr. Harold MacKenzie, our college placement officer at Delaware Technical and Community College, Southern Campus. Mr. MacKenzie thinks that my qualifications might be of special interest to you.

One June 10, I receive my Associate of Applied Science Degree in Architectural Design at Delaware Tech and will be available for employment. Throughout training, my interests have been directed toward industrial design, not only because I prefer it, but also because I was fortunate enough to gain some practical experience assisting designers of poultry construction during the last two summers and on weekends. (See attached resumé.)

This winter at B.A. Brewer, Inc., I worked independently at night and weekends making detailed shop and field drawings for welded and mechanically assembled steel structures and shop drawings from engineering sketches of grain elevators, screw conveyors, and storage silos.

One of my original designs for improving brooder construction was adopted and made standard equipment by Brewer. The design and model of a solar-heated brooder, which I developed as my term project at college, is now on display at the local Chamber of Commerce.

Could I have an interview with you? I am seeking a position outside the poultry industry because I would like to enter a broader field of design where I could gain wider knowledge and find more opportunities to apply my ideas. During the day my phone number is (302) 730-6434.

Your consideration of my application would be greatly appreciated.

Sincerely,

*Chris Freeman*

Chris Freeman

Enclosure

---

## ACTIVITY 14-E: Writing a Letter of Application

Use the Planning Form for the Letter of Application at the end of this module to outline your ideas; then write a letter applying for a specific position. Use your typewriter or a word processor with a letter-quality printer. Use good-quality 8½″ × 11″ stationery. Hand in Planning Form, rough draft, and revised draft.

## PART VIII: THE MEMO

The *memorandum (memo)* is a form of communication used to relay information within a company. Like the business letter used to send information between companies, the memo is an important part of business communications. By nature, the memo is usually concerned with one topic. and it should be kept as short as possible. It communicates a message best when it is concise and direct. The memo is usually conversational in tone and free of business jargon, clichés, and slang.

There are three main kinds of memos. The *informative memo* is the most common type, and it is used to relay announcements and to verify data. A second type, the *persuasive memo,* tries to persuade the reader to adopt a point of view through the use of logical argument and example. The third kind of memo, used to *seek information,* consists of specific questions to answer or checklists to mark, or it may simply ask for general comments.

The memo follows the same basic guidelines of all good business writing. It should be organized and have a beginning, a middle, and an end. It should be proper in tone and correct in form, and its message should be clear and concise.

**Form**

The unique characteristic of the memo is its use of the heading, which consists of four parts. Usually a company will have the four basic parts of the heading preprinted on company stationery. The format varies with the company, but the following is common practice:

> TO:      Name, Title
> FROM:    Name, Title
> SUBJECT: Treat Like a Title (capitalize all words of more than four
>          letters)
> DATE:    Write out (no abbreviations)

Sometimes the order of the heading will be different and placement on the page may vary, but all four sections should be present. Memos are usually typed and, unlike the business letter, are not signed. Instead, the sender usually initials the FROM line in ink to authorize distribution of the completed memo after checking it for accuracy.

> FROM:    Mary Jarvis      *MJ*

Memos use traditional paragraph format which may or may not be indented; most are not. There is no salutation or closing as in the business letter. The memo is single-spaced, with double spacing between paragraphs and three spaces between the heading and the first paragraph.

**Content**

The memo has three basic parts: introduction, body, and closing. A properly planned memo communicates the message clearly and eliminates wordiness and repetition.

The *introduction* of the memo should state the purpose and summarize the most important point. In other words, memos begin with the main message; there is no working up to the major point. To be effective, the memo should deal with one issue at a time. Once the purpose of the memo is established, the succeeding paragraphs can fill in necessary details.

The *body* of the memo supplies those facts or details the reader needs to make a decision, to understand the purpose of the memo, or to form an opinion. Included are facts, arguments, questions to be answered, historical background, charts, enumerated items, or other relevant material. The content depends on the purpose of the memo. Details should be presented logically, and therefore need to be stated only once. If the body is extremely long or complicated, headings at the left margin or centered will help to section the information.

The *conclusion* is a very important part of the memo that is frequently overlooked. It should leave the reader with some idea of a follow-up. It may give the reader something to think about or do; it may ask for a response by a given date; it may ask the reader to present ideas in writing or to get in touch with the sender of the memo. In a longer memo, it may be a summary of the main points. Frequently, the conclusion consists of an **IF** statement that will give the recipient some idea of the next step in the process.

EXAMPLES

If you cannot attend the meeting, please send a substitute.
If you have any questions, please contact me.

**Sample Memo**

This sample is an illustration of how a memo should look in form and how the content can be expressed.

TO: All Personnel

FROM: Jason Parker, Chief Security Officer *JP*

SUBJECT: Parking Permits

DATE: September 19, 1988

Due to the increase of illegally parked cars in the Company parking lots, new parking stickers have been issued and will be distributed to all Company personnel. As of October 1, any car parked in a lot without a proper sticker will be towed at the owner's expense.

Stickers are available at the Security Office and can be issued during working hours. Each department will be given released time before the end of the month so that all personnel can get needed stickers. To speed up the process, please bring the following information with you:

1. Car registration
2. Company identification card

You will need a separate sticker for each car you possess. You should place the new sticker on the back right bumper for easy verification in the lots.

If you have any questions, please contact me at Extension 32.

Before writing your memo assignment, study the charts on pp. 332–33 comparing the business letter and the memo.

## ACTIVITY 14-F: Writing a Memo

Choose one of the following situations and compose a memo using the correct format and tone. Outline your ideas by following the Planning Form for a Memo at the end of this module. The assignments listed below give only sketchy details. Supply all the specific information, such as names, dates, times, places, etc., necessary to make your memo complete and accu-

# COMPARISON OF BUSINESS LETTER AND MEMO

|  | BUSINESS LETTER | MEMO |
|---|---|---|
| AUDIENCE | person outside company | person inside company |
| FORMAT | heading or letterhead, date, inside address, salutation, body, closing, signature, reference notations<br>always has full signature<br><br>modified block style uses indented paragraphs, no indented paragraphs for block style<br>uses 8–½″ × 11″ stationery | to, from, subject and date lines; body; initials or signature<br><br>may have initials beside FROM line or full signature at end of body<br>no indented paragraphs<br><br>may use 8–½″ × 11″ stationery or half sheet if message is short |
| TONE | positive, conversational, "you" flavor, focus on reader—very few **I's** and **we's** | positive, direct, not personal, concentrates on message, not person |
| ORGANIZATION OF BODY<br>Introduction<br><br>Body<br><br><br>Conclusion | at least 3 paragraphs<br>cordial greeting and brief statement of purpose<br>background and details of message<br><br>cordial leave-taking | first paragraph<br>direct statement of purpose<br><br>background and details of message (often in numbered list)<br>request for action or follow-up |

## COMPARISON OF BUSINESS LETTER AND MEMO FORMATS

| BUSINESS LETTER | MEMO |
|---|---|

rate. Make sure your memo has at least three sections of content. Proofread your work. Finally, initial your memo when it is completed to indicate that it is ready for distribution. Hand in Planning Form, rough draft, and revised draft.

1.  You are the in-company Blue Cross representative. Write a memo to all company personnel to explain that everyone will be required to have a medical checkup every two years. The checkups will be paid for by the company. Announce a meeting (give specifics) at which a Blue Cross spokesperson will explain the new requirement for physicals.

2.  You are the in-company United Fund representative. Announce a meeting for all personnel to discuss the possibility of automatically deducting contributions from employees' paychecks.

3.  You are a part-time college student. Write a memo to your supervisor asking for a one-year leave of absence so that you can complete your associate degree.

4. You are in charge of company parking. Schedule a meeting to discuss the parking problems in the company lot and to arrive at a solution to improve the situation.

## PART IX: TRANSMITTAL LETTER AND TRANSMITTAL MEMO

Often in business, a report is written and must be sent to the proper people for review. It is important to have a transmittal (or cover) letter or memo to accompany the report.

The transmittal letter is used if the material is being sent outside the company. Because it is going to another establishment, it is in the form of a business letter and is typed on the firm's letterhead. The transmittal memo, using the standard memorandum form, is used if the material is being circulated within the company.

Because the primary purpose of the transmittal letter or memo is to identify an enclosed report, the correspondence should be relatively short. It should include the title of the report, the name of the person who requested it, and a one- or two-sentence description of the contents. The writer can also acknowledge the help that particular persons gave in compiling the report. Here are two samples.

### SAMPLE TRANSMITTAL LETTER

MEDICAL RESEARCH, INC.

SUITE 541

1012 ARCH AVENUE

ST. LOUIS, MO 63155

September 27, 1988

Mr. A. B. Jenkins

National Employment Agency, Inc.

4940 Bayview Drive

Chicago, IL 60600

Dear Mr. Jenkins:

We have completed the report, "Projection of Medical Laboratory Technicians' Employment 1990 to 1999," as requested by Mr. Hamilton Rose on May 17.

The survey was conducted among 1,409 recipients at 251 institutions, including public and private hospitals and commercial labs in 41 states. Variation in projected demand is broken down by geographic region.

Our interviewers are grateful for the assistance provided by Mrs. J. B. Brandor of the Health Department and Mr. James R. Glanding of the New York Laboratory Association.

Your comments will be welcome.

Sincerely yours,

MEDICAL RESEARCH, INC.

*Walter Lanahan*

Walter Lanahan
Director, Operations Division

WL/pm

Enclosure

pc: Mr. Harold Morakian

## SAMPLE TRANSMITTAL MEMO

TO: John Harr, National Director

FROM: Walter Lanahan, Operations Division *WL*

SUBJECT: Employment of Medical Laboratory Technicians

DATE: September 27, 1986

We have completed the report, "Projection of Medical Laboratory Technicians' Employment 1990 to 1999," as requested by Faye O'Hara on May 17.

The survey was conducted among 1,409 recipients at 251 institutions, including public and private hospitals and commercial labs in 41 states. Variation in projected demand is broken down by geographic region.

Our interviewers are grateful for the assistance provided by Mrs. J. B. Brandor of the Health Department and Mr. James R. Glanding of the New York Laboratory Association.

Your comments will be welcome.

After reviewing the guidelines for the transmittal letter and memo, proceed to Activity 14-G.

---
**ACTIVITY 14-G: Writing a Transmittal Letter or Memo**
---

Using the following details, write appropriate transmittal correspondence. Choose the transmittal letter format if the material goes outside the company or the transmittal memo format if the material is circulated within the company. Use the Planning Form at the end of this module to outline your information. Hand in Planning Form, rough draft, and revised draft.

1.  The report being sent is entitled "Analysis of Maintenance Costs of Cooperative Farm Machinery in Iowa." This material is being sent by Jordan Davies, chief analyst of the John Brix Implement Corporation, 118 Marriott Way, Des Moines, IA 50300, to the attention of Mr. Gentry Yves, Agri-Business Development Center, 496 Eden Avenue, Boston, MA 02165. The report was requested by Ms. Gale Roper.
2.  The report is also being sent to Jordan Davies' supervisor, Calvin Jarvis, president of the John Brix Implement Corporation.

After carefully proofreading the final draft of your assignment, submit it to your instructor for evaluation.

**Letter style:** (block or modified block)

**Return address:** (or letterhead)


**Date:**
**Inside address:**
    Name and title:
    Mailing address:

**Salutation:**
**Body:**
    Greeting and purpose:

    Appropriate details:

    Conclusion:

**Closing:**
    Complimentary close:
    Company name: (optional)
    Signature: (name and title)

**Reference notations:**


**Content Check:**
    Courtesy
    Clearness
    Completeness
    Conciseness
    Correctness

**Letter Style:**   (block or modified block)

**Return address:**   (or letterhead)

**Date:**
**Inside address:**
   Name and title:
   Mailing address:

**Salutation:**
**Body:**
   Acknowledge request:

   Include neutral statement:

   Give reasons for refusal:

   Refuse directly:

   Suggest alternate plan:

**Closing:**
   Complimentary close:
   Company name:   (optional)
   Signature:   (name and title)

**Reference notations:**

**Content check:**
   Positive tone
   Appreciation shown
   Door kept open
   No blame placed on reader

**Letter style:** Formal or Informal?

*FORMAL*                                    *INFORMAL*
**Return address:**


**Date:**                                   **Date:**
**Salutation:** (colon)                     **Salutation:** (comma)
**Body:**                                   **Body:**
    Purpose of letter:   Purpose of letter:

    Appropriate comments:   Appropriate comments:

    Conclusion:          Conclusion:

**Closing:**                                **Closing:**
    Complimentary close:   Complimentary close:
    Signature:           Signature:
    Typed name: (optional)
**Inside address:** (after closing)


**Content Check:**
    Appropriate tone for reader
    Informality
    Cordiality

**Name:**

**Address:**

**Phone:**

**Job objective:**

**Education:** (reverse chronological order—include degrees, dates, major courses, military training)

**Work experience:** (reverse chronological order—include full-time and part-time with dates, job titles, and brief description of duties)

**Special achievements:**

**Military service:**

**Personal qualities:**

**Professional memberships:**

**Letter style:**  (block or modified block)

**Return address:**

**Date:**
**Inside address:**
    Name and title:
    Mailing address:

**Salutation:**
**Introduction:**
    Position applied for:

    Knowledge of opening learned through:

    Interest-getting statement:

**Body:**
    Comments on education:

    Comments on work experience:

    Comments on personal data:

**Conclusion:**
    Summary of qualifications:

    Request for interview:

**Complimentary close:**
    Signature:
    Typed name:
**Reference notations:**

**To:** Name and Title

**From:** Name and Title

**Subject:** Brief phrase

**Date:** No abbreviations

**Introduction:** State purpose

**Body:** Give all supporting details

**Conclusion:** Give idea of follow-up. desired response, or summary of main points

**Content Check:**

Focus on one main point.

Use appropriate tone for reader.

Keep message simple.

Supply adequate supporting details.

Include all pertinent information.

State clearly the reader response you desire.

**Letter Style:** Block or modified block

**Return address:** (or letterhead)

**Date:**

**Inside address:**
Name and title:
Mailing address:

**Salutation:**

**Body:**
Title of report:
Who requested it:
Description of contents:


Acknowledgment of persons contributing information:


**Closing:**
Complimentary close:
Signature: (name and title)

**Reference notations:**


**Content Check:**
Brevity
Completeness
Proper business tone

**To:**    (name and title)

**From:**  (name and title)

**Subject:**

**Date:**

**Body:**
    Title of report:
    Who requested it:
    Description of contents:


    Acknowledgment of persons contributing:


    Concluding statement:


**Content Check:**
    Brevity
    Appropriate business tone
    Completeness

## State Abbreviations

| | | | |
|---|---|---|---|
| Alabama | AL | Missouri | MO |
| Alaska | AK | Montana | MT |
| Arizona | AZ | Nebraska | NE |
| Arkansas | AR | Nevada | NV |
| California | CA | New Hampshire | NH |
| Colorado | CO | New Jersey | NJ |
| Connecticut | CT | New Mexico | NM |
| Delaware | DE | New York | NY |
| District of Columbia | DC | North Carolina | NC |
| Florida | FL | North Dakota | ND |
| Georgia | GA | Ohio | OH |
| Hawaii | HI | Oklahoma | OK |
| Idaho | ID | Oregon | OR |
| Illinois | IL | Pennsylvania | PA |
| Indiana | IN | Rhode Island | RI |
| Iowa | IA | South Carolina | SC |
| | | South Dakota | SD |
| Kansas | KS | Tennessee | TN |
| Kentucky | KY | Texas | TX |
| Louisiana | LA | Utah | UT |
| Maine | ME | Vermont | VT |
| Maryland | MD | Virginia | VA |
| Massachusetts | MA | Washington | WA |
| Michigan | MI | West Virginia | WV |
| Minnesota | MN | Wisconsin | WI |
| Mississippi | MS | Wyoming | WY |

# Spelling Aids

OBJECTIVE: This Appendix is designed to help you review five fundamentals of spelling. It should be referred to whenever you are in doubt or need to brush up. Activities and Feedback are provided so that you may test yourself. Keep a log of the words that give you trouble, and review them until you master them.

Upon completion of this Appendix, you will be able:

To apply four fundamental rules that govern changes in spelling of root words when adding prefixes and suffixes.

To maintain a log of commonly misspelled words for practice and mastery.

**Prefixes**

Which is correctly spelled:

**displease** or **dissplease?**

**disatisfy** or **dissatisfy?**

Did you guess or did you know? It's very simple if you take the words apart:

**dis   please**

**dis   satisfy**

These words begin with the prefix **dis-** meaning *no* or *not*. A prefix is attached to the front of a word to change its original meaning.

**dis** + please = displease *(not to please)*

**dis** + satisfy = dissatisfy *(not to satisfy)*

A prefix never loses any of its letters when it is tacked on to the beginning of a word. That is why words like **displease** can have only *one* **s,** while **dissatisfy** must have *two:* one belonging to **dis-** and one to **satisfy.**

Let's look at a few more **dis-** words.

**dis** + similar = dissimilar

**dis** + regard = disregard

**dis** + possess = dispossess

**dis** + service = disservice

**dis** + appoint = disappoint

You simply attach the word to the prefix. Don't drop or add any letters.

Here are four more common prefixes that give a word a negative meaning. Note the spellings.

| MIS- | | IL | |
|---|---|---|---|
| **mis** + shape = misshape | | **il** + luminate = illuminate | |
| **mis** + step = misstep | | **il** + legal = illegal | |
| **mis** + spell = misspell | | **il** + literate = illiterate | |

| | | |
|---|---|---|
| **mis** + state = misstate | | **il** + legible = illegible |
| **mis** + print = misprint | | **il** + legitimate = illegitimate |
| | | **il** + logical = illogical |

| UN- | IM |
|---|---|
| **un** + neighborly = unneighborly | **im** + movable = immovable |
| **un** + natural = unnatural | **im** + mortal = immortal |
| **un** + necessary = unnecessary | **im** + material = immaterial |
| **un** + noticed = unnoticed | **im** + mobility = immobility |
| **un** + fair = unfair | **im** + mature = immature |
| | **im** + partial = impartial |

The following prefixes change a word's meaning in a different way. The same spelling rule applies: prefix plus word, without dropping or adding any letters.

### OVER

**over** + run = overrun (two *r*'s)

**over** + flow = overflow (one *r*)

### UNDER

**under** + rate = underrate (two *r*'s)

**under** + take = undertake (one *r*)

---

### ACTIVITY Ap-A: Prefixes

Follow the directions for each item.

1. Add the prefix **dis-** to the following words:
   a. similar _____
   b. advantage _____
   c. locate _____
   d. satisfy _____
2. Add the prefix **mis-** to the following words:
   a. spell _____
   b. pronounce _____
   c. step _____
   d. fortune _____
3. Add the prefix **un-** to the following words:
   a. natural _____

b.  afraid _____

   c.  noticed _____

   d.  necessary _____

4. Add the prefix **il-** or **im-** to the following words:

   a.  legal _____

   b.  logical _____

   c.  material _____

   d.  mobile _____

5. Add the prefix **over-** to the following words:

   a.  run _____

   b.  flow _____

   c.  rate _____

   d.  take _____

6. Add the prefix **under-** to the following words:

   a.  rate _____

   b.  take _____

   c.  stand _____

   d.  refined _____

Check your responses in Feedback Ap-A at the end of this Appendix. Study
any words you missed. Then proceed to the section on Suffixes.

**Suffixes**

A suffix is tacked on to the *end* of a word. Like a prefix, it affects
the word's meaning. If you know the suffix that is added and you know
the original word, in most cases you'll have no trouble with the spelling.
Simply combine the two, without dropping any letters.

### -LY

practical + **ly** = practically

accidental + **ly** = accidentally

sure + **ly** = surely

extreme + **ly** = extremely

actual + **ly** = actually

sincere + **ly** = sincerely

| -NESS | -AL |
|---|---|
| mean + **ness** = meanness | vocation + **al** = vocational |
| drunken + **ness** = drunkenness | occasion + **al** = occasional |
| clever + **ness** = cleverness | function + **al** = functional |

|  -MENT  |  -LESS  |
|---|---|
| entertain + **ment** = entertainment | heart + **less** = heartless |
| arrange + **ment** = arrangement | plan + **less** = planless |
| improve + **ment** = improvement | doubt + **less** = doubtless |

|  -FUL  |  -EST and -ER  |
|---|---|
| success + **ful** = successful | kind + **est** = kindest |
| doubt + **ful** = doubtful | kind + **er** = kinder |
|  | high + **est** = highest |
|  | high + **er** = higher |

Sometimes a word acquires two suffixes:

occasion + **al** + **ly** = occasionally

doubt + **ful** + **ly** = doubtfully

heart + **less** + **ly** = heartlessly

function + **al** + **ly** = functionally

## ACTIVITY Ap-B: Suffixes

Follow the directions for each item.

1. Add the suffix **-ly** to the following words. Add an additional suffix when you need to.
   a. practical _____
   b. vocation _____
   c. occasion _____
   d. sincere _____
2. Add the suffix **-ness** to the following words:
   a. soft _____
   b. mean _____
   c. smart _____
   d. drunken _____
3. Add the suffix **-ment** to the following words:
   a. improve _____
   b. ship _____
   c. disillusion _____
   d. entertain _____
4. Add the suffix **-less** to the following words:
   a. heart _____

b. care _____

c. fruit _____

d. pain _____

Check your responses in Feedback Ap-B at the end of this Appendix. Study any words you missed. Then proceed to Aid 2.

## AID 2: DOUBLING FINAL CONSONANTS

The final consonant of a word must be doubled when adding a suffix beginning with a vowel *in the following situations:*

1. When a word has one syllable
2. When a two-syllable word is accented on the final syllable
3. When the final consonant has a vowel before it

### EXAMPLE

**Plan**—one-syllable word ending in a consonant preceded by a vowel.
**Planning**—final consonant is doubled before **-ing.**
**Planner**—final consonant is doubled before **-er.**
**Planned**—final consonant is doubled before **-ed.**

#### One Syllable

| | | | |
|---|---|---|---|
| swim | swimming | sit | sitter |
| bid | bidder | sad | saddest |
| hot | hottest | rob | robber |
| star | starred | win | winner |
| step | stepping | rub | rubbed |

### EXAMPLE

**Admit**—two-syllable word accented on final syllable (*mit*); word ends in a consonant (*t*) preceded by a vowel (*i.*)
**Admitting**—final consonant is doubled before **-ing.**
**Admitted**—final consonant is doubled before **-ed.**
**Admittance**—final consonant is doubled before **-ance.**

This spelling aid applies to thousands of words, so it's a good one to know. Here are a few examples:

#### Two Syllables

| | | | |
|---|---|---|---|
| remit | remittance | prefer | preferred |
| defer | deferred | submit | submitter |

| | | | |
|---|---|---|---|
| regret | regretting | commit | committing |
| control | controller | occur | occurrence |
| begin | beginner | | |

Note that the rule does not apply when the suffix begins with a consonant. For example, the final consonant is *not* doubled before the suffix **-ment.**

| Not Doubled | Doubled |
|---|---|
| deferment | deferred |
| preferment | preferring |
| commitment | committed |

Note also that the rule does not apply if there is no vowel before the final consonant of the accented last syllable:

EXAMPLE

accept—acceptance (**t** is not doubled)

---

**ACTIVITY Ap-C: Doubling Final Consonants**

---

Add a suffix beginning with a vowel to the following words:

1. sit _____
2. win _____
3. remit _____
4. prefer _____
5. occur _____
6. defer _____
7. rob _____
8. regret _____

Check your responses in Feedback Ap-C at the end of this Appendix. Study any words you missed. Then proceed to Aid 3.

---

**AID 3: *IE* AND *EI***

---

The spelling **ei** is used after the letter **c:**

| | | | |
|---|---|---|---|
| conceited | inconceivable | receive | perceive |
| ceiling | deceive | receipt | deceitful |

After other letters, the spelling **ie** is usually used:

| | | |
|---|---|---|
| niece | achieve | shield |
| believe | reprieve | relieve |
| mischief | grief | fiend |
| pierce | belief | yield |
| sieve | chief | apiece |

When the sound is long *a,* as in *weight,* use the **ei** spelling:

weigh

neighbor

eight

Memorize the following exceptions and note the various pronunciations:

| | |
|---|---|
| **leisure** | **foreign** |
| **either** | **seize** |
| **neither** | **species** |
| **weird** | **financier** |

---

**ACTIVITY Ap-D:** *IE* and *EI*

Complete the words by adding **ie** or **ei**.

1. conc _____ _____ ve
2. n _____ _____ ce
3. w _____ _____ ght
4. rec _____ _____ pt
5. ach _____ _____ vement
6. n _____ _____ ghborhood
7. bel _____ _____ ve
8. c _____ _____ ling
9. _____ _____ ghty
10. y _____ _____ ld

Check your responses in Feedback Ap-D at the end of this Appendix. Study any words you missed. Then proceed to Aid 4.

When a word ends in **e** and you want to add a suffix *beginning with a vowel* (such as **-ing, -able, -ible, -ation, -ous**), you usually drop the **e.**

| | | |
|---|---|---|
| use | using | usable |
| argue | arguing | arguable |
| imagine | imagining | imaginary |
| come | coming | |
| write | writing | |
| refuse | refusing | refusal |
| segregate | segregating | segregation |
| recognize | recognizing | recognizable |
| invite | inviting | invitation |
| obscure | obscuring | obscurity |
| reduce | reducing | reducible |

**EXCEPTIONS:**

Words that end in **ce** or **ge** *do not* drop the final **e** before **-able** and **-ous.** The **e** is retained to keep the c and g sounds soft (that is, like s and j, respectively) as they sound in the original word.

| | | | |
|---|---|---|---|
| outrage | outrageous | advantage | advantageous |
| courage | courageous | knowledge | knowledgeable |
| service | serviceable | notice | noticeable |

When you add a suffix *beginning with a consonant* (such as **-ty, -ment, -ly, -ful, -less, -ness, -teen**), the silent **e** is usually retained.

| | | | |
|---|---|---|---|
| nine | ninety | definite | definitely |
| advertise | advertisement | separate | separately |
| like | likely | nine | nineteen |
| waste | wasteful | severe | severely |
| improve | improvement | hate | hateful |
| shame | shameless | commence | commencement |
| excite | excitement | aggressive | aggressiveness |

## ACTIVITY Ap-E: Dropping Final *E*

Follow the directions for each item.

1. Add the suffix indicated.
   a. refuse + ing _____
   b. knowledge + able _____
   c. examine + ing _____
   d. come + ing _____
   e. hope + ing _____
   f. imagine + ation _____
   g. reduce + ing _____
   h. notice + able _____
   i. courage + ous _____
   j. write + ing _____
2. Add the suffix indicated.
   a. nine + ty _____
   b. sincere + ly _____
   c. obscure + ly _____
   d. improve + ment _____
   e. excite + ment _____
   f. separate + ly _____
   g. waste + ful _____
   h. use + ful _____
   i. love + ly _____
   j. late + ly _____

Check your responses in Feedback Ap-E at the end of this Appendix. Study any words you missed. Then proceed to Aid 5.

## AID 5: CHANGING *Y* TO *I*

When a word ends in y, and a *consonant* comes before the **y**, change the **y** to **i** before all suffixes except those beginning with **i.**

EXAMPLES:

**Try** ends in **y**
A consonant (**r**) comes before the **y**
Change the **y** to **i** = **tri**
Add the suffix **-ed: tri** + **ed** = tried

**Rely** ends in **y**
A consonant (**l**) comes before **y**
Change the **y** to **i** = **reli**
Add the suffix **-es: reli** + **es** = **relies**

When the suffix begins with **i**, do not change the **y** to an **i**. The y is retained to avoid having two **i**'s next to each other.

EXAMPLES

**try** + **ing** = **trying** (*not* "triing")
**rely** + **ing** = **relying** (*not* "reliing")

Here are some other examples. Notice when the **y** changes to **i** and when it remains a **y.**

EXAMPLES

marry—married      happy—happiest      city—cities
lonely—loneliness  defy—defied         pretty—prettiest
carry—carrying     cry—crying          envy—envied

When a word ends in **y,** and a *vowel* comes before the **y,** the **y** usually does not change when you add a suffix.

EXAMPLES

**Enjoy** ends in **y**
A vowel (**o**) comes before the **y**
**enjoy** + **able** = **enjoyable**
**enjoy** + **ed** = **enjoyed**

Here are more examples:

EXAMPLES

boy—boyish      play—plays            lobby—lobbyist
key—keys        monkey—monkeying      pray—prayed

---

**ACTIVITY Ap-F: Changing _Y_ to _I_**

Follow the directions for each item.

1. Add the suffix **-ed** to the following words:
   a. rely _____
   b. volley _____
   c. defy _____
   d. vary _____
2. Add the suffix **-ing** to the following words:
   a. defy _____
   b. marry _____

c. try _____

d. enjoy _____

3. Add the suffix **-s** or **-es** to the following words:

a. play _____

b. jockey _____

c. vary _____

d. city _____

Check your responses in Feedback Ap-F at the end of this Appendix. Study any words you missed. If any of the five Spelling Aids gave you trouble, ask your instructor for additional practice before taking the Spelling Test.

## FEEDBACK FOR APPENDIX

### Feedback Ap-A

1. a. dissimilar
   b. disadvantage
   c. dislocate
   d. dissatisfy
2. a. misspell
   b. mispronounce
   c. misstep
   d. misfortune

3. a. unnatural
   b. unafraid
   c. unnoticed
   d. unnecessary
4. a. illegal
   b. illogical
   c. immaterial
   d. immobile

5. a. overrun
   b. overflow
   c. overrate
   d. overtake
6. a. underrate
   b. undertake
   c. understand
   d. underrefined

### Feedback Ap-B

1. a. practically
   b. vocationally
   c. occasionally
   d. sincerely
2. a. softness
   b. meanness
   c. smartness
   d. drunkenness

3. a. improvement
   b. shipment
   c. disillusionment
   d. entertainment
4. a. heartless
   b. careless
   c. fruitless
   d. painless

### Feedback Ap-C

1. sitting, sitter
2. winning, winner
3. remitting, remitted, remittance
4. preferring, preferred (in *preference,* do not double the consonant *r* because the accent is on the first syllable)
5. occurring. occurred, occurrence
6. deferring, deferred

357

7. robbing, robbed, robber
8. regretting, regretted, regrettable

**Feedback Ap-D**

1. conceive
2. niece
3. weight
4. receipt

5. achievement
6. neighborhood
7. believe

8. ceiling
9. eighty
10. yield

**Feedback Ap-E**

1.  a. refusing
    b. knowledgeable
    c. examining
    d. coming
    e. hoping
    f. imagination
    g. reducing
    h. noticeable
    i. courageous
    j. writing

2.  a. ninety
    b. sincerely
    c. obscurely
    d. improvement
    e. excitement
    f. separately
    g. wasteful
    h. useful
    i. lovely
    j. lately

**Feedback Ap-F**

1.  a. relied
    b. volleyed
    c. defied
    d. varied

2.  a. defying
    b. marrying
    c. trying
    d. enjoying

3.  a. plays
    b. jockeys
    c. varies
    d. cities

# GLOSSARY

**Action verb** (*See also verb*) An action verb shows physical or mental engagement. The action can be done.

> Examples: He *typed* the letter. (physical action)
> I *thought* about the experiment. (mental action)

**Active voice** A verb in the active voice shows the subject of the sentence performing or doing the action of the verb.

> Example: *Mr. Jones spoke* to the new employees.

**Address** (*See also noun of address* and *comma*) When an address appears in a sentence, place a comma after the name, after the street, after the city, and after the zip code. If no zip code is used, place a comma after the state. There is no comma between the state and the zip code.

> Example: Deliver the package to Dr. Marvin Bronson,
> 112 Oak Lane, Panhandle, Texas 76691, before 5 P.M.

**Adjective** An adjective describes or modifies a noun or pronoun. It answers the questions: what kind? which one? how many? how much? The articles *a, an,* and *the* are classified as adjectives.

> Examples: He dictated *a long* letter. (what kind)
> *That* syringe is sterilized. (which one)
> The department needed *five* typewriters. (how many)
> We ate *enough* lunch. (how much)

**Adverb** An adverb modifies or describes a verb, an adjective, or another adverb. It answers the question how, where, when, or how often. Adverbs frequently end in *-ly*.

Examples: She dresses *smartly*. (how)
I put the memo *there*. (where)
He will call the boss *soon*. (when)
The doctor makes rounds *frequently*. (how often)

**Agreement**   (*See subject–verb agreement or pronoun–antecedent agreement*)

**Antecedent**   An antecedent is the word a pronoun stands for.

Example: The *nurse* filled *her* syringe.

**Apostrophe**   The apostrophe (') is a mark of punctuation used to show possession or a contraction.

Examples: architect's drawing (possession)
can't (contraction)

**Appositive**   An appositive is a word or phrase that renames a noun or pronoun immediately preceding it. It is set off by commas.

Example: Mr. Green, *the electrician in charge,* supervised the wiring job.

**Body**   The Body is that part of a paragraph or report that develops or supports the Topic Sentence.

**Case of pronouns**   (*See pronoun case*)

**Clause**   A clause is a group of words containing a subject and verb. (*See also dependent clause or independent clause*)

**Clause signal**   A clause signal is a word that introduces a dependent clause. It is sometimes referred to as a subordinate conjunction.

Examples: if, when, although, etc.

**Cliché**   A cliché is an expression overused to the point that it loses its effectiveness.

Examples: six of one, half-a-dozen of another
pretty as a picture, sly as a fox

**Collective noun**   A collective noun refers to a group but is singular when the group is thought of as a unit.

Examples: family, team, committee, group, etc.

**Comma**   A comma (,) is a mark of punctuation used to indicate an address, an appositive, coordinate adjectives, a date, an interrupter, an introductory clause or phrase, a noun of address, or a series. A comma is also used to prevent misreading, to follow a transitional expression, and to separate two independent clauses with a conjunction. (*See also address, appositive, coordinate adjectives, date, independent clause, interrupter, introductory clause, introductory phrase, misreading, negative expression, noun of address, series, transitional expression*)

**Comparative degree**   (*See degree of comparison*)

**Comparison of adjectives and adverbs**   (*See degree of comparison, verb*)

**Complete verb**   The complete verb consists of the main verb and all of its helpers. (*See also helping verb* and *main verb*)

Example: The disk *has been sitting* in that spot for years.

**Compound subject**   (*See also subject*) A compound subject consists of two or more subjects linked by a conjunction.

Example: *Typing* and *shorthand* are essential skills for the secretary.

**Compound verb**   (*See also verb*) A compound verb consists of two or more verbs linked by a conjunction.

Example: A good secretary *types* rapidly and *transcribes* accurately.

**Concluding sentence**   A concluding sentence comes at the end of a paragraph or report and restates the topic sentence in different words.

**Conclusion**   A conclusion is the final paragraph in a report. It sums up the main ideas presented and restates the introduction in different words.

**Conjunction**   (*See also coordinate conjunction* or *subordinate conjunction*) A conjunction is used to join words or groups of words.

**Consonant**   The consonants are those letters of the alphabet that are not vowels. The vowels are *a, e, i, o,* and *u* (and sometimes *y*).

**Controlling idea**   A controlling idea is a word or phrase located in a topic sentence. It narrows the subject or tells the reader what will be said about the subject.

Example: Sponsoring a family of "boat people" can be a *rewarding experience.*

**Coordinate adjectives**   Coordinate adjectives are two or more adjectives that modify the same noun. They are separated by a comma.

Example: The treaty ended a *long, bitter* struggle.

**Coordinate conjunction**   A coordinate conjunction is a word used to join together two words, two phrases, or two clauses.

Examples: and, but, or, nor, for, so, yet

Example: He saw the file, *but* he did not touch it.

**Coordination**   (*See also coordinate conjunction, independent clause, subordination*) Coordination, in sentence structure, refers to connections of two independent clauses with a coordinate conjunction.

Example: The surveyors set up the transit, and they surveyed the property lines.

**Correlatives**   (*See also parallel structure*) Correlatives are pairs of conjunctions that are used together. They require parallel construction.

Examples: not only . . . but also
either . . . or
neither . . . nor
both . . . and

**Date**   In a date, the month and day are treated as a unit, and the year is treated as a unit. In the context of a sentence, follow the day and the year with commas.

Example: He applied for the job on August 12, 1980, after hearing of the opening.

**Degree of comparison**   When using an adjective or an adverb to compare items, the degree of comparison depends on whether you are comparing two items (*comparative degree*) or three or more items (*superlative degree*). The word referring to one item is in the *positive degree*.

| POSITIVE | COMPARATIVE | SUPERLATIVE |
|----------|-------------|-------------|
| good | better | best |
| smart | smarter | smartest |
| efficient | more efficient | most efficient |

**Dependent clause**   A dependent clause is a group of words containing a subject, a verb, and a clause signal. A dependent clause cannot make sense as a sentence when it stands alone; it is a fragment.

Examples: When the mail comes in. . . .
After the storm hits. . . .
While I was typing. . . .

**Direct address**   A noun of direct address is used when you use a person's name or title to speak directly to that person.

Example: *Mr. Basin*, here is the memo.

Call for the ambulance, *nurse.*

You can see, *Ms. Smathers*, we have complied with your request.

**Direct object**   (*See also object*) A direct object is a word that receives the action of the verb.

Example: The nurse gave the *shot.*

**First person**   (*See person*)

**Fragment**   A fragment is a part of a sentence, not a whole sentence. It may be a dependent clause, a prepositional phrase, a verbal phrase, a subject, or a verb.

Examples: Because the machine was broken. (dependent clause)
Out of the office and down the hall. (prepositional phrases)
Breaking the test tubes. (verbal phrase)
The executive of the plant. (subject)
Ordered the new safety policy. (verb)

**Future tense**   (*See also past tense present tense,* and *tense*) A verb in the future tense shows an action or state of being taking place at a later date.

Example: I *will type* the letter tomorrow.

**Gerund**   A gerund is the *-ing* form of the verb used as a noun. It is also called a verbal.

Examples: *Typing* is a necessary skill.
He is best at *calculating* interest.

**Helping verb**   (*See also verb*) A helping verb is used in conjunction with the main verb. It helps the main verb express action or make a statement.

Examples: She *will be* fired tomorrow.
The memo *has been* typed.

**Indefinite pronoun**   (*See also pronoun*) An indefinite pronoun refers to a general rather than a specific person, place, thing, or idea.

Examples: each, anyone, everyone, all, few, nobody, anybody, etc.

**Indefinite reference**   In an indefinite reference, a pronoun does not have a specific antecedent.

Example: *It* says in the paper that costs are rising.

**Independent clause**   An independent clause is a group of words with a subject and a verb. It is not introduced by a clause signal; therefore, it makes a complete sentence. An independent clause stand-

363

ing alone is punctuated as a complete sentence. Two independent clauses in the same sentence can be punctuated several ways: with a comma and a conjunction, with a semicolon, or with a semicolon and a transitional expression followed by a comma.

Example: The *mail arrives* at ten each morning.

**Infinitive** (*See also verbal*) An infinitive is a verbal that can be identified by *to* plus a verb.

Examples: to draw, to type, to work, to edit.

**Interfering words** Interfering words are phrases that come between the subject and the verb and often cause problems with subject–verb agreement.

Example: *Each* (of the secretaries) *types* well.

**Interjection** An interjection is one of the eight parts of speech. It usually expresses strong emotion and is not grammatically connected to the rest of the sentence.

Examples: Oh! Heavens! Well!

**Interview report** (*See also report*) An interview report is the written account of a personal interview. It can be written in the regular report format with an Introduction, Body, and Conclusion, or in a question-and-answer format.

**Interrupter** An interrupter is a word or phrase that breaks the grammatical flow of a sentence. It is set off by commas.

Example: Mr. Blandell, *on the other hand*, is an experienced draftsman.

**Introduction** The introduction is that part of a report or paper that indicates the subject and controlling idea. Coming at the beginning, it sets forth the purpose of the piece of writing.

**Introductory clause** (*See also comma* and *dependent clause*) An introductory clause is a dependent clause that comes at the beginning of a sentence. It should be followed by a comma.

Examples: While I was typing, the power went off.

**Introductory phrase** (*See also comma* and *phrase*) An introductory phrase comes at the beginning of a sentence. Usually followed by a comma, it may be a prepositional or verbal phrase.

Example: Typing the memo quickly, she made several errors.

**Irregular verb** (*See also verb*) An irregular verb is one that does not form its past tense by adding *-d* or *-ed* to the present tense.

Examples: wear    wore    worn
    eat     ate     eaten

**Linking device** (*See transitional expression*)

**Linking verb** (*See also subject complement, verb*) A linking verb joins the subject to a noun or an adjective that follows the verb. It does *not* show action; it merely shows a state of being. It acts like an equal sign and is followed by a subject complement.

Examples: The nurse *seems* efficient.
    The nurse *is* my friend.

**Main clause** (*See independent clause*)

**Main verb** In a sentence containing a verb phrase (the verb and its helpers), the main verb is the last word in the verb phrase.

Example: He *should have been writing* the report.

**Major clause** (*See independent clause*)

**Minor clause** (*See dependent clause*)

**Misplaced modifier** A misplaced modifier can be a word, phrase, or clause that is positioned incorrectly in the sentence so as to cause misunderstanding or confusion.

EXAMPLES
Misplaced: The draftsman looked for the pencil in his cabinet that was missing.
Correct:  The draftsman looked in his cabinet for the pencil that was missing.

**Misreading, prevention of** (*See also comma*) Use a comma after a phrase at the beginning of the sentence when it is necessary to prevent misreading.

Examples: By 1999, 25 of these computers will no longer be in use.
    After shooting, the policeman put his gun in the holster.

**Negative expression** (*See also comma*) A negative expression is a phrase coming at the end of a sentence. It either asks a question or shows contrast. It is preceded by a comma.

Examples: Today is bitterly cold, *isn't it?*

**Nonrestrictive element** A nonrestrictive element is a word, phrase, or clause modifier that is not essential to the clear identification of the word it modifies. It is set off by commas.

EXAMPLES
Nonrestrictive: Mrs. Landers, *who works in Dr. Burroughs' office*, is an excellent
    secretary.

**365**

**Restrictive:**   The lady *who works in Dr. Burroughs' office* is an excellent secretary.

**Noun**   (*See also collective noun, gerund, noun of address, subject, object*) A noun is a word that names a person, place, thing, or idea. It can be used in a sentence as a subject or as an object.

Examples: A *doctor* was summoned. (person)
He came into the patient's *room*. (place)
He was carrying a black *bag*. (thing)
His *desire* was to make the patient well. (idea)

*Note:*   In the above examples, *doctor* and *desire* are used as subjects, and *room* and *bag* are used as objects.

**Noun of address**   A noun of address is used in a sentence to speak directly to a person by using his or her name. It is set off by commas.

Example: I see, *Mr. Bowen*, that you have drawn the plans.

**Number**   (*See also shift*) There are only two types of number in the use of nouns and pronouns: *singular* and *plural. Singular* refers to one; *plural* refers to two or more.

Examples: She was reading a *book*. (singular)
She read several *books*. (plural)

**Object**   (*See direct object, object of preposition,* or *object pronouns*)

**Object of preposition**   The object of a preposition is the noun or pronoun following the preposition.

Example: He got a shot in the *arm*.

**Object of verb**   (*See direct object*)

**Object pronouns**   The object pronouns are used as direct objects, objects of prepositions, and objects of verbals.

Examples: me, you, him, her, it, us, them.
Take *it* to the office. (direct object)
Come with *me*. (object of preposition)
Calling *him*, I made the appointment. (object of verbal)

**Outline**   An outline is a bare skeleton or framework of the ideas to be included in a piece of writing longer than a paragraph. Items can be phrases or complete thoughts. Remember that if you have point 1, you must have point 2. If you have example *A*, you must have an example *B*.

Example:  I.  Introduction
              A.
              B.
     II.  Body
              A.
              B.
                    1.
                    2.
   III.  Conclusion
              A.
              B.

**Paragraph**  A paragraph is a group of related sentences with a Topic Sentence and Supporting Sentences. If it stands alone, it also has a Concluding Sentence.

**Parallel structure**  Parallel structure occurs when two or more words, phrases, or clauses are joined by a coordinate conjunction. The items linked in this manner must all be parallel in form; that is, they must all be nouns, all prepositional phrases, all clauses, etc.

    Examples: *Typing memos, alphabetizing mailing lists,* and *transcribing shorthand* were duties of the new receptionist. (parallel phrases)
    The copy editor was *fast, accurate,* and *creative.* (parallel adjectives)

**Parenthetic element**  (*See interrupter*)

**Participle**  (*See also present participle, past participle,* and *verbal*) A participle is one of the three types of verbals. It is the *-ing* form or past tense form of the verb used as an adjective.

    Examples: The *falling* rocks injured many tourists.
    The *barking* dogs kept us from sleeping.

**Passive voice**  (*See also active voice*) A verb in the passive voice shows the subject receiving (rather than doing) the action of the verb. The passive voice is signaled by a form of the verb *to be* as a helper.

    Example: The new employees *were spoken* to by Ms. Jones.

**Past participle**  The past participle is the form of the verb used with the helper *have* or *has* to show action or state of being completed.

    Examples: We *have walked* three miles.
    He *has gone* to work.

| PRESENT | PAST | PAST PARTICIPLE |
| --- | --- | --- |
| walk | walked | (have) walked |
| go | went | (has) gone |

**Past tense** (*See also future tense, present tense, and tense*) A verb in the past tense shows an action completed at a former time.

Example: I *typed* the letter yesterday.

**Person** Person indicates the division of pronouns into first person, second person, and third person.

EXAMPLES
*First Person*:  (person speaking) I (me, my, mine), we (us, our, ours)
*Second Person*:  (person spoken to) you (your, yours)
*Third Person*:  (person spoken about) he (him, his), she (her, hers), it (its), they (them, their, theirs)

**Persuasion report** A persuasion report is an essay designed to convince readers of a certain point of view and to urge them to take some form of action.

**Phrase** (*See also prepositional phrase, verbal phrase*) A phrase is a group of words used to convey a single idea. Although it does not contain a subject or a verb, it is a distinct part of a sentence.

Examples: The boss stamped out *of the office.*
*Hearing the phone,* she jumped up to answer it.

**Plural** (*See also singular*) The plural form of a word indicates more than one. Generally, a noun forms its plural by adding *-s* or *-es* to the singular; a verb forms its plural by dropping the *-s* or *-es* from the singular.

Examples: *Architects are* in great demand.
*Teachers* often *strike* for higher wages.

**Point of view** (*See also person, shift*) Point of view refers to the perspective from which a paragraph or a report is written. It may be told through the writer's eyes in the first person (I–we). It may also address the reader in the second person (you). Finally, it may speak about an individual or group in the third person (he/she, they). The important thing to remember about point of view is to be consistent throughout a piece of writing. Do not shift back and forth from first to second or third person. Also, be consistent with singular or plural throughout.

Examples: *I* was granted a loan. (first person singular)
*You* were granted a loan. (second person)
*They* were granted a loan. (third person plural)

**Positive degree** (*See degree of comparison*)

**Possession** (*See also apostrophe* and *possessive pronouns*) Nouns or pronouns can show possession or ownership. Nouns use an apostrophe or an apostrophe and an -*s* to show possession ('s). If the noun ends in -*s*, add an apostrophe only; if the noun does not end in -*s*, add an apostrophe and an -*s* ('s). Pronouns *never* use an apostrophe to show possession.

Examples: The *tree's* trunk was rotten.
The *trees'* trunks were rotten.
*Its* trunk was rotten.
*Their* trunks were rotten.

**Possessive pronouns**   (*See also object pronouns, pronoun, subject pronouns*) A possessive pronoun is used to show ownership.

Examples: my, mine, your, his, her, hers, its, their, theirs.
Hand in *his* report.
The report is *mine*.
*Their* desks are neat.

**Preposition**   (*See also prepositional phrase*) A preposition is a word used to show the relationship between one word and another in the sentence.

Examples: with, in, to, of, on, at, from, etc.
The woman *with* the briefcase is my boss.
(*With* shows the relationship between *woman* and *briefcase*.)

**Prepositional phrase**   (*See also preposition*) A prepositional phrase is a group of words composed of a preposition, its object, and any modifiers of the object.

Example: He wrote a script *for a children's television show.*

**Present participle**   (*See also participle, past participle,* and *verbal*) A present participle is the -*ing* form of a verb used as an adjective.

Example: The *fluttering* flags caught my eye.

**Present tense**   (*See also tense, future tense,* and *past tense*) A verb in the present tense shows an action or state of being occurring at that moment, not in the past or future.

Example: I *am typing* the letter now.
or I *type* the letter now.

**Pro and con paragraph**   A pro and con paragraph develops two opposing controlling ideas. In the concluding sentence of the paragraph, the writer does not take a stand; he or she merely restates both ideas of the issue.

**Process paragraph** or **Report** (*See also paragraph, report*) A process paragraph gives the reader a step-by-step procedure of how something is done.

**Pronoun** (*See also possessive pronouns, object pronouns, relative pronouns,* and *subject pronoun*)
A pronoun takes the place of a noun.

Examples: man    (*he, him, his*)
woman   (*she, her, hers*)
people   (*they, them, their,* theirs)
object   (*it, its*)
objects   (*they, them, their, theirs*)

**Pronoun–antecedent agreement** A pronoun must agree (be consistent with) its antecedent in number and person.

Examples: The actress checked *her* daily schedule.
(third person singular)
I will retype *my* notes.
(first person singular)
The students took *their* books home.
(third person plural)

**Pronoun case** (*See also possessive pronouns, pronoun, object pronouns,* and *subject pronoun*)
*Case* indicates the various forms of pronoun usage: subjective case (pronoun used as subject), objective case (pronoun used as object), and possessive case (pronoun used to show possession).

**Pronoun reference** (*See point of view*)

**Punctuation patterns**
IC, cc IC
IC; IC
IC; trans, IC
DC, IC
IC DC

**Reasons and examples paragraph** (*See also paragraph*) A reasons and examples paragraph develops its Topic Sentence by using supporting reasons and also giving examples for each reason.

**Reasons paragraph** (*See also paragraph*) A reasons paragraph develops its Topic Sentence by using supporting reasons.

**Recommendation report** A recommendation report is the written account of a comparative study, resulting in the recommending of one item or thing over another.

**Reflexive pronouns** (*See also pronoun*) A reflexive pronoun ends in

*-self* or *-selves.* It is used to show that someone did something to oneself or to show emphasis.

Examples: He questioned *himself* about his motives.
Melanie *herself* is in charge.

**Relative pronoun**    A relative pronoun introduces a dependent clause or a question.

Example: who, whom, that, which, when, where
The accountant *who* got the job was well qualified.
*Which* typewriter do you want?

**Report**    (*See also interview, process, persuasion, recommendation,* and *summary reports*) A report is an essay or paper composed of several paragraphs developing an idea more extensively than a single paragraph would.

**Restrictive element**    (*See also nonrestrictive element*) A restrictive element is a word, phrase, or clause modifier that is essential to the clear identification of the word it modifies. It is *not* set off by commas.

EXAMPLES
Restrictive:       The doctor *who treated me,* has office hours tomorrow.
Nonrestrictive:  Dr. Smathers, *who treated me,* has office hours tomorrow.

**Run-on sentence**    A run-on sentence is an incorrectly punctuated sentence containing two independent clauses. To correct a run-on sentence, separate the independent clause with a semicolon or a period, or insert a comma with a coordinate conjunction between the two independent clauses.

EXAMPLES
Run-on:  The new skating rink was completed, students began using it.
Correct:  The new skating rink was completed; students began using it.
Correct:  The new skating rink was completed, and students began using it.

**Second person**    (*See person*)

**Semicolon**    A semicolon (;) is a mark of punctuation used to indicate a division between separate elements in a sentence.

Examples: The clouds were dark and heavy,  a storm was brewing in the west. (between two independent clauses)
He had lived in Seattle, Washington; Boise, Idaho; and New Orleans, Louisiana. (between items of series with internal punctuation)

**Sentence**    (*See also independent clause*) A sentence is a group of words having a subject and a verb and making a complete thought.

**Sentence combining**    To vary sentence structure and to avoid short, choppy sentences, you can employ the techniques of sentence combining, which includes use of dependent clauses, prepositional phrases, verbal phrases, and adjectives or nouns to condense ideas.

EXAMPLES
Choppy:   Joe was in college.
            He studied architectural engineering.
            His professor was highly qualified.
            He enjoyed the course.
Better:   While Joe was in College, he studied architectural engineering, which he enjoyed, with a highly qualified professor.

**Series**    (*See also comma*) A series is a list of three or more items in sequence in a sentence. Use a comma to separate words, phrases, and clauses in a series.

Example: We ordered roast beef, baked potatoes, and broccoli for dinner.

**Shift**    (*See also point of view*) A shift is an unnecessary change within a sentence or paragraph or report. Be careful to avoid shifts in number, person, point of view, tense, and voice.

**Singular**    (*See also plural*) The singular form of a word indicates *one*. Generally, a singular noun does not end in *-s* or *-es*, whereas, a singular verb does end in *-s* or *-es*.

**Slang**    Slang is language that is highly informal or unconventional. It is not acceptable in formal or traditional writing or speaking.

Examples: high five (slapping of hands)
            fink (undesirable person)

**Subject**    (*See also noun, pronoun*) The subject of a sentence is what the sentence is talking about. It is usually a noun or pronoun.

Examples: *Coffee* increases nervousness.
            *He* is my supervisor.

**Subject complement**    (*See also linking verb*) A subject complement is the noun, pronoun or adjective that follows a linking verb and renames or describes the subject.

Examples: Mr. Borden is our new *guide*. (noun)
            The job applicant is *she*. (pronoun)
            The new secretary seems *competent*. (adj).

**Subject pronouns**    (*See also pronoun, subject*) The subject pronouns are *I, you, he, she, it, we, they*. These pronouns are used as subjects.

Examples: *I* would like to speak to the group.
            *They* are coming to work today.

**Subject–verb agreement** (*See also plural, singular*) A subject must agree with its verb in number. That is, a singular subject uses a singular verb; uses a plural subject uses a plural verb.

Examples: The *architect draws* house plans.
*Architects draw* house plans.

**Subordinate clause** (*See dependent clause*)

**Subordinate conjunction** (*See clause signal*)

**Subordination** (*See also coordination, dependent clause*) Subordination, in sentence structure, refers to the use of dependent clauses to make an idea less important to the thought in the independent clause. It is a useful method of varying sentence structure.

Example: After the surveyors set up the transit, they surveyed the property lines.

**Summary report** A summary report is a condensation of a larger piece of writing such as a magazine article. It attempts to capture the essence of the article in as brief a form as possible.

**Superlative degree** (*See degree of comparison*)

**Supporting sentence** (*See also topic sentence, concluding sentence, controlling idea*) A supporting sentence is one that gives factual detail to aid in proving a Topic Sentence for a paragraph or longer paper.

**Synonym** A word that has the same meaning as another word.

**Tense** (*See also shift*) Tense refers to time expressed by the verb—present, past, or future.

Examples: I *am typing* the lab report. (present tense)
I *typed* the lab report. (past tense)
I *will type* the lab report. (future tense)

**Third person** (*See person*)

**Topic sentence** (*See also concluding sentence, controlling idea, supporting sentence*) A Topic Sentence of a paragraph reveals both the subject (what the paragraph is talking about) and the Controlling Idea (what is being said about the subject).

Example: Large *computers* are *costly* to produce.

**Transitional expression** (*See also semicolon*) A transitional expression is a device used to link one idea to another.

Examples: (Therefore, on the other hand, consequently, for example, etc.)
There are many arguments for changing to the metric system; *however*, there are a number of opposing ideas as well.

**Unclear reference**   (*See indefinite reference*)

**Verb**   (*See also linking verb, helping verb, main verb*) The verb is the part of the sentence that shows the action or state of being of the subjects.

Examples: My boss *walks* five miles a day. (action)
My boss *is* considerate. (state of being)

**Verbal**   (*See also gerund, infinitive, participle*) A verbal is a word made from a verb, but is used in another way. The three types of verbals are gerunds, infinitives, and participles.

**Verbal phrase**   (*See also verbal*) A verbal phrase includes the verbal and its object and/or modifiers.

Examples: *Walking rapidly into the room,* he commanded attention.
*To be a state policeofficer* is his goal.

**Voice**   (*See active voice, passive voice, shift*)

**Vowel**   The vowels are *a, e, i, o, u,* and sometimes *y.*

# INDEX

# S

# T